John W Pratt

Given to Christ

And Other Sermons

John W Pratt

Given to Christ
And Other Sermons

ISBN/EAN: 9783337160265

Printed in Europe, USA, Canada, Australia, Japan

Cover: Foto ©Lupo / pixelio.de

More available books at **www.hansebooks.com**

AND

OTHER SERMONS.

BY
JOHN W. PRATT, D.D.

WITH A BIOGRAPHICAL SKETCH OF HIS LIFE AND LABORS.

NEW YORK:
ANSON D. F. RANDOLPH & COMPANY,
38 WEST TWENTY-THIRD STREET.

PREFACE.

If the writer of these sermons had published them himself, doubtless they would have had many imperfections removed; but as that could not be, in compliance with numerous requests, I give them just as they were prepared for the various congregations to which he preached; with the daily prayer that God will use them, and feeling assured that could his voice *now* be heard, his language would be that of Dr. Bonar:

> "Not myself, but the truth that in life I have spoken,
> Not myself, but the seeds that in life I have sown,
> Shall pass on to ages, all about *me* forgotten
> Save the *truth* I have spoken, the things I have done."

M. W. Pratt.

Louisville, Ky., 1888.

BIOGRAPHICAL SKETCH.

BY C. A. STILLMAN, D.D.

The Rev. John Wood Pratt, D.D., was born at St. Mary's, Georgia, on the 12th of May, 1827. He sprang from an honored ancestry; on his father's side from the grand old Puritan stock recognized as the chief glory of Old and New England, and on his mother's from the English gentry, that class which has been called more noble than "The Nobles."

His father, the Rev. Horace S. Pratt, was a Presbyterian minister and Professor of English Literature in the University of Alabama at the time of his death in 1840. His mother, Jane Wood, died when he was only one year old, so that his maternal training devolved upon his second mother—a most intelligent, godly, and in every way estimable woman. His early youth gave indications of the ability which marked his after-life. When only seventeen he graduated with distinguished honor at the University of Alabama. While a mere boy he consecrated himself to the service of Christ, and very soon resolved to prepare himself for that profession in which he became pre-eminent. Having completed his theological course at Princeton, N. J., he was licensed by the Presbytery of Tuscaloosa, Alabama, May 6, 1848, six days before he reached his majority. The youthful preacher soon attracted attention by his discourses, which were rich in eloquent diction and sound instruction. He was called to the church at Marion, Alabama, in October, 1849. Such was his aptness to teach that he was elected to the Professorship which had been made vacant by the death of his father ten years before, viz., that of English Literature and Belles-Lettres. He accepted this position and became distinguished for the clearness of his instructions, and at the same time an eminent example of the art of eloquence which he taught.

Prof. W. S. Wyman, of the University of Alabama, says of him at this period: "When the Rev. John W. Pratt became the Professor of English Literature at the beginning of the collegiate year 1850-51, I was a member of the senior class. After I was graduated in 1851 I became a member of the Faculty, and I continued to be a colleague of Mr. Pratt during the whole of his fifteen years' stay in the University. I feel, therefore, quite competent to speak of him during this part of his life. It was the duty of the Professor of English Literature to teach Rhetoric, Logic, Ancient and Modern History, and the History of English Literature, to supervise the writing of Essays and Orations by the three higher classes in the University, and to train the classes in Oratory. Mr. Pratt was only twenty-three years of age when he entered upon the important duties of this professorship. He had the enthusiasm of youth and a great love for his work. He was himself an eloquent orator, the master of a polished style, and remarkably well read for one of his age in the great masters of English Literature. At the outset he was fortunate enough to inspire his pupils with something of his own ardor in the study of the great exemplars of a pure English style. From causes not necessary to be mentioned here, the Department of English in the University had been for ten years previously in a languishing condition. The writing of Essays had been regarded by the students as a heavy task; and the revision of them by the Professors in charge for the time being had been for the most part perfunctory. Practice in oratory had been confined to the declamation of select pieces by the classes once a month before the President of the University. Mr. Pratt at once introduced a new and thorough system for the revision of original compositions, the result of which proved to be so excellent that the same system has been retained with but slight modifications to the present time. In Oratory he began to train every student separately and systematically. Prior to Mr. Pratt's time the Department of Rhetoric had been limited to the study of some short superficial book on literary criticism. His best work here was the introduction of a thorough treatise on the art of Invention, a book which required hard study to master, but the beneficial results of the hard study were soon manifested in the disciplined intellects of the advanced scholars. Mr. Pratt was deeply interested during his residence at the University in the moral and religious improvement of the students. He organized classes for the study of the Bible among the students, and trained them in the lessons. The students' prayer-meeting was, as I well remember, conducted by him, and was for a long time held at his house."

Mr. Pratt occupied this chair until 1865, when the University was suspended by the ravages of the Civil War. It was during this period he accumulated the store of varied learning which rendered his preaching so profound and instructive. He never made any display of it, for he despised pedantry, but it gave weight, accuracy, variety, and beauty to his exposition of divine truth. He by no means forsook the ministry while Professor. He loved to preach, and he was often called upon. He preached frequently in the city, but he was especially fond of his little rural charge, preaching with equal acceptability to all classes of people. He charmed and edified the most plain and unlettered, and attracted the most highly cultivated, because he preached the simple Gospel with transparent clearness and earnestness. Many have regretted that so much of the prime of his life was spent in the class-room, but he was thereby acquiring his higher education for the pulpit, and for those triumphs of sacred eloquence which crowned his usefulness and made him famous in after-life.

At the close of the war circumstances led him to open a school in Brooklyn, N. Y. In the second year of his stay there he received and accepted a call to the cultivated and important church in Lexington, Virginia.

Rev. James H. Smith, of Lexington, Virginia, writes of his work there: "It would have been difficult for him to find a centre more favorable for sending out his influence in wide and far-reaching streams, than he found in the church at Lexington. Washington and Lee University, situated there, held within her halls three hundred students, and the Virginia Military Institute three hundred more. His peculiar gifts were exactly those best calculated to attract and influence young men. Every resident of Lexington, and every student of either of these schools during the years of his ministry there, will remember without prompting, how intense was the interest excited and maintained by his preaching. All classes in the community, people of every differing faith, and people of none, were drawn to his services. Old men, whose time-seared hearts had grown callous with long indifference, exhibited an unwonted sensibility. Young men discovered with delight that the truths of revelation furnish worthier themes for a higher eloquence than can be inspired by subjects less supreme. It would be harder, perhaps, to calculate the harvest of this ministry than that of most others, for the sower planted, not in a single field, but stood as it were on a mountain and cast his seeds to the winds, which bore them wherever the Southern youth there congregated around him have made their thousand homes."

He continued to be a diligent student and prepared all his public exercises with extraordinary labor and care. The discerning stranger who happened to hear him at the weekly prayer-meeting on the stormiest night, had as fair an opportunity of estimating his powers as those who sat before him in the crowded church. He spoke words thoroughly credible when he declared that he *always did his best*. He prepared "beaten oil" for the sanctuary—hence the finished and enduring character of his discourses, which could stand the most rigid criticism, and which all his hearers and readers feel assured will secure them a place in the permanent literature of the pulpit. His sermons will live and will continue to delight and edify the Church. In place, however, of any further estimate of our own, we prefer to insert the following true and beautiful tribute from the Hon. J. Randolph Tucker, who had ample capacity and opportunity to form a correct judgment, having been a member of his church while he lived in Lexington, Virginia:

"The death of Dr. Pratt was sincerely a grief to me, for I had been privileged to know him for years as pastor, preacher, and friend. He was a very remarkable man in the endowments of his mind, as well as in the qualities which made up his character. He had an acute and subtle analytic power, which enabled him to discover the germs of truth, and to detect the concealed errors in the logic of his opponent. This keen insight into the subject of his criticism or of his discussion, made his discourse as clear as the sunlight. About his thought, and about his expression of it, there were no clouds of doubt or of uncertainty. No one could fail to see what he saw, to understand what he thought, for it was the pure diamond idea reflected in the mirror of a style which was simple, yet ornate in its strong, fervid, and classic rhetoric. He was logical, and yet imaginative, original, suggestive, and fertile in his conceptions, and powerful in setting them forth with all the beauties of expression with which a thorough education and refined literary taste could invest human thought.

"He was a genuine Calvinist, and so strongly held the Pauline type of the Christian faith that his mind never wavered in the most profound speculations, and his heart was anchored on the 'Rock of Ages,' with implicit and humble trust. The grand truths of the Bible he held with an intellectual enthusiasm which stirred his whole nature with a deeply sympathetic thrill, and which sometimes shook his bodily frame with visible emotion; and yet, though his mind was so nerved by the grandeur of truth, his sympathetic nature was alive to the appeals of distress and affliction. In the chamber of sickness and death he poured the oil of consolation upon the wounds of bereavement with gentleness, judgment, and tender sympathy. As a man he was brave, manly, candid, and sincere. He was liberal in his charity and generous without stint. As a friend he was constant and reliable, because while warm in his regard his feelings never swayed his judgment.

"As a preacher of the Gospel he was cogent in reasoning, luminous in expression, critical in exegesis, earnest in exhortation, and always and eminently instructive, practical, and Scriptural. He adhered to the written word with fidelity, and condemned with force and without compromise all the so-called rationalism which wandered from the Scripture into the mazes of a speculative and false philosophy. As a pastor he was discreet, conservative, and practical. He was not obtrusive of counsel, but ever ready to give it; nor intrusive into the domestic habits of his people, yet ever willing to advise in regard to them. He sought to lead men to the great Teacher to be taught by Him, and never did it by ignoble appeals to fear, nor by an unworthy play upon the animal emotions of his hearers. He preached the truth as it is in Jesus, as the best thing for the man; with which he would have peace and eternal rest, without which he must have unrest and eternal despair. Such is my imperfect estimate of Dr. Pratt. His memory is one of great value to me, in the instructions I received from him, in the guidance I derived from his counsel, and in the support I had from his friendship."

After six years in this important field he accepted the Presidency of Central University at Richmond, Kentucky, a young institution established by the Synod of Kentucky. To its organization and management he devoted himself for six years, and found an ample field for his large experience and eminent scholastic and practical ability. At the same time he occupied for three years the pulpit of the Presbyterian church of Richmond. This was his last connection with college work. Professor L. G. Barbour, of Central University, said of him:

"He had in a high degree two qualities not always conjoined, but both of them needful in the constitution of a first-class teacher: great quickness of apprehension and unusual breadth of view. He saw into the lesser and intricate points of a subject, and his eye swept over the broad relation of its parts and divisions; hence he gave clearness of detail and logical method in mass. When I first knew him at Princeton Theological Seminary he was noted for vivacity and humor. In his latter years a gleam of his old manner would occasionally flash out and remind me of his early manhood. Add to this his great geniality and unaffected goodness of heart which made him so popular among the students of Central University, and you will have some of the prime elements of a teacher."

Resigning his Presidency in 1878, he supplied for some time, during the absence of the pastor, Rev. T. H. Skinner, D.D., the pulpit of the Second Presbyterian church of Cincinnati, Ohio, where he fully sustained his already great reputation as a preacher. Indeed he so impressed himself upon a number of Christian gentlemen of that city that they induced him to attempt a novel enterprise, to bring into contact with the masses his strong and attractive presentation of Gospel truth without interfering with the regular exercises of the churches. For this purpose the immense Music Hall was rented, and a service held every Sunday afternoon. It proved all they had hoped for. The attendance was seldom less than three thousand, and often reached five, gathered from all churches and from all ranks in society, including multitudes not accustomed to attend any religious service. Here he found the grandest field for the exercise of his splendid powers. His noble intellectual face attracted every eye. He commanded perfect order and universal rapt attention. His strong, clear, melodious voice, always perfectly modulated, reached every ear and rung out with distinct enunciation, forceful emphasis, and often with tremulous notes as he proclaimed the glorious Gospel of the blessed God. He made no failures, was always equal to himself, and was manifestly made "a polished shaft in Jehovah's quiver," and doubtless pierced many a doubt-clad mind and many a sin-hardened heart.

In 1881 he became the successor of the distinguished Dr. Stuart Robinson as pastor of the Second Church in Louisville, Kentucky. It is needless to say that in this important charge he continued to exercise his extraordinary gifts and labors as Christ's minister for Christ's people and for the conversion of sinners. The following extract, taken from an address delivered at a congregational meeting by Col. Bennett H. Young, will best show the estimation in which he was held by this church:

"The Southern pulpit, in the past thirty years, has produced many widely renowned theologians and preachers. Part are dead and some remain with us, but Dr. Pratt, in some respects, was surpassed by none. As a writer of sermons, in my opinion he had no equal in the American pulpit. There was a pathos, tenderness, eloquence, combined with a comprehension of man's spiritual and moral forces, which placed him in the very front rank of modern preachers.

"In the elaboration of truth, as set forth in our standards; in the application of doctrine to daily life and as a solace in human sorrow; in the dignity and grandeur of the mental and spiritual powers of man, his sermons are a marvel, not only of oratorical finish, but of philosophical acumen and discrimination. His discourses on the value of human life in its relation to God, the resurrection, and man's destiny here and hereafter, are productions which will do credit to any age and any man.

"Confiding in his nature, tender and gentle in all his emotions, affectionate in disposition, firm in his Christian faith, with an unconditional consecration to the cause of Christ, he was a remarkable and unusual character, one the Church should reverence and remember, and one whom his friends will never forget.

"I am aware that these are strong terms I have used in reference to my departed friend, but he was worthy of all of them, and his life has been a blessing to the Church and a comfort and pleasure to those who knew his personal worth and his earnest, constant Christian testimony.

"In a less restricted field than was given him he would have shone with increased brilliancy. He possessed the power of stirring and developing the strongest and highest spiritual aspirations, and none ever heard his words who did not feel impressed with nobler ideas of God and truer and better conceptions of man's duties and responsibilities to his Creator and Redeemer. Wherever he preached, his pure gospel, his zealous, beautiful life, and his strong intellectual force will long be felt in the hearts and characters of his hearers.

"Nor should his efforts be permitted to die. The thoughts of such a mind justify and demand preservation and publication, and the force of his words will influence and direct a better life in those who may read, long after his name and his works are forgotten."

He supplied the Second Church in Memphis, Tennessee, for several months the last year of his life. In the eloquent words of Judge Heiskell we see the impression he made on this people: "My acquaintance with Dr. Pratt extended only through the few months he ministered to us last summer. In that brief period I learned to respect, to honor, and to love him. No man I ever met impressed me more profoundly. I do not hesitate to say he was one of the most scholarly men I ever knew. While his sermons were masterful in substance, his terse and elegant style made them always charming. His diction was ornate, chaste, and wonderfully graceful. His sentences, burdened with logical reasoning and rich and helpful thought, flowed easily and felicitously. He never paused for a word, and always chose the one most suitable to express his meaning, so that the profundity and dignity of his utterances were made thoroughly interesting and enjoyable by the appropriate language in which he clothed them. He was a rhetorician, an orator, and, what seems almost a lost art, he was an admirable reader. But these accomplishments were but the trappings of the sincere faith and Christlike spirit that breathed in every line and word that he uttered. If his prayers were always eloquent, it was because they were the simple pleadings of the child of grace, kneeling at his Father's feet, beseeching His favor, His help, and His protecting care. His daily life was a living epistle, 'known and read of all men,' of the beauty, symmetry, and power of our holy religion. Indeed, he came as near the perfect minister as any one I ever knew.

"With all this and through all, his deep humility and broad

Christian charity made him lovely and beloved by all. Such a man never dies. He only leaves us—to live. The good that he does lives after him and for ever."

The Rev. M. H. Houston, D.D., our Secretary of Foreign Missions, writes of him:

"In the removal of Dr. Pratt from among us we have lost one of the noblest, most generous and interesting men I ever knew. It was always a pleasure and privilege to me to be with him: he was always kind, always faithful as a friend, always instructive and stimulating, and I loved him. He was a prince among preachers and among men, and the whole Church must mourn his departure."

Dr. R. P. Farris speaks of him "as one of his dearest friends, a man who honored me with his confidence, a man in whom I could confide, whose naturalness I admired, whose high attainments I recognized and respected, whose grand preaching I enjoyed and boasted of."

The Rev. Dr. Basil Manly, of the Baptist Church, the friend of his youth, writes of him: "In the year 1837, at the reorganization of the University of Alabama at Tuscaloosa, when my father became President of the University, the only personal request he made of the Trustees was, to appoint the Rev. Horace S. Pratt, of Georgia, to be one of his colleagues. The intimacy and confidence already subsisting between them was only increased by their association in the work of the University. Their diverse characteristics and tendencies made each the complement of the other. It would sometimes be remarked, when Dr. Pratt had preached in the morning and Dr. Manly in the evening, that they had had first 'the feast of reason,' and then 'the flow of soul.' Boy as I was at the time of Professor H. S. Pratt's death, I was impressed by the fact that my father mourned over him as I do not remember his mourning over any similar bereavement; and one of my most distinct recollections of those early days is the funeral sermon which he preached in honor of his friend in the old capitol at Tuscaloosa, with the characteristic text, 'Alas, my brother.' The friendship of the parents was naturally inherited by John and myself as boys. Together in our plays, in our studies, in our plans and hopes, even occupying for a time the same room in college, we grew up in the utmost intimacy, notwithstanding he was a year or two my junior. And even subsequently to college life we spent the greater part of our time in the Theological Seminary together in the venerable shades of Princeton. From the time of leaving Princeton our lives necessarily drifted somewhat apart. Both of us have been busy men, deeply absorbed in important duties, and having little leisure for seeking social enjoyment outside of the immediate sphere of our labors. He soon became an honored and successful teacher, and occupied for years, under my father's presidency, the chair of English Literature which his father had filled, renewing and continuing the intimacy of those earlier years of which I have spoken. Subsequently, during the presidency of Dr. L. C. Garland, Professor Pratt continued to give his valued services to the University, and did as much as any man of his time to train the rising generation of Alabamians for meeting nobly the responsibilities of life. His impress is felt still on hundreds of students there. Of the latter periods of his life others can speak better and more appropriately than I. My memory clings to the picture of the genial, venturesome, affectionate boy, who was the most cherished friend of my boyhood's days, of the young man in college and seminary who shared and lightened my labors by his presence, and of the grand and impressive preacher, who thundered forth the terrors of God's law, or urged with eloquent persuasiveness the invitations and comforts of the Gospel; who made us forget ourselves, forget him, forget all our surroundings, and realize only the presence and authority of Almighty God, whose messenger he was. With a voice of remarkable clearness and force, a countenance that blazed with emotion while speaking, a delivery in which art had succeeded in concealing art, and nature spoke unimpeded; and above all, with a compactness and energy of thought, and a sacred fidelity to the Divine Word, which commanded at once the intellects and the consciences of men,—he was emphatically and eminently a Master of Assemblies. During the brief period of his afternoon services at the Music Hall in Cincinnati, the immense crowds which he attracted and held, and the profound impression produced, gave evidence of a power for popular effect which had hardly been suspected in the quiet and scholarly College Professor. I cannot but think it desirable that some of the choice discourses of such a preacher as he was should be preserved in a permanent form, not only as a memorial of him most dear and appropriate to preserve his memory among the friends that loved him, but as a means of extending and perpetuating his work, and of enlarging his influence, so that 'he, being dead, may yet speak.'"

These are the testimonies of men competent to appreciate the force, truth, and originality of Dr. Pratt's character and preaching. Yet if all the bereaved whose sorrows he consoled; if all the poor and humble ones, who helpless to explain the mystery of his power, were joyfully able to draw peace from his word; if all the souls whose doubts he drove back forever into the night from which they had come, and all the hearts whose indifference he melted, were to send up their tribute, it would be weightier by far, even than that of these thoughtful analysts of the secret of his success.

His pastorate at Louisville ended his regular work. His health gave way under his heavy pastoral duties. He went to Europe with the hope of restoration, but in 1883 he resigned this, his last charge. Yet even then he continued to preach whenever and wherever he had opportunity: sometimes for a few weeks, and sometimes for a few months at a time, for he was resolved to give his whole life to the cause of Christ, and to die in harness.

He died at his home in Louisville, Kentucky, March 24, 1888. There was no gloom in his sick-room, and we could not believe that death was really coming. When spoken to of dying, he said, "Why, I have no fear of death; it has no terrors to me. I have fixed all that years ago, and if I had not, on this bed would be no place to do it." He talked of dying in the same natural way he would speak of any other act he expected to perform. The evening before he died, in talking to a friend he said: It was such an inexpressible comfort to him now, when too weak to grasp any truth very strongly, to have these grand doctrines come unbidden to his mind. So long had his mind been stored with the consolations of Divine truth for the comforting of other hearts that he now found them adequate for his own supply. Dr. Pratt was twice married. His first wife was Mary Grace Crabb, of Tuscaloosa, Alabama. She left two children— Grace Winthrop, now Mrs. Clay Stacker, of Clarksville, Tennessee, and Edwin Alberti Pratt, of Louisville, Kentucky. His second wife was Maria Lindsay Waddell, of Lexington, Virginia.

She with two children, Harry Waddell and Nettie Wood Pratt, survive him. Of four sisters and one brother, only one sister is now living—Mrs. James W. Lapsley, of Alabama.

Dr. Pratt was a man of marked characteristics, not always understood—and perhaps he did not care enough for that—but his intimate friends knew, appreciated, and loved him. He was a man of large and free-hearted benevolence. An instance deserving record is that, after the emancipation of his slaves, he made generous provision for them, and some of them still enjoy that kindness, and will continue to do so while they live. All his former servants love and cherish him tenderly. In private life he presented the rare combination of a man full of common sense, eminently practical and systematic in all his business habits, and at the same time deeply absorbed in all the religious and literary work which engaged his thought and attention. He kept himself fully abreast of the times on all questions of interest before the public. With nothing of professional cant about him, he invited discussion on religious subjects with those who seldom met, and never sought the company of Christian people. There are two particulars in which he was unlike many great preachers: first, as a Pastor he was a methodical and conscientious visitor of his flock; and second, while his sermons were so grand and so grandly delivered, he by no means slighted the other parts of the public worship, but filled them all with beauty and power. He was a dear lover of sacred music, and showed great taste in the selection for the service of song. His Scripture-reading was equal to an eloquent commentary. But the prayer surpassed all. It was more than a sermon, simple, humble, reverent, earnest, comprehensive of all classes and topics, yet never tedious, but always refreshing and helpful to devotion. These were never in his view the mere preparatory services to the sermon, but were with him the solemn worship of God. He heard himself, and he strove to make his people hear, "the stately steppings of Jehovah" in His sanctuary.

The sermons which follow give a true idea, not of his delivery, which cannot be reproduced, but of the substance of his preaching. The reader of these sermons who never heard him preach can never be brought up to the vantage-ground on which they will read for whom every sentence will be informed and interpreted by the memory of that matchless voice and irresistible delivery. He always preached the grand and profitable themes of the Gospel. This selection is made not to bring out his greatest efforts, but to present a comprehensive and systematic view of evangelical truth.

Tuscaloosa, Alabama, 1888.

CONTENTS.

	PAGE
I.—GIVEN TO CHRIST, OR ELECTION	25

"All that the Father giveth me shall come to me; and him that cometh to me, I will in no wise cast out."—JOHN vi. 37.

II.—GOD'S SOVEREIGNTY 39

"The Lord reigneth; let the earth rejoice."—PSALM xcvii. 1.
"The Lord reigneth; let the people tremble."—PSALM xcix. 1.

III.—REGENERATION 50

"Verily, verily, I say unto you, Except a man be born again, he cannot see the kingdom of God."—JOHN iii. 3.

IV.—FAITH 57

"Precious faith."—2 PETER i. 1.

V.—JUSTIFICATION 65

"Being justified by faith, we have peace with God."—ROM. v. 1.

VI.—CONVICTION 72

"I remembered God and was troubled."—PSALM lxxvii. 3.

VII.—PEACE 82

"Acquaint now thyself with Him and be at peace."—JOB xxii. 21.

VIII.—PARDON 89

"For Thy name's sake, O Lord, pardon mine iniquity; for it is great."—PSALM xxv. 11.

IX.—LOOK AND LIVE 97

"And as Moses lifted up the serpent in the wilderness, even so must the Son of Man be lifted up; that whosoever believeth in Him should not perish, but have everlasting life."—JOHN iii. 14, 15.

		PAGE
X.—Grace Reigning		105

"For sin shall not have dominion over you; for ye are not under the law, but under Grace."—ROMANS vi. 14.

XI.—True Freedom 117

"If the Son therefore shall make you free, ye shall be free indeed."—JOHN viii. 36.

XII.—Light 131

"Ye are the light of the world."—MATTHEW v. 14.

XIII.—Preparing an Ark 142

"By faith Noah, being warned of God of things not seen as yet, moved with fear, prepared an ark to the saving of his house; by the which he condemned the world, and became heir of the righteousness which is by faith."—HEBREWS xi. 7.

XIV.—The Sabbath 155

"The Sabbath was made for man, and not man for the Sabbath."—MARK ii. 27.

XV.—What is Life? 165

"Man shall not live by bread alone."—MATTHEW iv. 4.

XVI.—Fragments 180

"Gather up the fragments that remain, that nothing be lost."—JOHN vi. 12.

XVII.—The Glory of God 189

"Whether therefore ye eat, or drink, or whatsoever ye do, do all to the glory of God."—1 CORINTHIANS x. 31.

XVIII.—The World and the Soul 201

"What shall it profit a man, if he shall gain the whole world, and lose his own soul? or what shall a man give in exchange for his soul?"—MARK viii. 36, 37.

XIX.—Special Providence 210

"And a certain man drew a bow at a venture, and smote the king of Israel between the joints of the harness."—1 KINGS xxii. 34.

XX.—Influence 223

"And that man perished not alone in his iniquity."—JOSHUA xxii. 20.

	PAGE
XXI.—STEWARDSHIP (A New-Year's Sermon)	238

"Give an account of thy stewardship."—LUKE xvi. 2.

XXII.—CONSOLATION	257

"And the cup was found in Benjamin's sack."—GEN. xliv. 12.

XXIII.—RESURRECTION	265

"The Power of His Resurrection."—PHILIPPIANS iii. 10.

XXIV.—HEAVEN	279

"In my Father's house are many mansions: if it were not so, I would have told you. I go to prepare a place for you."—JOHN xiv. 2.

PRAYERS	296

"MOREOVER, WHOM HE DID PREDESTINATE, THEM HE ALSO CALLED: AND WHOM HE CALLED, THEM HE ALSO JUSTIFIED: AND WHOM HE JUSTIFIED, THEM HE ALSO GLORIFIED."—Rom. viii. 30.

I.

GIVEN TO CHRIST.

"All that the Father giveth me shall come to me; and him that cometh to me, I will in no wise cast out."—John vi. 37.

It is a very general, but erroneous, belief that Calvinists get all their "hard" theology from the Apostle Paul. I would, therefore, have you observe that the text is the language of our Lord himself.

In it, He mentions a class of persons who seem to enlist His special affection. They are those whom God the Father had given Him. He mentions them again in the thirty-ninth verse of this chapter. "And this is the Father's will, which hath sent me, that of all which He hath given me, I should lose nothing, but should raise it up again at the last day." And, in the seventeenth chapter of this same Gospel, He refers to this same class five times, in the following words: "That He should give eternal life to as many as Thou hast given Him"; "I have manifested Thy name unto the men which Thou gavest me out of the world; Thine they were, and Thou gavest them me; I pray not for the world, but for them which Thou hast given me"; "Those that Thou gavest me I have kept"; "Father, I will that they also whom Thou hast given me be with me where I am." And, in the tenth chapter of this same Gospel: "My sheep hear my voice, and I know them, and they follow me, and I give unto them eternal life; and they shall never perish, neither shall any man pluck them out of my hand; my Father which gave them me is greater than all."

Now, here is a most interesting class of persons of whom our Lord is speaking. Let us see what can be said about this class on the authority of Christ himself.

1. All that the Father giveth Him shall come to Him; *i. e.*, shall have faith in Him; for this is what coming to Christ means.

2. Of all these, He should lose none, but would raise them up at the last day.

3. He would give eternal life to as many as the Father had given Him.

4. He would manifest the Father's name to them, and they should keep His Word.

5. They alone were the objects of His prayer to the Father. He expressly excludes the rest of the world. "I pray not for the world, but for *them*."

6. They are "kept," so that none of them is lost.

7. It was the will of Christ that they should be forever with Him to behold His glory.

8. As His sheep, He knew each individual of the flock; they hear His voice, and they follow Him, and they are safe in His care, so that no man can pluck them out of His hands.

Thus, we see, in regard to this interesting class of men whom Christ describes as given to Him, that they have faith in Him; that they follow and obey Him; that they are secure in the possession of eternal life; that they will be raised in a glorious resurrection at the last day; and that they will be forever with Christ in heaven to see His glory. Now, it is perfectly clear that all this can be said only of those who are saved through the atonement of Christ. These things cannot be said of any men except those who, having believed on the Lord Jesus Christ, have eternal life. It follows, then, inevitably, that all those who are saved were, in some sense, given to Christ by God the Father. The only point that I insist on here is, that the description of those given to Him by the Father corresponds in every particular with what the Scriptures say in regard to those who are finally saved. The statement, you see, does not touch the question whether few, or many, or all are saved. It only asserts that all who are saved are designated by Christ as *given to Him by God the Father*. If all men are at last saved, as the Universalist maintains, then all men were given to Christ. If only a portion of the race is saved, then that portion was, in some sense, given to Christ. The two classes, "*the saved*" and "*the given to Christ*," are exactly coterminous and identical, like two circles of the same diameter put one above the other. Whoever belongs to the one class belongs to the other. Whoever is excluded from the one class is excluded from the other.

Now, in regard to this class of persons, who may be indifferently designated as "*the saved*" or as "*the given to Christ*," there are some things that are self-evident.

1. If they were *given to Christ*, it must have been as individuals that they were thus given, and not as a class. As men are not saved in masses as such, neither could they have been given to Christ in an indistinguishable mass. They must have been given to Him as individuals. This is made evident by the fact that He says: "*I know my sheep.*" The figure is drawn from pastoral life. In Palestine, the shepherd was identified with his sheep far more than is the case in this country. He knew all his sheep by sight, and each sheep had a name; and when he called them by name, they knew him and recognized his voice. Now, although the shepherds of our country know their sheep by sight, and say there is as much difference in the faces of sheep as of men, they have not, as a rule, attained the art of teaching their sheep to recognize their names. But it is not so in the East. There the shepherds can call any particular sheep by name, and it will leave its pasturage and its companions and come to him. Hence, our Lord refers to a well-known fact when He says: "The sheep hear his voice, and he calleth his own sheep by name and leadeth them out." Then, immediately afterward, He says: "I am the good Shepherd *and know my sheep, and am known of mine*," implying that He knows all those whom the Father hath given Him *by their names*.

2. But, if all those whom the Father gave Him were given to Him *by name*, then it follows, of necessity, that this class must consist of a definite number. To conceive of an indefinite number of names is an absurdity. The way in which we arrive at an enumeration of the men in an army, or in a congregation, or in

a country, when the census is taken, is by setting down their *names*. As soon as the names were enrolled, we can fix the number exactly; we know precisely how many are in the list. This is perfectly clear, so that I need not dwell on it a moment.

3. Another thing seems to follow just here. If *all* men had been given to Christ by the Father, such careful specification of them by name would not have been necessary. If the whole race, without exception, had been included in the gift, it would have been enough to designate them simply by the generic title of *men*. But our Lord distinctly says that all men were not thus included in the paternal gift, for He says to the Jews: "*Ye believe not, because ye are not of my sheep*," and, in another place, He says: "I pray not for the world, but for them which Thou hast given me," clearly showing that all men were not included in this gift; and, in another place, still more distinctly, He designates them as "*the men whom Thou gavest me out of the world*," i. e., they were separated from the mass of mankind. Now, from the fact that those given to Christ out of the world are known by name, it follows, of necessity, that they must have been *selected* out of the mass of mankind. The only way in which it was possible to give to Him a definite number of individuals, whose names were known, was to call their names, *one by one*. And this implies a selection—a passing by of others whose names were equally known to God, but whom He did not choose to give His Son from out of the world.

Now, everything that I have said thus far is based directly on the very language of Christ himself. Let us, before we go a step farther, see what we have established.

(1.) That Christ speaks of a body of men given Him by the Father, selected from out of the mass of men whom He calls "*the world*."

(2.) That this body of men given to Christ is identical with those who are *saved*, inasmuch as the description given of them corresponds exactly with that elsewhere given of those whose names are written in the Lamb's Book of Life.

(3.) That they were given to Christ as individuals, and not as a class.

(4.) That they were given to Him *by name*, and that He knows the *name* of each.

(5.) That the number of them must be definite.

It is impossible to deny any one of these propositions if all that Christ says about those "given to Him by the Father" is kept in mind.

I. And now the question arises, *When were these men given by the Father to the Son?*

This is to be answered by referring to another name which our Lord applies to this class of men. We have seen that they are composed of those whom God selected from among the mass of mankind. Now our Lord calls this class of men His "*elect*." He speaks of the "elect whom God hath chosen." As there can be no other class of men in whom God delights except those whom He hath given to His Son, it is clear that the "elect whom He hath chosen" must be the very same men whom He hath *given to Christ*. No amount of ingenuity in the torturing of Scripture to suit a purpose can evade the conclusion that the "elect" of whom our Lord often makes mention are the same men selected by name and given to Him by the Father as "*His sheep*." The elect, according to our Lord, are those for whose sake the days of trouble and darkness at the end of the world are to be shortened; they are those whom, of all mankind, it will be impossible for false christs and false prophets to deceive; they are those whom the angels are to gather together from the four winds and from the uttermost part of the earth at the day of judgment. It is clear, then, that they are the very same men whom God selected out of mankind to give to His Son. The question, when they were given to Him, is to be answered then by answering this question, "When were they selected or chosen?" This question the other Scriptures answer in a hundred different forms. The elect were selected "before the foundation of the world"; *i.e.*, from all eternity. Paul tells us all we can desire to know on this subject. He says, Eph. i. 4, that they were "chosen in Him before the foundation of the world"; and in another place he speaks of them as those whom God hath "*chosen from the beginning.*" And the Apostle John, in the Revelation, speaks of those whose "names are written in the Book of Life from the foundation of the world" (Rev. xvii. 8). From these Scriptures we learn definitely that those whom the Father gave the Son were selected from among men before the foundation of the world. If they were selected from among men from all eternity in order *to be* given to Him, they were given to Him *then*, and promised as His inheritance then, *being then mentioned by name.*

II. But God knew that these men, chosen out of the world, would be sinners exactly like those from among whom they were selected.

On what ground, then, could a God of inflexible justice elect them to life and glory? The answer to this question brings to view what is known as the "COVENANT OF REDEMPTION." According to this covenant, entered into between God the Father and God the Son, in the counsels of eternity, Christ engaged to take the place of all God's elect, and fulfil for them obedience to the law they had broken, and suffer for them the penalty which they had incurred. He becomes the Shepherd of His flock through an express agreement made between Him and the Father, by which, as a good Shepherd, He "lays down His life for His sheep." And now you will be able to understand that passage in the thirteenth of Hebrews: "Now the God of peace that brought again from the dead our Lord Jesus, *that great Shepherd of the sheep, through the blood of the everlasting covenant.*" He became the Shepherd of the flock in virtue of a covenant; and this covenant was sealed with blood; and although His blood was not yet actually shed, yet its virtue was already recognized by God the Father; for His engagement to shed His blood in the fullness of time was regarded by the Father the same as its actual shedding, and hence He is called a "Lamb slain from the foundation of the world."

The purpose of election is very comprehensive. "It was the purpose of God to bring His people to holiness, to sonship, and to eternal glory. But He never intended to do this irrespective of Christ. On the contrary, it was His purpose, as revealed in Scripture, to bring His people to their exalted privileges through a Redeemer. It was in Christ as their head and representative they were chosen to eternal life; and, therefore, in virtue of what He covenanted to do in their behalf. There is, therefore, a federal union between Christ and His people—*i. e.*, a union arising out of His covenant with the Father by which they become His sheep, His possession—which is antecedent to their actual union with Him, and which is the source of the actual union. God gave a people to His Son in this Covenant of Redemption. Those included in that covenant, and *because* they are included in it—in other words, because they are in Christ, as their head and representative—receive in time all the benefits of redemption. Their subsequent *voluntary* union with Christ by *faith* is not the *ground* of their federal union with Him, but, on the contrary, their *federal* union is the ground of their *voluntary* union. It is, therefore, *in Christ;* *i. e.*, as united to Him in the Covenant of Redemption that the people of God are elected to eternal life and to all the blessings therewith connected. Much in this same sense the Jews are said to have been chosen in Abraham. Their relation to Abraham and to God's covenant with him were the ground and reason of all the peculiar blessings they enjoyed. So their covenant union with Christ is the ground of all the benefits which the people of God possess or hope for. *They were chosen in Christ as the Jews were chosen in Abraham.*"—(Hodge.)

Let us stop just here and recapitulate the propositions established, to wit:

That there is a definite number of men, whose names have been written in the Lamb's Book of Life from the foundation of the world, whom God the Father gave to His Son, to constitute His flock, in an everlasting covenant, by the terms of which Christ engaged to take their place, and by the shedding of His blood redeem them from the punishment due to their sins; and by thus taking their place He became their representative and federal head. As their representative, He receives promises for them, even the promise of eternal life, and claims for them, as rightfully belonging to Him, all the blessings promised in His Covenant with the Father.

III. The question now arises, and it is perfectly pertinent: Why should God the Father elect some of our race to these unspeakable blessings, and pass others by? Why did He write certain names in the Lamb's Book of Life from the foundation of the world? Why did He leave out of the list of the myriads who are saved, the names of thousands who are lost? Why did He choose some and not all? There can be no doubt of the fact that He did do it; now why?

In reply to this question, I remark that we are to look for the reason, why God does one thing rather than another, to the same source of information from which we learn that He does it at all. In other words, there is no room for speculation on a subject which is a matter of pure revelation. God tells us why He did this thing of which we are speaking; He elected some and passed others by, "according to the good pleasure of His will." *He did it simply because He chose to do it,* and He does not see fit in His Word to give any other reason. Men have undertaken to vindicate the justice of God in the purpose of election on philosophical grounds. God himself does not seek thus to vindicate His own character. He claims the right of selection, and that without rendering any other reason than this: "*I will have mercy on whom I will have mercy, and I will have compassion on whom I will have compassion.*"

As in the case of Esau and Jacob, before either was born, or had done any good or evil, God said: "Jacob have I loved, but Esau have I hated"; "That the purpose of God according to election might stand, not of works, but of him that calleth"; just so in the case of those given to Christ, God prefers one to another, without any reference to the character which they will have after they are born.

But some man will say, "This is a frightful doctrine." That depends upon circumstances. It is not frightful to the true people of God.* But no matter how the doctrine may be regarded

---

* On the train from Cincinnati to Lexington, an old man took his seat be-

by you, here it is in the Bible. And the true Church of Christ in all ages has held this doctrine as one of the most precious in the Word of God. I shall not quote from our standard authors what they say on this subject, because you expect to find Presbyterian writers speaking strongly upon it; I shall simply quote from the Book of Common Prayer of the Episcopal Church, just to show you what those who are usually supposed to hold all strong doctrine in its mildest form say in regard to election:

"Predestination to life is the everlasting purpose of God, whereby (before the foundations of the world were laid) He hath constantly decreed by His counsel, secret to us, to deliver from curse and damnation those whom He hath chosen in Christ out of mankind, and to bring them by Christ to everlasting salvation as vessels made to honor." This is the statement of the doctrine. Now for the comment upon it. "As the godly consideration of Predestination, and our Election in Christ, is full of sweet, pleasant, and unspeakable comfort to godly persons, and such as feel in themselves the working of the Spirit of Christ, mortifying the works of the flesh and their earthly members, and drawing up their mind to high and heavenly things, as well because it does greatly establish and confirm their faith of eternal salvation to be enjoyed through Christ, as because it does fervently kindle their love toward God: So, for curious and carnal persons, lacking the Spirit of Christ, to have continually before their eyes the sentence of God's Predestination, is a most dangerous downfall, whereby the devil doth thrust them either into desperation, or into wretchedness of most unclean living, no less perilous than desperation." (Art. xvii.)

IV. And now the questions which have given a great many very serious concern are: If the number of elect is fixed and definite; if their very names have been recorded in a book

---

side me. In the course of a long conversation he said: "Sir, if the doctrine of Election is eliminated from the Bible, you might as well blot out all Scripture." He was unknown to me, nor did he know who I was. I afterward learned from him that he was a preacher in the Christian (Campbellite) Church.

opened before the foundation of the world, how am I to know whether *my* name is among the number? if it should happen not to be included among them, what is the use of my trying to secure salvation? and if it is among them, why should I give myself any uneasiness on the subject? To this I answer that the *whole* list of the elect is among "the secret things that belong unto the Lord our God." It is none of your concern who constitute the whole body of those given to Christ. "But those things which are revealed concerning them do belong to you and to your children forever." Now, the text reveals concerning the elect the only thing important for you to know. This is it, "*All that the Father hath given me shall come to me.*" To come to Christ is only another form of statement for faith in Christ. This is a perfectly clear matter of revelation—that the moment a man believes in Christ, that very moment it is proved, so far as he is concerned, that he is one of the elect. If you want to settle the question definitely * and prove that you are one of the elect, all you have to do is to accept Christ as your Saviour. *Just come to Him*, and the question of your being among the number of those "*given to Him*" is forever at rest. Here, you see, is the visible mark which Christ has fixed upon all who are chosen in Him; *they come to Him;* and He adds the assurance, "Him that cometh to Me (the Greek is more encouraging than the English; "*Him who is coming*"—Him who is on his way to me), I will in no wise cast out." That is to say, if you ever come to Christ, you are secure in His hands; for your coming only once proves that you are among the number given to Him, and He says: "Of all those that Thou hast given me *I have lost none*." † Mark

---

* *i. e.*, If you want to "make your calling and election sure" (2 Peter i. 10). On this passage Alford makes the following comment:

"Both *calling* and *election*, in as far as we look on them from the lower side, not able to penetrate into the counsels of God, are insecure unless established by holiness of life. In *His* foreknowledge and purpose there is no insecurity, no uncertainty; but in *our vision* and *apprehension* of them as they exist in and for us, much, until they are made secure in the way here pointed out; for doing these things, 'if ye do these things, ye shall never fall (stumble).'" It is not to the real security of the elect that Peter has reference, but to their own assurance of security.

† "None of them is lost, but the son of perdition," (John xvii. 12). The

the form of statement. He does not say, *None are lost*, though this is true, and He does say this in another place; but, "*I have lost none.*" As if He had said: "Their being kept in my hands is my work now, after they come to me. I hold them safe in my Almighty grasp. Mine they are, *I hold them fast*, and no man is able to pluck them out of my hands." We may without irreverence fancy the great Redeemer standing with the Book of Life in His hands, in which the names of those given Him have been written; and, as one after another emerges from the mass of unbelievers and professes faith in Him, we may imagine Him, as it were, checking off their names, and to the designation "elect of God," adding His "*own new name*," "*saved and redeemed by the blood of my everlasting covenant.*" So that the record will now stand, not only "*elect of God,*" but "*justified by faith,*" "*to whom there is now no condemnation.*"

V. Now you are prepared to see how this doctrine is adapted and intended by God to console His people in their hours of spiritual darkness and despondency; how in the language of the Episcopal symbol, which I have quoted, it is "full of sweet,

---

mistake which Arminians make in regard to this passage consists in supposing that this part of the verse contains an exception to what is declared in the words coming immediately before. A reference to the original will at once show their error. If "but" meant *except*, the Greek would read *plen tou huiou*, instead of "*ei me ho huios.*"

Compare with this passage Luke iv. 25: "Many widows were in Israel in the days of Elias, but unto none of them was Elias sent save unto Sarepta, a city of Sidon, unto a woman that was a widow." Again, verse 27: "Many lepers were in Israel in the time of Eliseus, the prophet; and none of them was cleansed saving Naaman the Syrian." Again, Revelation xxi. 27: "There shall in no wise enter into it anything that defileth, neither whatsoever worketh abomination, or maketh a lie; but they which are written in the Lamb's book of Life."

In each of these texts, the latter clause is not an exception to what is asserted in the former, but asserts a different fact. The following is plainly their meaning: "Many widows were in Israel in the days of Elias, but unto none of them was Elias sent; but (he was sent) to Sarepta, a city of Sidon, unto a woman that was a widow." "Many lepers were in Israel in the time of Eliseus, the prophet; and none of them was cleansed, but Naaman the Syrian" (was cleansed). "There shall in no wise enter into it anything that defileth, etc., but they (shall enter in) which are written in the Lamb's book of Life."

pleasant, and unspeakable comfort to godly persons." For it is often the case that the true believer walks in great darkness. Sometimes such is the state of his health that he is overwhelmed with religious despondency; or sometimes he is surprised into sin by Satan's getting the advantage of him; and, judging of his state of grace by his own feelings, he fears that he is no child of God. Well, he can look back and remember that once in his life he did really and truly come to Christ. He can have no doubt about that fact in his experience; he knows as well as he can know anything that *once* he did have real communion with his Redeemer. But now all is changed. He walks in darkness and sees no light. At such a time in his experience is it not a blessed thing to know that, although his feelings have changed, so that he has no sensible experience of divine love, Christ's love to him is unchangeable? to know that, having once really come to Christ, he is surely among the number whom He will never cast out? that "having loved His own which were in the world He loves them unto the end"? to be persuaded that "neither death, nor life, nor angels, nor principalities, nor powers, nor things present, nor things to come, nor height, nor depth, nor any other creature, shall be able to separate him from" Christ's love for him? This is the triumphant reply which he can make to Satan when he would tempt him to despair. This is the rejoinder he can make to his own accusing conscience. With the assurance that no one can "lay anything to the charge of God's elect" he can hurl defiance at hell and devils and all his accusers. God has justified him, and He who alone has the right to condemn him *has died for him*, and is at the right hand of God making present intercession for him.

It is said by some that the preaching of this doctrine will encourage men to sin, and lead to licentiousness. To this I have two answers to give, either of which by itself ought to be sufficient.

First: Christ was not afraid of this result when He taught this doctrine.

Second: I appeal to history. Do the men and the churches that hold this doctrine exhibit any laxity in their lives? Was

Paul a licentious, careless Christian? was Luther? was Calvin? was the saintly Toplady, who wrote the hymn, "Rock of Ages, cleft for me"? was John Knox? or Bunyan? or Chalmers? or Hall? Or the men who heard their preaching and believed their doctrines—were they men who continued in sin that grace might abound? Is Calvinistic Scotland—where the covenant of grace and the eternal election of God's people are the key-notes to all the theology they learn and the preaching they hear—is Calvinistic Scotland inhabited by a people who are distinguished by laxity of morals and looseness of life? Oh, no! It is too late in the history of the world to say that this doctrine leads to licentiousness; for wherever it has been enshrined in the heart of a people's piety, there you find the most moral, grave and pious people on earth. Why, what is it that has impressed upon the people of the Valley of Virginia characteristics, which make them a people peculiar for their hardy virtues, their indomitable courage, their purity of morals, their integrity of character? How are we to account for this *homogeneousness in virtue?* Partly by the fact that this valley was peopled so generally by a race of men who hold in its entireness the great and impregnable system of doctrine, for which their ancestors, the "Men of the Covenant," shed their blood at Bothwell Bridge. Were the men with whom Stonewall Jackson * prayed before going into battle, the men of whom Jackson was the type and leader, the "patient infantry," behind whom Bee commanded his fleeing battalions to rally—were they men of dissolute or immoral lives? "Men do not gather grapes of thorns, or figs of thistles." My brethren, when these great doctrines shall lose their hold on the heart of the Presbyterian people of this country, you may write "Ichabod" on their banners, for their glory will have departed.

But this doctrine is not only a source of great peace and comfort to the believer in his hours of spiritual darkness and desertion; it is a panacea for all the ills of life. For it is a part of the doctrine that "all things work together for the good of those" who are the elect of God. It banishes the word calamity

---

* This sermon was preached to the church in Lexington, Virginia, in which Stonewall Jackson had been an elder.

from their vocabulary. Nothing can be to them a disaster. The fire, the storm, the earthquake, the pestilence, and the famine; war, poverty, sickness, and death; the loss of friends, the destruction of property, although to the eye of sense they may seem evils, can be to them productive only of good. "All things work together for good to them that love God, to them who are the called according to His purpose." Nothing can really harm them. All holy angels are commissioned to be their ministering spirits: all devils are commanded, "Touch not mine anointed and do them no harm." All things are theirs; the world, life, death, things present and things to come; all are theirs, because they are Christ's and Christ is God's. Do you not see that the man who holds this truth in his heart is really superior to all the ills of life? How is it possible to disturb the peace of that man who knows upon the authority of God that all the events of his life are ordered for his good, and that he himself is safe in the arms of Jesus? How is it possible to make that man unhappy who persists in construing every dispensation of Providence as an evidence of the divine favor? How can you ruffle the repose of a man whose faith is a talisman by which he transmutes everything into a blessing bestowed by paternal love? Oh! whatever else you relinquish, never give up your faith in this great doctrine which you receive direct from the Bible, and which your ancestors cherished with passionate devotion. Think of the loving-kindness of your God now in the midst of His temple. "Walk about Zion, and go round about her, tell the towers thereof. Mark ye well her bulwarks; consider her palaces; that ye may tell it to the generation following. For this God is our God forever and ever: He will be our guide even unto death."

II.

GOD'S SOVEREIGNTY.

"The Lord reigneth; let the earth rejoice."—Ps. xcvii. 1.
"The Lord reigneth; let the people tremble."—Ps. xcix. 1.

THESE two texts teach the same doctrine; but from the doctrine two opposite lessons are derived,—a fact which illustrates the principle that the same truth when looked at from different points of view, is adapted to produce very different effects in the mind of the beholder.

The doctrine of these texts is the *Sovereignty of God*. In view of this Sovereignty the earth is called to rejoice and to fear.

"The Lord reigneth; let the earth rejoice"; "let the people tremble."

I shall first explain the doctrine, and then show why it may be the occasion of joy and of fear.

"The Lord reigneth" is an ascription of unlimited dominion to Jehovah. If there were one spot in the vast universe which is free from His control; if there were but one atom floating in the far-off realms of space which is not pervaded by His presence and moved by His finger, it would be impossible to say with truth, "The Lord reigneth." This doctrine of absolute and universal dominion of God is affirmed more explicitly in other passages, which entering into minuter detail describe the empire of God as extending through every portion of the universe.

I. What is the nature of this dominion? Is it simply a *physical* control? That is, does God, in the simple exercise of His omnipotence, work His will only in *things* He has made? Is it general, or is it also special? Does it extend to thoughts as well as to things? Does it embrace men and angels, as well as worlds and sidereal systems? Is it a dominion of right only, or is it also a dominion of power? That is, has God only a moral right to govern His universe? or does He invariably secure the accomplishment of His will?

When all these questions come to be answered by different schools of theology, you will find some disposed to deny some of the logical consequences of the general doctrine that the Lord reigneth.

Without mentioning any of the erroneous views which men have advocated in reply to these and similar questions, I proceed to unfold the true Scriptural doctrine in regard to the Sovereignty of God.

Two elements are contained in the Sovereignty of God: *unlimited power* and *absolute authority*.

The power of God is called His omnipotence—His strength to accomplish any of His purposes. His sovereignty includes not only this, but also His moral right to exercise His power. The first is, so to speak, His physical power; the second is His moral power or authority. The distinction is intelligible, because it is one constantly recognized in human relationships between the governor and the governed. Now, as it is essential to the stability of every human government that *power* and *authority* shall be vested in the same person in order to constitute him *as* a sovereign; so we must concede to God infinite power and absolute moral right, in order to conceive of Him as the sovereign of the universe. If power without right rules over a kingdom, we call it usurpation. If legitimate authority without power to enforce its claims undertakes to rule a kingdom, anarchy must follow. In the dominion of God, in which there can be neither usurpation nor anarchy, He sits sovereign in virtue of infinite power and absolute authority concentred in Him.

A third element in the Sovereignty of God is evolved in answer to the question, "According to what law does God exercise His power and authority?" If God is controlled in the exercise of His power by any considerations that lie outside of Himself, the Psalmist could never have said: "The Lord reigneth." Now the Apostle Paul in so many words affirms that God works "all things after the counsel of His own will"; *i. e.*, that He is *self-determined*.

More specifically, the *work of creation* is ascribed to His sovereign pleasure. "Thou hast created all things, and for Thy pleasure they are and were created." "The Lord made all things for Himself." So also the work of redemption and the publication of the Gospel into the world, are ascribed to the same motive; as the Apostle tells us in the Epistle to the Ephesians: "Having predestinated us unto the adoption of children by Jesus Christ according to the good pleasure of His will"; "having made known unto us the mystery of His will, according to His good pleasure which He purposed in Himself."

He created the world just because He chose to create it; He preserves it just because He chooses to preserve it; and He redeems His people just because He chooses to redeem them. "For of Him, and by Him, and through Him are all things."

The Sovereignty of God, then, consists in His infinite power and right to execute a will determined solely by His good pleasure.

II. Who and what are the subjects of God's dominion? The Scriptures say "all things." Does this mean only the material universe, or does it include rational creatures? The Scriptures are full of assertions of God's control as reaching to *all* the creatures He has made. If this is so, of course His dominion extends over the whole race of men, over all angels and over all worlds.

Now, while it is easy enough to believe that all physical nature is under His supreme control, so that He orders the movements of every atom and the revolution of every orb, some minds find it very hard to understand His sovereignty in reference to man. The difficulty may be stated thus. Inanimate nature is passive, incapable of resisting the plastic hand of its maker. But in creating man, God made a being endowed with a free will of his own; and when this free being fell from his first estate, in which his will was always coincident with the Divine will, he, retaining his freedom of will, instead of delighting to do the will of God, now delights in frustrating it and refusing to obey it. Thus it would seem that by endowing man with free agency, God has conferred upon the creature the power of limiting His absolute sovereignty—first, by doing what is contrary to His will; and secondly, by refusing to do what He enjoins. If it is true that men in the exercise of their free agency can frustrate the Divine will, then whatever may be God's *authority*, He cannot secure the accomplishment of *all* His will. He has made a machine that has gotten away from Him so that He cannot control it.

Now, although this is a very difficult problem, one that has never been solved, I ask your attention to the following considerations, which, although they do not solve the problem, may lead you to believe the doctrine of God's absolute sovereignty over the free wills of His creatures.

1. If you deny this doctrine, you are compelled to deny the explicit statements of God's Word. "He turneth the king's heart as the rivers of water are turned." "It is God that worketh in you, both to will and to do of His own good pleasure."

2. To deny the free agency of man is equally opposed to Scripture and to the consciousness of the whole human race. No amount of argument to the contrary could convince any human being that in all his conduct he does not act freely.

3. But why should men believe the latter proposition and reject the former? When both truths are taught in the Word of God, and stand on the same authority, why not receive them both as true?

The doubter is ready with the answer. He cannot see how these propositions can be made to agree with each other.

I have somewhere read that among the many wonderful endowments of Napoleon Bonaparte, he possessed an extraordinary power of vision, so that he could discern objects that were visible to ordinary eyes only with the aid of the telescope. On one occasion, while discussing with his marshals the plan of a campaign from which he expected most brilliant results, they confessed themselves unable to *see* how his plans could be executed. He stepped to the window, and pointing to the planet Jupiter, he said, "Do you see the four satellites of that planet?" "No," they replied. "But," said he, "I see them." Thus it is with us short-sighted men. God reveals truths in His Word which we find it hard to reconcile; and in opposition to the clearest teachings of His Word, we dare to doubt, because we, the pigmy insects of a moment, cannot *see* how they can be made to harmonize. It may be our duty to believe some things that we cannot see. Since God has said so, it is one's duty to believe that He is a Sovereign and man a free agent, although we cannot see how these things consist with each other. His thoughts are not as our thoughts. As the heavens are higher than the earth, so are His thoughts higher than our thoughts.

III. The Sovereignty of God being clearly taught in Scripture, the question is pertinent, How does God manifest or exhibit it?

I answer—

1. By the giving of a *Law*, God claims to be a great king: and by giving the law to all His creatures without any exception, He proclaims Himself a universal King—King of kings.

2. The arbitrary character of some of God's laws is a claim of sovereign authority. Some of God's laws are founded in the nature of things; such, for example, as the obligation to love Him and to worship Him, and to love our fellow-men and to do them no harm; but there are others which have no such natural congruity, and are founded on no other ground than that so He wills it. The prohibition to Adam to eat of the fruit of a certain tree, the law of the Sabbath, the Jewish ceremonial law, were arbitrary in their nature, and were striking exhibitions of God's sovereignty.

3. The abrogation of some of the laws He has given; *e. g.*, the revoking of the ceremonial law, or the change in the method of His dealing with mankind by the substitution of the Covenant of Grace for the Covenant of Works, is one of the highest displays of His Sovereignty.

4. God manifests His Sovereignty by punishing every transgression of His law. In human governments some criminals escape punishment. This is a sign of a weak government. But

in the Divine government all sin is punished; and this proves it to be infinite and absolute.

5. God manifests His Sovereignty in His Providential government of men. Why does He make one rich and another poor; one robust, another invalid; one white, another black; one free and another a slave; one wise and another foolish; one an American and another a Hottentot? Why does He give you the Gospel and withhold it from the Bushmen? Are you any better by nature than the uncivilized heathen? Why then? Simply because He is a Sovereign and does whatsoever He chooses. All the inequalities among men and among nations, all calamities and all prosperity, all promotion and all dishonor, all the vicissitudes of human life, must be referred to the "good pleasure" of God, and are exhibitions of His Sovereignty.

6. The Sovereignty of God was most conspicuously displayed in His sending His Son into the world for the salvation of sinners. Nobody will dare affirm that God was compelled to do this. He might, if He had chosen, have left us to perish in our sins. Or if we suppose that something in the character of God or in the claims of the Divine glory made it necessary for Him to make some illustrious display to the intelligent universe of His mercy, why did He select fallen men instead of fallen angels as the objects of His mercy? Herein was a striking exhibition of His sovereign good pleasure.

7. The Sovereignty of God is manifested in the fact that only some men are chosen to be saved in Christ, while others are suffered to perish. This predestination of some men to eternal life is the *most* distinguished manifestation of the Sovereignty of God. Just here I fancy I hear an objector lift up his voice in protest. He says, "I do not deny the general doctrine of God's Sovereignty; but I must dissent from this particular aspect in which you now present it." In short, he holds to God's Sovereignty in everything but the matter of man's salvation. He cannot *see* how sovereignty in election can be reconciled with God's impartiality. Neither do we. I agree with him at once. I admit that for God to choose from among guilty beings, all equally ill-deserving, some to everlasting life, while He passes others by, is a

striking exhibition of *partiality;* and I claim for God, *as sovereign,* the right *to be partial.* "But," says the objector, consulting the dictionary, "partiality is a preference springing from the *will* and *affections* rather than from a sense of *justice.*" Precisely so. The election of God's people is an act of preference springing from His own will and from His own good pleasure, without any reference to the claims of justice, which concludes all alike under condemnation. "But then," says the objector, "this discrimination is unjust." To this I reply, It would be unjust in a *judge,* but not in a sovereign. A judge could not condemn one criminal while he suffered another equally guilty to escape. But this very thing a *sovereign* may do, and does, without being called in question. And so may God, the great Sovereign, choose some whom He intends to save, while He leaves others to their just condemnation. "But then," says the objector, "the ends of *justice* are defeated if only one offender goes free." True, the ends of justice would be defeated if any solitary transgression of the law of God goes unpunished. How, then, does God vindicate His justice, while He thus exercises His sovereignty? I answer, By providing an atonement, a sacrifice, a fulfiller of the law, both as to its precepts and penalty, to stand in place of His elect ones, in the person of Jesus Christ our Lord. When God as Sovereign elected some unto life, He did not forget His character as judge; the solemn demands of justice were too sacred for even Him, the Sovereign, to set the law aside, (as is done in every act of executive clemency among men); He still required that the penalty of His law should be paid, if not by the guilty themselves, in the person of His own dear Son. And thus the Sovereignty of God is further illustrated by His setting aside the old covenant of works, the terms of which were, "Do this and live," and putting in its stead the covenant of grace, the terms of which are, "Believe on Christ and live."

Thus, you see, God, as Sovereign, chooses from among guilty men some whom He has determined to save; as Sovereign, changes the covenant of works for a covenant of grace, (by which arrangement alone the salvation of any can be made possible), in order that He may save His elect ones: as Sovereign, accepts the work of Christ in their behalf in place of their obedience and punishment; and then, as *Judge*, justifies all who believe in Jesus;—thus showing to all men and all angels and all devils how God the Judge may be just and yet a justifier of the ungodly. And now, "Who shall lay anything to the charge of God's elect?" God has justified them. "Who is he that condemneth?" But the objector answers, "There is no dispute between us as to the ground of sinners' justification; but we differ as to the ground of God's election of the sinner to justification." The objector is bound to admit that the Scriptures speak of *an election;* but he says God elects men because He foresees that some will believe on Christ and become holy, while others will reject Christ and remain impenitent. This is a very plausible and very intelligible explanation of the matter; but it is liable to the fatal objection that there is not one line of Scripture to support it, and numberless Scriptures that deny it. The Scriptures have a great deal to say about faith as the *result* of election; of holiness as the *consequence* of election; but never in a single instance of the relation as reversed. The same thing cannot be the cause and the effect of some other thing. Faith and holiness cannot be the foreseen cause of our election by God and the result of that election. The one surely must precede the other. And when the Scriptures say, "According as He hath chosen us in Christ before the foundation of the world in order that we should be holy," they cannot mean that He has chosen us *because He foresaw that* we would be holy. If this was what the Apostle *meant,* why did he not say so? Why does he everywhere say just the opposite? Why does he say, "hath predestinated us that we should be holy," "that we should be conformed to the image of His Son," "that we should be to the praise of His glory"? Why does he, guarding against this very error, say, "not of works, *lest any man should* boast," "that the purpose of God according to election might stand, not of works, but of Him that calleth"? What does the Apostle mean when he says, "Whom He did foreknow, He also did predestinate *to be* conformed to the image of His Son"; "Moreover, whom He did predestinate, them He also called, and whom He called, them He also justified; and whom He justified, them He also glorified"? Is the daylight the cause of the sun? or is the sun the cause of daylight? Now faith and holiness are the *result* of election, just as day is the result of the rising sun.

The objector now shifts his ground and says: "But faith and good works are the conditions of salvation, and God certainly saves some and condemns others, because some believe and others do not." To this I reply, True, but why do some believe and others reject Christ? He will reply: "Because God not only gives the means of grace, but accompanies them by the efficiency of His Spirit." I press the question: "But why does He give the influences of His Spirit to some and not to all?" He will reply: "Because He has decreed by grace to prepare men for glory." But why decree to prepare some and not all? And he must at last admit that it is all because of God's good pleasure; and if at last driven to the wall, he is still ready to rebel against the sovereignty of God, I can go no farther in argument, but must adopt the language of Paul in his argument with this very objector and say: "Nay, but oh! man, who art thou that repliest against God? Shall the thing formed say to him that formed it, Why hast thou made me thus? Hath not the potter power over the clay, of the same lump to make one vessel unto honor, and another unto dishonor?" Oh! my hearer! it is only in moments of rebellion against God that men do thus reply against Him. We know with the certainty of intuition that we are as clay in the hands of the potter, and when we ask, Why was I made the subject of converting grace? Why did the Spirit strive with me and not with them? your hearts will acknowledge the Sovereignty of God, and you will say: "Because He hath mercy on whom He will have mercy, and whom He will He hardeneth." And when you sit at the table of the Lord, you must sometimes inquire:

> "Lord, why am I a guest?
> Why was I made to hear Thy voice
> And enter while there's room,
> While thousands make a wretched choice,
> And rather starve than come?"

And your hearts must respond:

> " 'Twas the same love that spread the feast
> That sweetly forced us in ;
> Else we had still refused to taste,
> And perished in our sin."

Yes! it is all of sovereign grace. "It is not of him that willeth nor of him that runneth; but of God that showeth mercy." And therefore in the salvation of men, God makes the most signal display of His Sovereignty.

IV. I have left but little time for showing why the Sovereignty of God should be the occasion of rejoicing to His people and of trembling to His enemies. In conclusion I remark that God's Sovereignty should make us rejoice, because it is exercised in perfect harmony with infinite goodness, wisdom, and love. Amidst our perplexities, cares, sorrows, disappointments, and bereavements, how sustaining, how exhilarating the reflection that the Lord reigneth! In the dark days of the Reformation, Luther stayed his soul on this great doctrine. He said: "The Lord reigneth, and I know He loves His Church better than I love it; and why should I fear that He will not take care of it? All the dispensations of God's providence and grace are only so many straightforward steps to the accomplishment of good for us. Like the wheels and bands in a great machine, some of which are turning one way, some another; some going up and some going down, yet all contributing to produce the perfect result; so all things in the great machinery of Providence are co-operating to accomplish God's purposes of good to His people. What a source of rejoicing to know that He reigns over all!"

Some of you do rejoice that you have such a Sovereign. But I fear there are some here who are saying, I do not like this doctrine. It presents God in such a terrible aspect to me, that instead of winning my love, it makes me hate God. Well, you know the Apostle says: "The carnal mind is enmity against God." If this is the effect of the doctrine on your heart, it only proves that you have that carnal mind that hates the God of the Bible. If the doctrine of God's Sovereignty is terrible to you, don't you see that this proves the doctrine true? for the Psalmist says: "The Lord reigneth, *let* the people *tremble*." "Ah!" you say, "we could rejoice in the Sovereignty of God, if we were only good; but we are wicked; and as such we cannot delight in the thought that we are in the hands of a sovereign God." Well, then, why remain wicked? Why not be good? Why not make friends with this Almighty Sovereign? Why not lay hold upon His strength, and be at peace with Him?

I appreciate the full force of the reply which I know is in your minds. You are saying, How can we change our hearts and love God, and accept Jesus Christ as our Saviour, if it is true, as you just now told us, that God sovereignly bestows the grace of faith, and that it is not of him that willeth nor of him that runneth, but of God that showeth mercy? Well, my dear friend, I cannot help it; I cannot help you out of the terrible difficulty, and it is for this very reason that you are helpless in the hands of a sovereign God, that you have need to tremble. Your only help is to be found in God himself. If you will only bow before His Sovereignty, and, like the publican, cast yourself on His mercy, He will graciously incline His ear to you and grant you His converting grace that your soul may live. Shall I give you the words wherewith you may approach Him in prayer? Come to Him with language like this:

> Pass me not, O gracious Father,
>   Sinful though my heart may be;
> Thou might'st curse me, but the rather
>   Let Thy mercy light on me,
>   Even me.
>
> Pass me not, O tender Saviour,
>   Let me love and cling to Thee;
> I am longing for Thy favor,
>   When Thou comest, call for me,
>   Even me.
>
> Pass me not, O mighty Spirit,
>   Thou canst make the blind to see;
> Witnesser of Jesus' merit,
>   Speak the word of power to me,
>   Even me.
>
> Love of God, so pure and changeless,
>   Blood of God, so rich and free,
> Grace of God, so strong and boundless,
>   Magnify them all in me,
>   Even me.

III.

REGENERATION.

"Verily, verily, I say unto thee, Except a man be born again, he cannot see the kingdom of God."—John iii. 3.

There is a wonderful harmony between all the doctrines of a sound system of theology. It is no insignificant proof of the truth of any science that all its doctrines are consistent with each other, and cohere in one compact harmonious whole. The Scriptures contain religious truths, which being arranged in scientific form, constitute what is called a system of theology. If any one of these great truths or doctrines is omitted, the whole system falls to pieces, just as an arch tumbles down if one of the bricks is taken out.

The text contains one of the great truths which is essential to any correct theory of the plan of redemption,—viz.: the necessity of the "new birth." But this doctrine would be utterly unintelligible and incredible were it not that we learn from the Scriptures another doctrine—viz.: the depravity of the whole human race. Deny this doctrine, and the doctrine of the necessity of regeneration, or being born again, is an absurdity. Hence those who teach that infants are born innocent and perfect, and fall into sin simply through the force of example, are perfectly consistent in teaching that the new birth of which the text speaks is simply a reformation of life and habit. Those who teach this error hold that this result is brought about by "moral suasion"; *i. e.*, a persuading of the sinner to abandon the error of his way.

I should despair of convincing any man that he must be born again in order to see the kingdom of God, who is not persuaded of the total depravity of human nature. I shall not undertake to show that this is the doctrine of the Bible. David says: "Behold, I was shapen in iniquity, and in sin did my mother conceive me." "The wicked are estranged from the womb; they go astray as soon as they be born." The doctrine pervades the whole Bible. It is one of the constructive ideas of inspiration, which are not so much here, or there, as everywhere. It is like the blood in the human body. Draw it out of the system and you may as well bury the system in the grave. The doctrine reverberates from the first chapter in Genesis to the last in the Revelation. Expunge it, and you may as well vacate the office of the Holy Ghost in the work of man's redemption.

If any holy being were asked, what is the distinctive characteristic of man? his answer would be, "Sin." It is not weakness, it is not misfortune, it is not suffering, it is not death; it is sin. And indeed, if there is one truth on which the mind of the whole human race is agreed, it is the fact of depravity and sin, and the necessity of a radical change in his nature to fit man for the presence of God.

Assuming as conceded the depravity of all men without exception, I desire now to enforce the doctrine of the text.

What is regeneration? It is a work done in a man by the Spirit of God. It differs from justification in this, that the latter is done only *for* a man, and changes his state in relation to God's law. Regeneration is not a change in relations, but a change in the man himself; it gives him a new character.

As the change is in the soul, and not in the body, it is perfectly clear that no mechanical operation performed on the body can produce this change. Many persons have a vague idea that in some mysterious way baptism can secure this result. But our Lord distinctly teaches that a man must be born of "water *and* the Spirit."

There is one aspect of this truth which is of great practical value. Let me illustrate it by the case of the converted drunkard. Before his conversion he was the victim of two diseases: one a corrupt and depraved heart; the other, a disordered bodily condition, brought about by long intemperate indulgence. Now when the Spirit of God entered his soul and changed his spiritual nature, this mighty work did not cure his diseased body. He has the same insatiable longings for the intoxicating bowl which he had before his conversion. If now, by the grace of God, he has the strength to persevere in habits of sobriety, his body will in the end regain its healthful tone, and he will become a sober man. But the cure of the nervous disorder is not the direct work of the Spirit; it is the result of his being "strengthened with all might by the Spirit in the inner man." If, however, at any time the nervous disorder should again conquer the regenerate nature, and the man should be overtaken in his old fault, this is no decisive proof that he is not a true child of God. I make this remark not to encourage any one to dally with temptation, but to encourage any who may have fallen back into a vicious habit from which he once was rescued, and who now fears that God has cut him off, to rise up again and with humble reliance on Divine grace to fight his old enemy.

Again, regeneration does not change the faculties or susceptibilities of the soul. The man loves, desires, hopes, fears, rejoices, grieves, proposes, and wills just the same as before his change of heart: but these emotions, passions, and purposes are now fixed on new objects. Hence, the Apostle says to the Thessalonians: "The Lord direct your hearts into the love of God." They had been worshippers of idols and they had "turned to God from idols to serve the living and true God." The act of worship was the same, but it was now directed to God.

In reply, therefore, to the question: What is regeneration? I say that it is a real, mighty, miraculous renovation of the soul by the direct agency of the Spirit of God, which reverses the whole current and bent of the affections, desires, and purposes, so that the man who experiences it may say, ' Old things have passed away; behold, all things have become new."

The text declares that without this change no man can see the kingdom of God. There are only two destinations in the great future which awaits you beyond the grave. Exclusion from the kingdom of God implies inclusion in the kingdom of Satan. "Except a man be born again, he cannot see the kingdom of God."

I think the reason why the fulfilment of this condition is indispensable can be made apparent to any reasonable mind.

1. Admittance into heaven is an immediate introduction into the presence of the Holy One, to hold familiar intercourse with Him, to attend upon His court, and to serve Him continually. To be qualified for this near and intimate association with Him who is of purer eyes than to behold iniquity, the man must be not only a pardoned sinner, but must be personally holy in character, presenting nothing offensive to the eye of the divine holiness. Hence David says, "Lord, who shall abide in Thy tabernacle? Who shall dwell in Thy holy hill? He that hath clean hands and a pure heart." "For Thou art not a God that hath pleasure in wickedness; neither shall evil dwell with Thee; the foolish shall not stand in Thy sight." The Apostle says that "the carnal heart," that is, the unregenerate man, "is enmity against God, and is not subject to the law of God, neither indeed can be." Think of the manifest incongruity of the Divine Being surrounding His throne with those who hate Him and despise His government, and you will readily admit that "except a man be born again, he cannot see the kingdom of God." "Holiness becometh Thy house, O Lord, forever"; "and there shall in no wise enter into it anything that defileth, neither whatsoever worketh abomination, or maketh a lie."

2. But we are forced to the same conclusion by considering the character of the unregenerate man and the character of the society in heaven. The kingdom of God is peopled by perfectly holy beings. Their constant occupations are such as are congenial to pure and holy spirits. An unregenerate man is not a fit associate for those holy intelligences that stand around the throne. Let me illustrate. Here is a family reared amid the kindliest influences. It is composed of a father, who is the type of everything noble, refined, and elevated; a mother, the model of all that is pure and beautiful in woman; daughters that are lovely beyond their sex, just budding into womanhood, and sons who have been kept unspotted from the world.

On the other hand, here is a base, corrupt, unprincipled libertine; a man without education, culture, or refinement; with low tastes and depraved appetites. Now, why is he excluded from this family circle? Manifestly, because he is not a fit associate for the elevated and good. Why does he not desire or seek to enter there? Simply because he has no taste for the society he would meet within the precincts of that Christian home. Why would he be miserable if compelled to enter that household as an inmate, and engage in the employments of its members? Simply because he could take no pleasure in the pursuits that engage the refined, the elevated, and the good.

Now heaven is a holy place, and those who dwell there delight in holiness. The angels are "holy angels." Glorified saints are said to be as the angels of God in heaven. Is an unrenewed, depraved man a fit associate for them? Would they not turn their backs on him, and, fleeing from his presence, leave him in the solitude of his own vileness?

These holy angels and spirits of just men made perfect are constantly engaged in acts of adoration, in studying the perfections of God, in the exercise and expression of supreme love to God, in the vocal utterance of His praises. How can a man whose heart is unholy engage in these services? If he does not delight to do the will of God here, will he delight to do it there? If he does not take pleasure in the study of God here, will he take any more pleasure in the study of His perfections there? If his language now is, "Depart from me, for I desire not the knowledge of thy ways," can such a temper be fit for heaven, where nothing but thoughts of God will fill the minds of glorified spirits? Then, again, how can he engage in the worship which constitutes so large a part of the employment of saints and angels? What is the angels' song? "Holy! holy! holy! Lord God of Hosts." Can the corrupt, depraved man join in this chorus? What is the song of the saints? "Hallelujah! Salvation, and glory, and honor, and power unto the Lord our God! Hallelujah! For the Lord God omnipotent reigneth." How can the heart that hates God echo this hallelujah? The tongue can never be tuned to praise while the heart is evil. God must be glorified in us before He can be glorified by us.

Don't you see that the unrenewed man would be miserable in

heaven if forced to enter there? Is he not unhappy in the society of the pure and holy here on earth? Why should he be happy in their society hereafter? Is not the occupation of the pious a weariness to him here? Why should it be any more agreeable to him there? Is not the Sabbath as a day of holy rest an object of aversion to him? How then will he delight in the eternal Sabbath? He would be miserable in heaven; for heaven consists in nearness to God and in the beatific visions of His Son. Could *he* delight in nearness to God who all his life has lived without God, or be happy in looking upon Jesus Christ who all his life turned his back on Christ? No! no! He would be wretched in heaven. Chain him to the foot of the Eternal Throne, and he would cower beneath the gaze of the Holy One. Bind him with fetters to the very right hand of Him in whose presence is fullness of joy and pleasures for evermore, and he would shriek in agony and call on rocks and mountains to fall on him and hide him from the face of Him that sitteth on the throne. That burning eye which looks on sin with abhorrence would blanch his cheek with terror; that awful frown would kindle hell in his bosom, and he would pray to be released from imprisonment in the presence of a holy God, that he might flee from the brightness of His glory as darkness flees before the rising sun. "Verily, verily, I say unto you, Except a man be born again, he cannot see the kingdom of God."

One thought more and I have done. Hell is a place of misery. And one of the bitterest drops in the cup of woe is, that, while the lost soul longs after the enjoyment of sensual delights, there will be a total privation of them. Heaven is the perfect gratification of holy tastes which have begun to be cultivated on earth. Does the drunkard expect that heaven will afford him the excitement of the intoxicating cup; or the libertine that it will be a Mohammedan paradise; or the covetous man that it will be a place for him to buy and sell and get gain? Certainly not. Yet they all hope in some way to be finally happy. But happiness consists in the satisfaction of the desires and appetites, in the gratification of the tastes and propensities of the soul. They know full well that heaven cannot gratify these sensual and sordid tastes and desires. Is it not true that even those who do not admit the necessity of regeneration do in fact expect in some mysterious way to be so changed at death that heaven will be a place of happiness even for them? And what is this expectation but an unconscious affirmation of the doctrine of the text, "Ye must be born again"? Ye must be changed in your tastes, desires, and character before ye can enjoy the kingdom of God. Oh! my hearer, abandon the unfounded hope that at death you will undergo any such change as will make you "meet to be a partaker of the inheritance of the saints in light." There is no sanctifying power in death. "As the tree falleth, so shall it lie." "He that is unjust will be unjust still; he that is filthy will be filthy still; he that is righteous will be righteous still; and he that is holy will be holy still." If you would see the kingdom of God you must be born again this side of the grave; for "except a man (a *man*, not a disembodied spirit,) be born again, he cannot see the kingdom of God."

IV.

FAITH.

"Precious faith."—2 Pet. i. 1.

In this discourse I shall answer two questions:
First, What is Faith?
Second, Why does the Apostle call it precious?

I. The word faith is used in several distinct senses in the Scriptures. Sometimes, it means simple assent to the truth of the Bible; sometimes, a temporary impression in regard to God and His love; sometimes, the power to work miracles; while "*the faith*" means the whole summary of Christian doctrine.

The text has reference to none of these, but to that specific act of the soul by which a sinner is justified at the bar of God on the ground of the righteousness of Christ imputed to him, and which to distinguish it from all other acts of the soul, is called "saving faith."

1. Saving faith differs from every other act of the soul, in that while each of the others may be produced or caused by natural means, it is the result of *supernatural* inworking of the Holy Ghost, mysteriously accompanying the truth with His own powerful demonstration, and divinely convincing it of the excellence, beauty, and all-sufficiency of Jesus Christ.

2. Saving faith differs from every other act of the soul, in that while one is simply an act of the intellect assenting to truth, and another, a state of the emotions, *it* is the act of the intellect, the heart, and the will—the act of the whole soul with all its powers harmoniously discharging their appropriate functions in relation to the object.

3. Saving faith differs from all those acts of the soul sometimes mistaken for it by a diversity as to the object on which it terminates. Thus, he who believes that the Scriptures are true, simply assents to a logical proposition; he who thinks he is in a state of peace because he has felt so happy in attending upon exciting religious services, simply believes a proposition which may or may not be true. The object upon which saving faith terminates, is not a historical fact, nor a proposition nor a form of words, but a *person*, a living being, to whom we may say, "I believe Thy word, I approve Thy law, I embrace Thy precious promises, because Thou hast spoken the word, Thou hast enacted the law, Thou hast uttered the promises; I love Thee, because Thou hast loved me; I give myself to Thee, because Thou hast given Thyself for me; I cast myself upon Thine everlasting arms, for in the Lord Jehovah is everlasting strength; I trust my life, my soul, my all to Thee forever: for I know whom I have believed, and am persuaded that He is able to keep what I have committed to Him against that day."

The expressions used in Scripture to describe the exercise of faith show that it is something very different from simple belief in a proposition.

"Have faith in God," "Believe in the Lord Jesus Christ," "Look unto Me," "Receiving Christ," "Eating of Him," "Coming to Him," "Embracing Him," "Fleeing unto Him," "Laying hold of Him,"—all clearly show that Faith is differentiated from all acts of belief by involving as its essential element *confidence in a person*, as distinguished from belief in a truth embodied in words.

Now we may have confidence in a human as well as in a Divine person. Hence there is a human faith and a Divine faith.

When a client commits a cause to an advocate and relies on his professional skill for a favorable verdict, there is something different from mere *belief;* and this "something" is *faith*—faith terminating on a *person* as its object.

An American man-of-war was once lying becalmed in the Mediterranean. The son of the captain, a playful boy, amused himself daily by climbing the rigging. One day, with the thoughtlessness of childhood, he ascended to the very top of the mainmast, and stood upon the giddy summit swaying to and fro with the gently-heaving billow. His father saw him from the deck, and knowing from experience that it would be impossible for him to stoop down from his perilous perch to regain his hold upon the mast, without falling headlong to the deck, he shouted to him, "JUMP! I command you, *jump into the water!*" The boy looked down to assure himself that it was his father that spoke, and then, with an instantaneous bound, he leaped, cleared the deck, plunged into the sea, and was saved. Here was something different from belief. It was faith manifesting itself in prompt obedience. Precisely the same act of the soul terminating on God is that Divine faith of which the Bible speaks. Faith in the last analysis is the act of confiding in a person;—human, when the person is a man; divine, when the person is God.

This explanation of faith will enable you to understand the 11th chapter of Hebrews—in which faith is represented as underlying all those heroic doings and sufferings of the Old Testament saints, "of whom the world was not worthy." "By faith, Abel offered a more acceptable sacrifice than Cain; by faith, Enoch was translated; by faith, Noah built an ark; by faith, Abraham obeyed, and went from his own land, not knowing whither he went; by faith, he offered up Isaac; by faith, Moses refused to be called the son of Pharaoh's daughter; by faith, the Israelites passed through the Red Sea; by faith, heroes, kings, and prophets subdued kingdoms, wrought righteousness, obtained promises, stopped the mouths of lions, quenched the violence of fire, escaped the edge of the sword, out of weakness were made strong, waxed valiant in fight, turned to flight the armies of the aliens; by faith, women received their dead raised to life again; and others were tortured, not accepting deliverance. And others had trial of cruel mockings and scourgings, yea, moreover, of bonds and imprisonment. They were stoned, they were sawn asunder, were tempted, were slain with the sword; they wandered about in sheep-skins and goat-skins, being destitute, afflicted, tormented; they wandered in deserts and mountains, and in dens and caves of the earth."

Regarding faith as a principle implanted in the soul by the Holy Spirit, the essence of which is confidence in a person, we can see how it is the germ of the many developments ascribed to it by the Apostle in the foregoing enumeration of Faith's conflicts and victories. This we could not understand, if faith were merely a belief of truth. So that I am justified in saying that Faith is not belief, but it is a cause of which belief is only one of the many effects:—the root out of which belief and many other graces grow.

You believe one man's statement, because you have confidence in the man himself; you disbelieve another's, because you lack confidence in the man himself. And so the Christian believes the Word of God, because he has confidence in God—the personal God—the God of Abraham, of Isaac, and of Jacob.

Now, as any fundamental principle in the soul makes itself known in various ways;—as benevolence, for example, may wear a thousand smiling semblances; so faith exhibits itself outwardly in various forms—sometimes by believing the truth, because it is revealed by God; sometimes by relying on His promises; sometimes by prompt obedience to His commands; sometimes by filial love and reverence; sometimes by acceptance of Jesus Christ as a Saviour. Faith is confidence in God, in all His offices, as Creator, Preserver, and Benefactor; or as Moral Governor, Redeemer, and Sanctifier. And justifying, or saving, faith is that specific act of the soul, in which, fixing upon God, the Redeemer, as its object, it flees to His cross, trusts to His righteousness, bows to His will, and clings to His everlasting arm.

II. I come now to the second question I propose to answer: Why does the Apostle Peter call faith " precious " ?

1. Because it cannot be obtained in the way other valuable acquisitions are made. Gold cannot buy it. Labor will not procure it. Birth, talents, learning, will not acquire it. It is precious, because nothing which has a tangible value in this world

can be exchanged for it. By grace ye are saved through faith, and that not of yourselves, it is the GIFT of God.

Let me illustrate. A great banquet has been provided through the munificence of a merchant prince. The invitations cost nothing to those who receive them. They cannot be purchased with money. So precious are they, that if they could be bought, hundreds would pour out gold for the privilege of admission to the great supper. None can enter except the favored few. Is the invitation worth nothing because it costs nothing? Nay, it enhances its value that it can be obtained only as a gift.

Belief in the truth of the Bible may be attained by a study of the overwhelming proof of its authenticity and inspiration; but "precious faith," the "faith of God's elect," as the Apostle calls it, comes not "of the will of the flesh, nor of the will of man" (John i. 13), but of the "demonstration of the Spirit."

2. But if faith is precious on account of its origin, it is no less precious on account of its results.

(1.) It is the instrument of our justification before God's law. We are justified by faith in the atoning Saviour. In order to realize the full meaning of these words, you must in imagination project yourself forward to that great day, when on a great white throne, the Judge of all the earth shall sit to pass sentence upon men for the deeds done here in the body. The question that will then agitate every bosom will be, "Wherewith shall I come before the Lord, and bow myself before the high God?"

One shall say, "Lord, in Thy name have I prophesied, and done many wonderful works"; another, "I have sacrificed burnt-offerings and poured out rivers of oil"; another, "I have given my first-born for my transgressions—the fruit of my body for the sin of my soul"; another, "I have been charitable, amiable, philanthropic"; another, "I have fasted and prayed, have worn hair-cloth, and scourged myself with bloody rods, have done many 'works of supererogation,' and many penances." Oh! my friends! in the blazing light of eternity, all these "righteousnesses" will look like "filthy rags."

But there shall appear another before that august tribunal,

who will say: Lord, if Thou art strict to mark iniquities, O Lord, who shall stand? And when God shall open the book of judgment, his faith shall say, "Lord, I place the death of Jesus between me and Thy judgment; otherwise I will not contend or enter into judgment with Thee." And if God shall say, "But thou art a sinner," his faith shall reply, "Lord, I put the death of the Lord Jesus between me and my sins, and I offer His merits in place of my own, which I ought to have, but have not." And if God shall say, "But I am angry with thee," his faith will reply, "Lord, I put the Lord Jesus between me and Thine anger." And then his faith shall be counted to him for righteousness. But in reality, the believer shall not wait till that great day to be vindicated before that high court. Even now, while on earth, his sins are cancelled and his justification is complete. He does not walk in chains expecting *future* deliverance. The moment he trusted in Jesus as a Saviour his chains were struck off, his sins were blotted out, and his name was written in the Lamb's book of life; and then his faith was "the substance of things hoped for, the evidence of things not seen." "Precious faith!"

(2.) Faith is precious, because it gives conscious peace with God. The believer is no longer afraid of God. Why should he be afraid of God? It is God that has justified him; and shall his justifier lay anything to his charge?

Then, as a necessary consequence, comes peace of conscience. For when God is pacified, his own conscience is also pacified, and then through faith, he realizes the "peace which passeth all understanding." "Precious faith!"

(3.) Faith gives *communion* and *fellowship* with God. As the mutual intercourse between men depends upon the confidence subsisting between them, so our communion with God depends upon our affectionate confidence in Him as Preserver and Redeemer. And as it is the first impulse of our nature to flee to the person in whom we most confide, to whisper our sorrows in his ear or to claim his sympathy with our joys, so the soul that trusts in God communes with Him in secret, or talks with Him by the wayside. Although he may use no speech or language, and his voice be not heard, yet, like Enoch, he "walks with God," holding sweet, but mysterious colloquy.

(4.) Once more. Faith gives a man power with God; because one of the strongest principles of a rightly constituted nature is never to disappoint any confidence justly reposed in it. Why, who is there that would not protect a fawn pursued by the hunter, if it should leap into his arms and with liquid eye appeal for succor? or a dove, pursued by a hawk, if it should fly into and nestle in his bosom? An appeal by innocence, by helplessness, or by distress, in which the individual abandons himself with entire confidence to us, is the very strongest appeal that can be made to our nature; and very often it will be met by the greatest sacrifices not only of individuals but of great nations. Let any refugee from political European tyranny come to our shores and confide himself to the American people for protection, and let him be pursued by Austria or Russia, or by the world in arms, and the whole people would arise like a living wall around him, and he would be taken only when they had trampled down a nation of dead men.

Shall men do this? and will not God stretch forth His arm over those who nestle under the shadow of His wing? Heaven and earth may pass away, but not a hair of the head of that man who puts his trust in God shall ever fall to the ground. Sooner, far sooner, would God blot out the universe than He would disappoint the *authorized* confidence of the most insignificant of His creatures. Precious faith! which gives to feeble man such power with God! Learn then where to look to-day. Don't harass yourself with the question, "Do I really have faith?" You do yourself harm by this self-inspection. Turn away from yourself and look to Jesus, the author and finisher of faith. Look aloft! Look aloft! If with the penitential Psalmist you say, "But my sin is ever before me," turn away from it and gaze on that Saviour whose glory and whose grace are most conspicuously illustrated in that He is able and willing to save even you.

"Cling to the Mighty One ;
　Cling in thy grief.
Cling to the Holy One ;
　He gives relief.
Cling to the Gracious One ;
　Cling in thy pain.
Cling to the Faithful One ;
　He will sustain.
Cling to the Living One ;
　Cling in thy woe.
Cling to the Loving One ;
　Through all below.
Cling to the Pardoning One ;
　He speaketh peace.
Cling to the Healing One ;
　Anguish shall cease.
Cling to the Bleeding One ;
　Cling to His side.
Cling to the Risen One ;
　In Him abide."

V.

JUSTIFICATION.

"Being justified by faith, we have peace with God."—Rom. v. 1.

This text assumes that by nature men are not at peace with God. I shall not consume time in proving this. In your hours of quiet reflection, you all confess that all is not right between you and your Maker. "The soul that sinneth, it shall die"; and as all have sinned, all must die, unless some means can be devised by which they can escape the penalty of sin.

God cannot abolish His law to suit your case. He has declared that He will "by no means clear the guilty." There is no hope in this direction. Yet the Gospel comes to you and says, Here is a scheme devised by God, and executed by His Son, by which you who are really a guilty sinner, may be treated as if you had never sinned at all. This scheme is called a plan of Justification. Now what is Justification? It "is an act of God's free grace, wherein He pardons all our sins and accepts us as righteous in His sight only for the righteousness of Christ, imputed to us, and received by faith alone."

It is very clear from the use of the word "Justification," both in Scripture and in our common talk, that it has respect to the violation of law. We never speak of our being justified in doing an innocent act. We always say it in reference to something contrary to law. If a man kills another, he is at once arrested. Why? Because he has done what the law forbids. But suppose he did it in self-defence? He is at once released on the ground that he was justifiable. But even though everybody knew this beforehand, this does not exempt him from arrest and trial. He is liable to punishment until he shall be by law pronounced "justified." Observe, the Court does not say that the man did not kill his neighbor; it simply declares that although he did kill he cannot be legally punished.

Now the Bible uses the word "justify" in the same sense exactly. In Scripture usage a justified man is not one who is not a sinner; but one whom for good reasons God will treat as if he had never sinned. Justification is an act of God. "It is God that justifies," says Paul. It is an act of God declaring the sinner *Just*—*i. e.*, declaring him released from the clutches and the penalty of the Law. Now listen carefully to a very important statement. God stands in two different relations to all His creatures on this earth. First, He is their King; secondly, He is their Judge.

As King, He makes the Law.

As Judge, He administers and executes the Law.

Now, although I have been preaching to you constantly about the "pardon" of sin—and this use of the word is right, as it is the Scripture term—yet, speaking accurately, I say, God never pardons sin. Pardon is the act of a sovereign who forcibly steps in between the criminal and the execution and sets the law aside. Justification is the act of a just judge who declares that the law has no claim upon the accused. Pardon releases the criminal at the very moment that he is acknowledged to be guilty.

Justification releases him on the ground that he is accounted just. Pardon supposes guilt; Justification is a formal declaration of freedom from guilt. In Pardon the law is set aside. In Justification the law is satisfied. Pardon remits a just penalty. To justify is to declare that the infliction of the penalty would be unjust. In no language spoken on earth do the words to pardon and to justify mean the same thing. If they did mean the same thing, then we must admit that the law of God may be dispensed with. For a pardon is the remission of a sentence the execution of which justice demands; of course the law would be set aside if justification and pardon were identical. But the Bible is uniform in the declaration that the law is immutable both as to its commands and its penalty,—that there can be no remission of the penalty without a complete satisfaction of the demands of the law. As, therefore, the law cannot be set aside, that act of God which justifies the sinner must be something different from pardon. Now the account which the Scriptures give of Justification shows that this view is correct. Justification is a dispensation from the penalty of the law, and a restoration to the favor of God, on the ground of the sinner's presenting a righteousness—that is, presenting before the law the very thing that the law demands. Pardon is the act of mere sovereignty, and does not demand any satisfaction to the law. Justification is founded on a full satisfaction to the law ; and, *ergo*, it cannot be pardon. Another important distinction is this : Pardon simply remits a penalty. The pardoned criminal is an outcast from society. He is looked upon with suspicion and distrust. Have you never seen how hard it is for a pardoned felon to regain the lost confidence of his fellow-men ? But justification not only remits a penalty ; it actually confers a title to the rewards of actual holiness : so the justified are not only delivered from hell, but have a clear title to heaven. This is in perfect consistency with strict justice. The law demands a perfect righteousness, and promises eternal life to every one who complies with this demand. Now in justification the sinner is provided with a perfect righteousness—the very thing that the law demands—therefore he who is justified has a right to demand admission into heaven. The everlasting doors are thrown open wide, and the ranks of the angels give way ; the fiery cherub sheathes his sword to allow any one to enter and ascend who appears clothed in the righteousness of God, the Son. Who dares bar his entrance now ? It is God that has justified him. Who dares condemn him ?

Thus you see that pardon and justification have only one point of resemblance, in this—that both release the criminal from punishment.

Here are the *points of difference:*

Justification is the act of a just judge. Pardon is the arbitrary act of a sovereign. Justification recognizes the claims of justice. Pardon tramples on justice. Justification rewards. Pardon simply releases. To justify the sinner is the only way in which God, as a just Judge, can save him. Do you not see that I was right in saying that in the strict use of words God cannot be said to pardon?

Now you ask very pertinently: How can God remain just and yet be a justifier of a man who is acknowledged to be ungodly?

This brings us to the very marrow of the Gospel.

The Apostle tells us that Christ, who knew no sin, was made sin for us, that we might be made the righteousness of God in Him. The Scriptures say distinctly that nothing we can do will avail to make us just before God; that we are justified solely on the ground of the righteousness of Christ. This is the doctrine of the Old Testament as well as of the New; for Isaiah, the prophet, calls Christ the "LORD OUR RIGHTEOUSNESS."

Now, I want to answer another question that has come into your minds: "How can the righteousness of one person be the ground of the justification of another?" "God requires *me* to be holy." "How can the righteousness of Christ satisfy this demand upon me?" I answer, it *cannot*, unless it can be "*imputed*" to me: unless I can be accounted to have it though inherently destitute of it. You ask again, "Is not this a mere sham? Can a just and holy God give me credit for what I do not really have?" I answer, He can, provided you are so united with Christ, that He stands as your representative. You all understand this doctrine of representation; what the Senator from Kentucky does in Congress the people of Kentucky are accounted as doing. The world holds you responsible for his acts; although you may not know at the time what he is doing. They are imputed to you. You know the old law maxim, What one does by an agent, he himself is accounted as doing.

But how does Christ become your representative? I answer, by your electing Him to take your place. This election of Jesus Christ as your representative in the high court of heaven is called "faith." By this act of faith, you become united with Him. His righteousness is your righteousness. His bearing the penalty of your sin is your bearing it. By means of this union with Christ as your representative, you are legally accounted as doing and suffering all that He did and suffered for you. It is to this the Apostle refers when he says, "I am crucified with Christ"; and again, "Therefore we are buried with Him by baptism into death"; that is, as our baptism is the outward sign of our profession of faith in Christ, when we are baptized we become so united with Him, that His death is our death, His burial our burial.

Thus faith, union with Christ, imputation of His righteousness to us, and justification, are all distinct, but essential links in the great chain of man's redemption. And as these two,—faith, the act of man, and justification, the act of God,—are at the two ends of the chain, the one on earth, the other in heaven; the Apostle, omitting the intermediate links of the series, says: "Therefore, being justified by faith, we have peace with God." I have been answering your questions, now I want you to answer mine. Will you accept salvation on these terms? Do not say, "I will think about it and tell you some time soon." You must come to this at last, if you are ever saved at all. You must consent to be saved as a sinner, without a ray of your own righteousness. If you ever feel good enough to *merit* salvation, you may be sure that this self-righteousness will make you stumble before you reach the cross. A man never feels so vile as at the instant he casts himself on Christ. By grace ye are saved through faith. Now, I want every unconverted man, woman, and child, before he leaves this house, to answer this question to his own heart: "*Am I willing to abandon every other ground of hope and trust to the righteousness of Christ?*" There is nothing mysterious or unintelligible in what I ask you to do. It is exactly like any other determination you may form. It needs no long preparation, no praying, no humbling of yourself before God, no fasting, no moaning, no laceration of soul or body. You do not need to prepare for it by long and bitter penitence, by painful and protracted self-examination, or by a month or a week spent in the endeavor to break off bad habits. You *cannot* prepare yourself to receive the righteousness of Christ. Christ holds out no hope to the man who tries to make himself righteous. He did not come to save the righteous. A righteous man does not need salvation. The salvation of the Lord Jesus is a salvation for sinners. Such an idea as salvation by works, by merit, by making yourself worthy to receive the righteousness of God—why, this frustrates the grace of God; it subverts the Gospel. It would reverse the song of the redeemed in heaven; for that song is, " Unto Him who hath loved us, and washed us from our sins in His own blood, be glory and dominion." But if you are to prepare yourselves for grace, your song would be, " Unto myself, who have made myself fit for salvation, and worthy of God's mercy; unto me be all the praise and the glory." What a travesty of the Gospel this would be!

A missionary among the Indians was visited by a proud chief, who had been deeply convicted of sin by the Spirit of God. The savage, while trembling under a sense of guilt, was unwilling, like a great many civilized people, to take of the water of life freely. He brought his wampum to the missionary and tendered it as a peace-offering to God. The man of God shook his head and said, " No, God will not accept this as an atonement for sin." He went away, but came again, bringing his wife and all the peltry he had taken in hunting. The missionary still shook his head, and again the wretched sinner withdrew. But the Spirit gave him no peace, and he returned once more to offer his wigwam, his wife, his children, and all that he had, to have " peace with God." The missionary still shook his head. The chief stood for a moment, his head bowed down in despair, and, raising his eyes to heaven, his heart poured forth in a cry of unreserved surrender, " Here, Lord, take poor Indian too."

To this, my friends, *you* must come at last, if you would " have peace with God."

> " But drops of grief can ne'er repay
> The debt of love I owe;
> Here, Lord, I give myself away,
> 'Tis all that I can do."

One word of counsel:

I never preach the Gospel without confidently expecting some soul to be converted. I have no doubt that some of you have accepted Jesus Christ this day. Now, hear what Jesus says:

"Whosoever confesseth me before men, him shall the Son of Man confess before the angels of God; but he that denieth me before men shall be denied before the angels of God." But one way to confess Christ before men is to do so publicly in the Church of God. Come, then, to the church of your father and of your sainted mother, or to the church where your wife has been praying for you, lo! these many years, or to any Christian church near which you live, and cast in your lot with it, saying:

> "People of the living God,
>   I have sought the world around,
> Paths of sin and sorrow trod,
>   Peace and comfort nowhere found:
> Now to you my spirit turns,
>   Turns a fugitive, unblest;
> Brethren, where your altar burns,
>   Oh! receive me into rest."

VI.

CONVICTION.

"I remembered God and was troubled."—Ps. lxxvii. 3.

ALL men seek congenial objects of meditation. If at any time unpleasant subjects are forced upon their attention, either by accident or by the mysterious law of the association of ideas, they are speedily expelled from the mind as unwelcome intruders. As the happiness of most men depends upon their peace of mind rather than upon their external surroundings; and as all men seek happiness by an instinct of nature, it is natural that they should endeavor to banish from their minds all thoughts that might endanger their wonted tranquillity. This will account for the aversion to serious meditation which characterizes the larger part of mankind. It fully explains that habitual lethargy in regard to matters of religion which we find so common among men of the world. Men cannot reflect upon their origin, their duty, and their destiny, without thinking about God; and thinking about God is adapted to produce trouble—not metaphysical trouble—that intellectual travail which attends the comprehension or the solving of some mystery or some perplexing problem; but that trouble which comes from a restless, disquieted conscience; the uneasiness of a wounded spirit, which inspired wisdom tells us is hard to bear. Hence the Psalmist says: "The fool hath said in his heart, 'there is no God'"; *i. e.*, he says so in his desires, not in his intellect. It is only in his heart that the atheism resides. He *wishes* that there were no God; hence he would fain believe that there *is* no God, and his practical life is moulded insensibly into an habitual forgetfulness of God. For the same reason, as the Apostle says, the heathen "did not like to retain God in their knowledge."

This aversion to God of the natural heart manifests itself in every class of men. When they "remember God they are troubled," and therefore they banish thoughts of God from their minds. The expedients by which they seek to do this, may be all reduced to two classes.

First, there is speculative Atheism. Among men of a reflecting turn of mind, the questions, whence am I? and whither am I going? often suggest themselves. These questions at once bring God to the mind. If the thought of God thus suggested is distressing, they often seek a refuge in what they regard a rational scepticism; or, if they cannot force themselves into the absurdity of Atheism, they deny the God of the Bible, and make for themselves a god of whom they may speak without fear, and whom they may remember without "being troubled."

But a far more common as well as a more invulnerable forgetting of God is the Atheism of the fool who says in his feelings and desires, "There is no God." It is the practical ignoring of God in His distinctive character—not the theoretical denial of His existence—a knowing of God and yet not glorifying Him as God—the outward acknowledgment, the habitual, inward forgetting of Him. This is the most prevalent form of Atheism, and the secret cause of it is disclosed in the text: When men "remember God *they are troubled*"; or as Job expresses it, "When I consider, I am *afraid* of Him." A calm, deliberate analysis of the Divine character, and of our relations to the Divine Being, is adapted to awaken the emotion of fear in the breast of the natural man.

Wicked men seem to think frequently of God. They do not hesitate to utter His name on the most trivial occasions; and, so far from being troubled by them, such recollections of God give them no concern whatever. It is not to such impious recollections of God that the Psalmist alludes, nor even to the common recognitions of God that flit through the minds of all men. So far from exciting a sense of uneasiness, such transient reminiscences familiarize the mind with His august and reverend name, and only aggravate the habitual irreverence. But if men could only be induced to replace these transient and unmeaning thoughts of God by one hour's serious contemplation of the Divine character, they would find that the experiment is adapted to disturb their quiet, to harrow up their fears—in short, to give them "trouble."

If any of you who hear me, doubt this, let me invite you to such a remembering of God; and if you will faithfully and intelligently follow me in the course of thought which I shall suggest, you may perhaps be ready to echo the language of the text: "I remembered God and was troubled."

Arrest the current of your listless thoughts, and "consider and be afraid of Him."

In order to think profitably of God so as to be affected by a meditation upon His character, we must think of His several attributes as they are revealed in His Word. I invite you, therefore, to think of some of those Divine attributes, the remembrance of which is adapted to produce uneasiness in the mind of a sinner.

1. The God of the Bible is a Being of immaculate holiness and purity. Now it is the instinct of an unholy being to dread the presence and shun the approach of one that is holy. It is not necessary to explain why this is so. It is enough to know that it *is* so. It accords with the observation and experience of every one of us. The aversion between the holy and the unholy is mutual. The antipathy is equal. And as a being of perfect purity can regard a sinful being only with abhorrence, the sinner knows that the pure eye of the Holy One is looking on him with disapproval. Hence a vivid recognition of the holiness of God is always followed by the pungent and painful conviction of sin. We cannot look at His purity without the immediate consciousness of our own vileness. As soon as Adam heard the voice of a holy God in the garden, he looked upon his own nakedness with shame and *fear;* so when we fix our minds upon a holy God, we at once look inward at our own uncleanness. In the broad glare of the sunshine, we see filthiness on our garments that was invisible in the darkness of the night. But this is not all. The

sense of sin awakened in the human bosom by the contemplation of a holy God, is immediately succeeded by the sense of guilt. The sinner then feels like stubble before consuming fire. This experience is not confined to the wicked man. The best and holiest men upon a vivid perception of this Divine attribute are filled with trepidation and dismay on account of the contrast presented in themselves. When Isaiah saw the Lord sitting upon His throne high and lifted up, and heard the seraphim lauding this attribute, crying one to another, " Holy, holy, holy is the Lord of Hosts," he cried, smitten with fear and with deep conviction of personal sin, " Woe is me, for I am undone : because I am a man of unclean lips," and he had no peace until he received angelic assurance of the purgation of his iniquity. This conviction of sin and consequent sense of guilt produce mental trouble, because the sinner knows that a holy God must of necessity abhor him. He can have no pleasure in wickedness. He is of "purer eyes than to behold evil, and cannot look upon iniquity." He "hates all workers of iniquity." And even though His hatred of the *persons* of believers is removed by their faith in the atonement, yet His hatred of their sin is not in the least abated thereby. Now the distinct recognition of this Divine attribute involves the recognition of all these truths. Think of the fact that the greatest Being in the universe is looking down from His high and lofty throne upon you with a disapprobation so intense that He is represented in a figure as averting His gaze from you, because He cannot bear to look upon you in your vileness; and is not the thought adapted to produce such a state of mental perturbation as would lead you to echo the language of the text, "I remembered God and was troubled "?

2. Intimately connected with the remembrance of God's holiness is the recognition of His justice. For His justice is only another aspect of His holiness. His holiness is that attribute by which He loves the right and abhors the wrong. His justice rewards the good and punishes the evil. It is an essential attribute of God. He cannot be other than just. He *must* punish sin. Hence the Bible represents this attribute as like fire. As it is essential to fire to burn, so it is essential to the Divine nature to

punish all iniquity. " Our God is a consuming fire." Consider, then, what God's justice will compel Him to do. Having promulgated His Law, He must abide by His declaration that He will by no means clear him that is guilty of its violation. To reward the good and to punish the bad is the rule of the just administration of Law. It is not optional with God to deviate from this rule in His moral government of His creatures. And of His determination to deal with you according to His immutable purpose, He has fully and frequently advised you in His Word : " I will render vengeance to mine enemies and will reward them that hate me" (Deut. xxxii. 41). " He will not be slack to him that hateth Him ; He will repay him to his face" (Deut. vii. 10). " The Lord is slow to anger, and great in power, and will not at all acquit the wicked" (Nahum i. 3). To all holy beings, this consistency of character and purpose, this harmony of purpose with the execution of it, must be the objects of continual admiration, love, and praise. But alas for the sinner ! that very Justice which decks the Seraphim with beauties and fills the Cherubim with joy is a sword, a terror, and a curse to his shrinking, cowering spirit. It weighs him in the balances, and he is found wanting. It restlessly pursues him. Its sword, like that of Damocles, hangs suspended over him by a hair, while he reclines at his banquet ; while he journeys, it sits behind the rider. In all his daily walks, the emissary of Justice is dogging his footsteps, bearing the scroll of his sentence on which is inscribed in dreadful capitals, " Condemned Already ": while by his side the recording angel bears the indictment containing the accumulating catalogue of offences which swell the vast aggregate of ill-desert. His best deeds all contribute a quota of guilt ; and so far from extenuating aught or cancelling any, there is enough in what he deems his "*good works*" to justify the reiteration and confirmation of the sentence, " Condemned Already." Let him try to draw around him the mantle of a moral life, and thus hide his secret sins ;—Justice inexorable tears away the flimsy veil, and tramples on it as " filthy rags," and thus disclosing the hidden deformity, points with rigid finger to the writing on the scroll of judgment, " *Guilty before God*," " Condemned

Already." This transition in thought from the justice of God to a man's sense of his own ill-desert is inevitable; the two are inseparably associated in consciousness, and the man seeks in vain to divorce them. The consciousness of being amenable to the penalty of the just law of a holy God is the source of intolerable disquietude; and hence he who thinks of God in reference to His inexorable justice, can truly say, " I remembered God and was troubled."

3. While the soul is thus perturbed by reflecting upon God's justice, its agitation is exasperated by the remembrance of God's knowledge.

The man who has sinned against the law of the land, or against the conventional rules of society, feels a sense of security as long as he thinks his act is unknown to the magistrate or to those whose condemnation would put him under the ban. The very moment he has reason to think he is even only *suspected* by either, that very moment they become to him objects of aversion or of fear. If, however, he knows that they not only *suspect* but *know* him to be guilty, the thought of this knowledge on their part becomes to him a source of the most harassing agitation; and as often as the picture of those who he fears will become his accusers is presented to his mind, so often is the presentation a cause of mental uneasiness and of aversion toward those whom he fears. Now it is precisely this state of mind and this attitude toward God which are produced by the calm consideration of the Divine Omniscience. For this *knowledge* of God is *absolutely* all-comprehending, extending over the whole of the past and stretching out over the limitless future; terminating, not only on the vast concerns which by themselves would tax the most towering created mind to hold them, but upon the thoughts and intents of every created heart; piercing through the thick darkness of the night, and through the thicker veil that enshrouds the inner recesses of the human soul; bringing out into bold relief before the infinite Eye those more subtle shades of emotion and those half-formed, furtive purposes which escape the grasp of a man's own consciousness; catching every idle word that falls from thoughtless lips; and stamping on the Eternal Memory every act, thought, word, and feeling of the man from the very dawn of consciousness till the present moment. The sins of youth, forgotten by the man himself; the sins of manhood and of riper years palliated and excused before the bar of conscience; the sins now premeditated, but not yet consummated; sins of omission, sins of commission; sins against God, against neighbor, against husband, against wife, against self, all "naked and open before the eye of Him with whom we have to do." The multitude and multiplicity of His concerns do not and cannot avert His eye or divert His attention for one moment from the ceaseless contemplation of the guilt of every individual human soul. It is as if that one human being were the only being in the universe that attracts the attention of his Maker, and as if the burning eye of the Almighty were glaring only upon him in its fierce wrath and hot displeasure. As it is the triumph of the painter so to delineate the eye in the portrait that it shall seem to gaze steadily upon each one of a hundred persons in the same room, so that each feels himself to be the only one to whom the gaze is directed, so the eye of God rests upon each one of us. "Thou, God, seest *me*," is the confession of every man who has a right conception of God. Can any man, then, thus remember God without crying out with the Psalmist, "*I* remembered God and was troubled"?

4. Turn now to the contemplation of the Power of this Holy, Just, Omniscient God. It is by His power that He accomplishes all the decrees of His justice and His goodness. His power extends to every part of the universe, and to every event actual or possible. It reaches to the utmost star, and yet finds a field for its exercise in the mote that sparkles in the sunbeam. It holds the hard round world in its orbit, and it shapes the dew-drop into a sphere. It rides the circle of eternal change, while it propels the vital current through every vein and artery of organized life. Its finger measures the interminable periods of the comet, while it counts the pulsations of the heart of the oyster. His power flashes in the blazing band of Orion, while it lights up the meadow with the mild lustre of the glow-worm. It holds the canopy of heaven upon its ethereal pillars, while it distends the

bubble that sparkles on the rim of the beaker. If we stand terror-struck in the rush of the whirlwind, or smitten with awe in the presence of the strong torrents which in their own gladness fill the hills with hollow thunder, if the earthquake makes our hearts quake, how much more really adapted to awaken the emotion of terror is the bare thought that our breath is in the hands of God, and that a single touch of His finger could stop the beating of our hearts; nay, that if He should only for one instant withdraw His sustaining hand, we would sink and die. If thus the weakness of God is so much stronger than we, when we remember that all Nature is but His laboratory filled with an infinite number of occult forces, any one of which He can in an instant commission to become our destroyer, this reflection upon His infinite resources and the "hiding of His power" is adapted to deepen our conception of the frailty of the tenure by which we stand upon the confines of life. Think, then, of an infinitely holy, just, omniscient and all-powerful God who hates sin, whose justice condemns you, and whose knowledge searches your inmost being, and who holds in His hand an omnipotent rod of punishment, and you can but cry out with David, "I remembered God and was troubled."

5. If such thoughts as these about God are adapted to give the sinner trouble, he is apt to console himself by thinking of God's goodness. Like the sublime vision which Moses saw, God makes all His goodness pass before us in the daily pageant of Nature's shifting beauty: in the changing seasons, in golden harvests, in fruits and flowers, in cooling zephyrs, and refreshing waters. But suppose that every star and every flower could become vocal, and could utter a voice of reproach to man's ingratitude; suppose that every morsel of food were endowed with a sting, and every cup of water were drawn from a well of Marah, in order to remind you that you have forgotten God's goodness, for the very reason that the bread is given and the water sure; suppose that God's Providence should become intermittent, in order to show you that your gratitude to the Giver of every thing good has ceased, for the very reason that the constancy of His protection had assumed the semblance of natural law; you might then

confess in view of even His goodness, "I remembered God and was troubled." And shall the remembrance of this goodness, forgotten and unrequited, give you less uneasiness though seasons roll on, stars ever shine and the fountains perpetually flow? When you remember that the goodness of God was designed and adapted to bring you to repentance, but that after thy hardness and impenitent heart thou hast been treasuring up unto thyself wrath against the day of wrath; oh! when you think of God's distinguishing goodness abused and perverted, can you remember God without being " troubled "?

6. But the favorite refuge from all such mental perturbation, is the remembrance of God's mercy. Unquestionably the only solid ground of peace for any man is to be found in the mercy of God. But what vague and incorrect ideas most men have of God's mercy! They attribute to Him a weak and sentimental softness of character which forbids His dealing harshly with His wayward, erring children. They think He is too kind and gentle to inflict pain upon His feeble creatures, and this is what they mean by the mercy of God. But let us hear what God says about Himself. "The Lord God, merciful and gracious, long-suffering, and abundant in goodness and truth, keeping mercy for thousands, forgiving iniquity, transgression and sin, and that will by no means clear the guilty." What is the meaning of this? "will by no means clear the guilty." Does this teach that He is too tender-hearted to punish sin? Now the mercy of God is revealed only in the plan of redemption through Jesus Christ. He can be good to the sinner without Christ. He can be just in all His dealings with him without Christ; but the great and glorious Jehovah cannot be merciful to him except through Jesus Christ, His Son. Hence the plan of redemption has been called a "scheme of mercy." Mercy originated and devised it. Mercy achieved it. Mercy proclaims it. Mercy applies it. Mercy gives it effect. If then you refuse Christ, if you turn your back on Him, if you look with indifference on His insulted anguish, who died to make God's mercy available for you; if you can derive comfort from God's mercy while you thus scoff at and reject God's Son, your hardihood surpasses that of the devils;

for while they believe, they tremble. God without Christ has no mercy for you. God without Christ is a "consuming fire." If thus you think of God, you have abundant reason to go home from this house of God's mercy soliloquizing in the language of the text—"I remembered God and was troubled."

> "Till God in human flesh I see,
> My thoughts no comfort find;
> The holy, just, and sacred Three
> Are terrors to my mind."

In conclusion I ask, Are you content to think thus of God always? Are you willing to live always afraid of God? Can you endure always to stand in such an attitude toward God that a calm contemplation of His character will fill your soul with trouble? Do you intend always to walk with your eyes fixed on the ground afraid to look up, lest you should see God? "We then as ambassadors for God, as though God did beseech you by us, we pray you in Christ's stead, be ye reconciled to God." Oh! if you would only be reconciled to God by faith in His Son, you would become sons of God, and with the spirit of adoption you would cry, "My Father! My Father!" And you would appropriate the language of another Psalmist, "My meditation of Him shall be sweet, when I remember Thee upon my bed in the night-watches." Then you will no longer say in your heart, "There is no God"; for you will have found a God of whom you may think without fear, and whom you may remember without being troubled—a God under the shadow of whose wings you may rejoice, a God in the light of whose countenance you may forever bathe, a God who will be your refuge and your strength, a very present help in trouble—a God in whose bosom your weary soul may eternally repose.

VII.

PEACE.

"Acquaint now thyself with Him and be at peace."—JOB xxii. 21.

THIS morning I tried to show you that a calm and deliberate analysis of the character of God is adapted to produce trouble in the mind of the natural man. I hope those who heard me were so troubled that they are now inquiring, How shall we get rid of this uneasiness of mind? How shall we be able to remember God without being troubled? To such an inquirer I answer in the language of Eliphaz the Temanite, "Acquaint now thyself with Him and be at peace."

Two things are implied in this utterance:

1. That a distant knowledge of God, like that to which I referred this morning, can never be other than a source of disquietude.

2. That a man *may* obtain such a personal knowledge of God as will dispel his fears forever and give him peace.

I desire, this evening, to introduce you, as it were, to God; to bring you, so to speak, into personal contact with Him.

Philip said to Jesus, "Show us the Father, and it sufficeth us." Jesus replied, "Have I been so long time with you, and yet hast thou not known me, Philip? He that hath seen me hath seen the Father."

Before Jesus Christ came in the flesh, a few favored individuals had been personally acquainted with God. Abraham had interviews with Him, and was called by God himself, "my friend." Moses had met Him in the mount, and received from Him the law. Others had heard His voice, and in other ways had held direct communication with Him. But all these were transient, brief seasons of intercourse, which only deepened the awe felt for the ineffable majesty of Jehovah. The vast mass of the chosen people had no personal acquaintance with God, and the pious Israelite felt, like Philip, that a sight of the Father would suffice him. And now that Christ has come in the flesh, whoever knows Him, from henceforth knows God and has seen Him. For He is the brightness of the Father's glory and the express image of His person. If, then, Christ is God, we shall find that an analysis of His character will correspond in every respect with the analysis we have made of the character of God.

1. Christ was a holy being. "For Him no friend ever apologized, and no enemy convinced Him of sin. Infidelity itself has never ventured to cast any reproach upon His name, which is above every name, full of an ideal light." Yet this perfectly holy man, instead of repelling, attracted sinners to Him in crowds. So winning were His ways that it was a cause of reproach to Him that "this man receiveth sinners and eateth with them."

2. In like manner, it may be shown that Christ, when He shall sit upon the throne of His glory, will sit as an infinitely just Judge, who shall judge the quick and the dead at His appearing and His kingdom.

3. So, too, it is equally clear from Scripture, that Christ is infinite in knowledge. He knew the thoughts and the hearts of all men. The woman of Samaria who met Him at Jacob's well, said: "Come, see a man which told me all things that I ever did." "He needed not that any should testify of man, for He knew what was in man."

4. He was all-powerful. He demonstrated His omnipotence over the elements of nature; for the winds and the seas obeyed Him: over the diseases and calamities of human nature; for at His word, the lame walked, the deaf heard, the lepers were cleansed, and the dead came to life.

He claimed the power to summon twelve legions of angels to rescue Him from His foes, and declared that all power was given to Him in heaven and on earth.

Here, then, is God in human flesh, holy, just, omniscient, all-powerful: the image of the invisible God, by whom and for whom all things were created.

This God I present to you and say, "Acquaint now thyself with Him and be at peace."

You may ask in what respect you are better off in becoming acquainted with God in Christ than you were in remembering the invisible God, if the *man* Christ Jesus has all the attributes of the great and glorious God of the Old Testament. To this I answer that the very object of the mission of Christ into the world was to reveal God as a God of love. This God, holy, just, and powerful, so loved the world as to give His only begotten Son to die for the salvation of men.

You need to be continually reminded that God does not and never did hate our race. You cannot too often be told that God was not pacified toward sinners by the interposition of Christ. There was no opposition between God the Father and God the Son. The plan of redemption originated in the loving heart of the Triune God. The love of God the Father was the same love that thrilled in the heart of God the Son and God the Holy Ghost. This is what is meant by the Gospel: Peace on earth and good-will toward men. Whose "good-will"? Why, God's good-will. Gospel means *good news*. You all know what is meant by good news. If you have been waiting to hear from an absent child whose life has been despaired of; or if you have been startled by the intelligence that an accident has happened to the train that was carrying your loved one to a distant city, you remember the thrill of joy you experienced when the telegraph announced that the child was getting well, or that the dear one had escaped unhurt. Precisely similar is the emotion when you can be made to realize that God does not hate, but really loves you. The whole life of Jesus was a reiteration of the song of the angels at His birth, "Peace on earth and good-will toward men."

He held in His hand the sceptre of omnipotence; and He swayed it never to destroy, but always to bless. Virtue went forth from Him to those who might only touch the hem of His garment. He was the angel of consolation to every saddened home that He entered. In all the forms in which it was possible did God, "manifest in the flesh," display His love for men. But while the testimony of His words and the evidence of His works of beneficence were cumulative proofs, the demonstration that God loves men was not complete until the final act of His great heroic life. Other men have been philanthropists and benefactors of the race. But "scarcely for a righteous man will one die, yet, peradventure, for a good man, some would even dare to die; but God commendeth His love to us in that, while we were yet sinners, Christ died for us." Christ, who is God, dies, suffers for sinners, on account of their sins. He in whom the fullness of the Godhead dwelt bodily, sacrifices Himself in the agonies of a human death, that man, though a sinner, may live forever. Do you ask me to explain how *God* can suffer? I answer that it is a thing which cannot be explained. It is a matter of simple revelation to be believed without explanation that the eternal Son of God "entered into vital union with human flesh, in order that the Godhead might present a vulnerable side to the powers of evil for suffering in life and for the suffering of death." It is enough for you to know that God loved you enough to die for you, though you may never be able to understand how God *could* suffer.

Now this is the God you need to become acquainted with, because if He loved you to such a degree as this, you may expect to get from Him everything necessary to give you peace. Why need you try to go back of Him to think of another and different manifestation of God? Is He not the very God whom your fallen, helpless, sinful nature demands? Is there any one of the thousand questions that torture the human bosom with anxiety that He does not answer satisfactorily? Do you ask, Is there a life beyond the grave? He answers, "Yes, I am the resurrection and the life." Is there a place where I may meet my lost ones who have gone before? "Yes, in my Father's house are many mansions." But can any one know the Father? "Yes, having seen Me, from henceforth ye have seen Him and know Him." Does God regard my daily wants? "Yes, your Father knoweth what things ye have need of." Does He who made me care anything for me? "Yes, He has actually numbered the hairs of your head." Is it of any use to pray to Him? "Yes, ask, and ye shall receive." Can I expect forgiveness for my sins? "Yes, the Son of Man hath power on earth to forgive sins." But how am I to know that this power will be extended to me? "Because whosoever believeth in Him shall never perish. If any man thirst let him come unto Me and drink." But how am I to know but that these things were intended only for the persons who heard Him and constituted His disciples? Hear His answer: "Neither pray I for these alone, but for them also who shall believe on me through their word."

Now, it is clear that if you can become personally acquainted with a God who uttered such words of cheer as these, you will be at peace.

Among the ancient Romans it was part of their religion to cherish faith in an inferior class of deities whom they called *Lares*. These Lares were originally human beings, men like us in every respect, who had lived upon the earth, and becoming pure spirits after death, loved to hover around the dwellings they once inhabited, to watch over their safety. Having been once partakers of our mortal condition, they were supposed to know better the quarters from which to expect danger, and what assistance to render. Images of these Lares were kept in every house, in a little private chapel consecrated to their worship. They were sometimes called "household gods." This beautiful conception of the heathen mind was only an unconscious expression of the yearning of our human nature after a god with human sympathies and a god near to us. The God with whom I want you to become acquainted is such a God. His name is Immanuel, which means God with us—a God who has lived on this earth, who has trodden all the paths of human sorrow, who was tempted to commit every sin you ever committed, and who, because He was compassed with infirmity, can have compassion on the ignorant, and on them that are out of the way.

Now hear what He says: "If a man love me, he will keep

my words, and my Father will love him, and we will come and make our abode with him." He will be a "household God" to you, living under the same roof with you. This is no fanciful idea in regard to the presence of Jesus Christ in the house and in the chamber. This is the true doctrine of the "real presence." There are many blessed homes where Jesus is a constant guest. There are many Christians in this house who will tell you that they talk with Him every day and every hour. There are those who, having heard Him knock, have opened the door, and He has come in and supped with them. The language of their heart is:

> "Abide with me, fast falls the eventide;
> The darkness deepens; Lord, with me abide;
> When other helpers fail and comforts flee,
> Help of the helpless, oh! abide with me.
>
> "I need Thy presence every passing hour.
> What but Thy grace can foil the tempter's power?
> Who, like Thyself, my guide and stay can be?
> Through cloud and sunshine, oh! abide with me."

He is the Immanuel, the God with us, with whom you must become acquainted, if you would be at peace. But how? You cannot see Him. You cannot hear His voice. Here comes in the office which Faith has to perform—faith which is the evidence of things not seen. It is the grace which brings the soul into personal contact with an unseen Saviour, "in whom though now we see Him not, yet believing, we rejoice with joy unspeakable and full of glory."

It is one of the miracles of modern chemistry by which the artist may impress upon a plate of glass a beautiful portrait invisible to the ordinary observer. But he who knows the secret breathes upon it with the warm breath of love, and lo! the image of the loved one stands out in bold relief. Thus it is that Christ manifests Himself to those who love Him as He does not unto the world. This secret of the Lord is with them that fear Him. Do not call this fanaticism. It is the blessed experience of thousands. Even young children have it. A little girl was lying in bed with a disease that had made her blind. Her teacher said,

"Are you blind, Mary?" "Yes," she replied, "but I can see Jesus." "How do you see Jesus?" "With the eye of my heart." It is irrational to discredit the testimony of good men that they hold personal intercourse with Jesus. Ray Palmer has embodied the experience of every true Christian in the following lines :

> "Jesus! these eyes have never seen
> That radiant form of Thine;
> The veil of sense hangs dark between
> Thy blessed face and mine.
>
> "Yet though I have not seen, and still
> Must rest in faith alone,
> I love Thee, dearest Lord! and will,
> Unseen, but not unknown."

"Acquaint now thyself with God," "manifest in the flesh," "and be at peace." I close this discourse with a warning from one of the greatest of American preachers. "Bear in mind that the grand anti-Christian movement of our day is not open and bold attack, but a flank movement to get into possession of the citadel of faith, which for near two thousand years has proved impregnable to the gates of hell. Discovering that humanity must have a gospel to satisfy its longings, and that therefore the assaults of open Atheism and Deism were unsuccessful from the disregard of the necessities of humanity, the assault by the infidelity of our age is chiefly by strategy to substitute 'another gospel which is not another,' but really no gospel at all. And the favorite strategy of all is to impose upon the people a gospel of Jesus with the part of Jesus left out. And while it may seem to be Christianity, and to construct an attractive form of the Gospel for literary men, yet in the day that sorrow and trouble of conscience shall drive you in search of a gospel to rest your soul upon, this will surely prove the baseless fabric of a vision. 'Other foundation can no man lay than that is laid in Christ Jesus,' however brilliant the genius and profound the reasoning powers of him that attempts it. And any foundation that pretends to be in Christ Jesus, while ignoring His true Divinity, is but a cheat and delusion of the human spirit." "Acquaint now thyself with God manifest in the flesh, and be at peace."

VIII.

PARDON.

"For Thy name's sake, O Lord, pardon mine iniquity; for it is great."—Psalm xxv. 11.

I DESIRE to present the subject suggested by this text with the greatest simplicity and plainness of speech.

As is evident from what follows this prayer of David, he was in great distress. He says he is desolate and afflicted, that the troubles of his heart are enlarged, and that he is suffering affliction and pain. His troubles, whatever they were, had brought him to a deep conviction of sin; and this was a cause of greater anguish than all the outward calamities that had overtaken him. There is no greater suffering of which the human spirit is susceptible than that which accompanies a profound conviction of sin. "The spirit of a man will sustain his infirmity, but a wounded spirit who can bear?" In his grief he flees to God. There is no other refuge for any sin-sick soul. Unless it can get assurance of pardon it must be miserable. The reason so many really great sinners are comparatively cheerful and happy is that they have lost sight of their sins and guilt, and their minds are occupied with other things that crowd out all serious reflections.

It is only when some faithful Nathan comes, saying, "Thou art the man," and awakes their consciences, that they see their sins in all their naked deformity; and then, for the time, they can see nothing else, and they say with David, "My sin is ever before me." Then they have no rest. New conceptions of the purity and breadth of God's law, of His inexorable justice, of their own ill-desert, and of their lost and helpless condition, arise in their minds, and they cry out and roar all the day long. It is a happy thing for us, that while we share the experiences of

David, he was divinely guided in framing his prayers for deliverance; so that in adopting his language, we are using words put by the Holy Ghost upon his lips; and may rest assured that all his utterances convey lessons of Divine instruction recorded for our benefit.

Observe, then, the extraordinary plea for pardon which he presents before God. When we plead for pardon from a fellow-being, it is our endeavor to palliate our offence, to seek to make it appear less heinous than it seems to be. When the friends of a condemned criminal apply for executive clemency to the Governor, they hunt up all the extenuating circumstances to show that the man was not as bad as he seemed to be at the time he was sentenced.

How different David's plea: "O Lord, pardon mine iniquity, because it is *great*." I am not a little sinner, but a great sinner. I have broken all Thy commandments. In me there is nothing good. Pardon mine iniquity, for it is great. Now, as no man not divinely guided would ever have thought of presenting such a plea as this, we must conclude that the Holy Spirit dictated this prayer, because God will admit it as a valid plea offered by any sinner who comes to Him for pardon.

Observe, in the next place, the ground upon which he bases his plea. "For Thy name's sake." David had not, as we have, a clear and full revelation of the plan of redemption through Jesus Christ; and he could not have explained the rationale of the mode by which God can be just and be a justifier of the ungodly; but he looked back over the history of the chosen people, and saw that in all His dealings with them God's mercy had been conspicuous. He remembered that when Moses had besought God to show him His glory, He had announced Himself by this name: "The Lord, the Lord God, merciful and gracious; keeping mercy for thousands, forgiving iniquity, transgression, and sin." And he reminds God of His great name, and grounding his plea on the character of God himself, as revealed of old, appeals to Him to be consistent with Himself, and for the sake of the glory of His own great name to answer his prayers for acceptance. He makes no promise of amendment. He derives no hope from anything he can do in the future. He feels that he can make no reparation to the broken law; that he cannot atone for the sins he has committed. He cannot blot out his past record, and he casts himself solely on the mercy of God. Although he had but a dim insight into the means of pardon through the righteousness of the Messiah to come, yet he prayed up to the light which he had, believing that God would graciously incline His ear.

The great doctrine which the Holy Ghost, who inspired this prayer, would have us derive from it is this: That if a sinner applies in the right way for pardon, the greatness or enormity of his sin constitutes no obstacle in the way of his receiving pardon.

The question of the greatest importance in this connection is, what is the right way in which to approach God to sue for pardon? I answer:

1. There must be a consciousness of real need of mercy. For those who do not experience this deep necessity of a Saviour, there is practically no Saviour.

No man ever calls out for help unless he is conscious of the helplessness of his case. He must realize that he is a wretch undone without the interposition of a Divine helper to save him.

2. He must feel that he does not deserve any mercy, that he is totally unworthy to receive anything from God but the merited punishment of his sins. This sense of unworthiness, and this self-condemnation, were what characterized the publican who would not so much as lift up his eyes toward heaven, but stood smiting on his breast and saying, "God, be merciful to me, a sinner."

3. The man who truly comes to God for pardon, must totally abandon all reliance upon himself. This renunciation of self-dependence is the most difficult of all lessons to learn. If the sinner could only be induced at first and at once to believe that nothing he can do will render his offended Maker more placable than He is already, more than half the work of his salvation would be accomplished. But he cannot divest himself of the idea that he must have some hand in the matter. Oh, if I could only convince you that the work of your redemption can in no

way be aided by your own efforts, I should know that it would not be many days or hours before you would be rejoicing in having found peace with God. But as long as you undertake to be your own saviour, how can Christ be of any use to you? Paul says Christ is of none effect to those who seek for justification by the works of the law. David evidently derived no hope from his performance of even those ceremonial rites which were prescribed by God in the worship of the sanctuary. He says: "Thou desirest not sacrifice, else would I give it; Thou delightest not in burnt-offerings." As if he had said, There is nothing I would not do to gain Thy favor, no costly oblation or expensive sacrifice I would not offer; but I know all this would be unavailing to propitiate the offended Majesty of heaven.

> " Just as I am, and waiting not,
> To rid my soul of one dark blot,
> To Thee, whose blood can cleanse each spot,
> O Lamb of God, I come."

4. The fulfilment of this negative condition in a genuine application to God for pardon will inevitably lead to the fulfilment of a fourth and positive condition; viz., a coming to Him in the name of Christ. This coming to God through Christ, is simply coming to Christ himself. The forms in which this act of the soul is described in Scripture are very various, and all equally expressive of the idea of going out of one's self to find help in another. Looking to, as the dying Israelite looked at the brazen serpent in the wilderness; receiving, as one who receives with pleasure the friend who knocks at his door; eating, as one appropriates food for his nourishment; coming to, as one goes to meet one whom he loves, or seeks one in whose ability to relieve him he has confidence; embracing, as one throws his arms around a strong swimmer who has leaped into the water to save him; fleeing unto, as the Israelite fled to the city of refuge to escape from the blood avenger; laying hold of, as one grasps a friendly hand stretched out to him in the hour of peril—all these are only strong figures, intended by the Spirit of God to convey to our minds what is meant by believing on Christ to the salvation of

the soul. They are intended to turn the mind of the sinner away from himself, and to encourage him to put his trust in One mighty to save.

Ah! but just here lies his difficulty. He may be convinced of his ill-desert, his helplessness, and his inability to do aught to secure the favor of God; but he finds it hard to believe that this simple act of reliance on Christ can secure the boon of pardon, and bring peace to his tortured soul. This difficulty experienced by every awakened sinner, God foresaw, and to meet it has condescended to set forth in every possible form the great doctrine that He does not desire the death of the sinner, and that the remedy He offers him in Christ is the very remedy which, being provided by Himself, must be the only one adapted to meet the necessities of the case. Hence all the lessons of His Word, all the ministrations of prophet and priest under the Old Testament, and of Apostle and Evangelist under the New, are aimed at the one single object of inducing the sinner to put his confidence in One mighty to save. The Prophet Isaiah looking down over the lapse of centuries, and catching a vivid view of the coming Messiah as He makes triumphal progress on His mission of redeeming mercy, cries out, "Who is this that cometh from Edom, with dyed garments from Bozrah? This that is glorious in his apparel, travelling in the greatness of his strength?" And the answer comes back to him, as if uttered from the cross of His triumphant agony, "I that speak in righteousness, mighty to save." Yes, it is because He is mighty to save that every sinner may, without hesitation, put his trust in Him. And the Apostle Paul, with sublime confidence in the divine power of the great Redeemer to whom he owed his own deliverance, declares, "This is a faithful saying, and worthy of all acceptation, that Christ Jesus came into the world to save sinners, of whom I am chief"; while the Apostle John, taking up the words of the glorious evangel, extends the offer of pardon to all mankind in the catholic utterance, "And He is the propitiation not for our sins only, but also for the sins of the whole world."

Who is this Jesus that invites all men to come to Him? Who is this man that challenges the world to heave its mighty mass of guilt upon His shoulders? Which of the angels would dare expose himself to the perils of bearing such a heavy load? It is none other than He upon whom God laid our help, mighty to save; a Being who had no sins of His own to bear; a Being above all law, who had no obedience to render; a Being of infinite dignity, whose voluntary obedience outweighs our disobedience, and whose voluntary death for us more than pays the penalty due to a world of sinful men. Take the sins of all the saints, and also all the sins of all the sinners in the world, and lay them on Him, and you could not exhaust His power to bear them. Lifting His mighty shoulders under the incumbent load, He would not "fail nor be discouraged," but "cast them all into the depths of the sea." Can you not afford to trust a Saviour like this? Are you alone, of all the world of sinners, so vile a transgressor that "He whom God has highly exalted with His right hand to be a Prince and a Saviour for to give repentance and forgiveness of sins," cannot reach the extremity of your case?

I tell you that if you fulfil the conditions which I have been explaining, the greatness of your sin cannot stand in the way of your pardon.

One of the most common forms of unbelief directly injected into the mind by Satan may be expressed thus: "It is true that Christ died for sinners, but not for me. Mine is a peculiar case; there is no one sinner whose state is like mine." Therefore when I offer you Jesus Christ as a Saviour, I know you say to yourself, "Now that man does not know what sort of a sinner I am; if he did, he would see that Christ does not meet my particular case."

One of you is saying: "I am an old sinner; I have slighted the Gospel all my life; I fear God will not accept the poor service which I can render Him during the remnant of my miserable, wasted life."

Well, to this I reply that God does not accept men for the sake of the work they do for Him; He saves men for the sake of glorifying His own abounding mercy. And in order to show that age is no obstacle in His way, He has recorded in the Bible the story of the conversion and pardon of a very old sinner. Manasseh was a very wicked king, even down to old age. An idolater, a man of violence and blood, in his old age he repented, was pardoned, and saved. Old men are less likely to turn to God than young men; but if they do, their age and their accumulated crimes are no impediment to their acceptance.

Another is saying: " I have sinned with peculiar aggravations to my guilt. I once was numbered among Christians; my name was on a church roll; I often led God's people in prayer; but, alas! I disgraced my profession; I am a backslider; I never pray, nor read my Bible, nor go to church, nor do any pious act; I have cast God away, and I fear He has cast me off forever." But you are not the first backslider, and you need not remain a backslider forever. " Take with you words and turn to the Lord and say unto Him, Take away all iniquity and receive us graciously." Hear what He says in answer to this prayer: " I *will* heal your backsliding; I will love you freely." If you were mistaken in thinking you were a Christian before, and never did truly come to Him, come now, and you will see how freely Jesus can forgive.

Here, perhaps, is another, some trusting woman, betrayed in the innocence and ignorance of her youth, and cast off by her father and mother, and abandoned to " the tender mercies of the wicked," and only those who have experienced them can tell how cruel they are. She has come here and heard of Jesus, and she wants to love Him and cast herself on His bosom; but she is " such a wicked sinner" and " knows herself to be the vilest of the vile," and " don't see how He ever can forgive her."

Oh, let me tell you, it is because I got your letter and did not know how else to answer it, that I am preaching this plain sermon for you this afternoon.*

---

* This sermon, preached in the afternoon service in the Music Hall in Cincinnati, was occasioned by Dr. Pratt's receiving an anonymous letter from " a woman who was a sinner," evidently under deep conviction of sin, but whom he could only answer in this public way. Like the woman in the Bible, nothing more was heard of *this* woman, but may we not hope that the same Spirit who prompted the letter also led her to hear its answer and accept her Saviour ?

Don't you remember the story of the "woman of the city who was a sinner," who wept on the feet of Jesus, and wiped His feet with the hairs of her head? You remember His loving words to her, how He said, "Her sins, which are many, are forgiven." Ah! if you will only truly come to Him, you need not fear that He will repel you.

We never read anything more about this woman who was a sinner; she sunk into social obscurity, and probably never was recognized by respectable society in her city; but what of that? She was forgiven. And now she is in the society of Jesus and among the spirits of the just made perfect in heaven. This Gospel which I am commissioned to preach would be a failure if it could not avail for such a case as yours.

Thus I might describe every class of sinners in this Hall, and show it is adapted to all. Oh! then stay no longer away from Him who came to call not the righteous, but sinners to repentance. With all your guilt and helplessness fall down at His feet, crying out, "For Thy name's sake, O Lord! pardon mine iniquity, for it is great."

IX.

LOOK AND LIVE.

"And as Moses lifted up the serpent in the wilderness, even so must the Son of Man be lifted up; that whosoever believeth in Him should not perish, but have everlasting life."—JOHN iii. 14, 15.

THERE are some things so vast that the words which stand for them do not, when uttered, produce the conception of them in our minds. Take the word ocean as an example. How few of its marks do we realize in consciousness when we utter the word! Its vast extent; its bottomless depth; its currents; its tide-waves; its storms; its monsoons; its cyclones; its typhoons; its coral islands and reefs; its icebergs; its immense meadows of seaweed; its deep abysses teeming with animal life; its sea-urchins, and starfishes with their thousand strange forms and tints; its yellow, green, and purple-striped limpets; its jelly-fishes, floating softly like spirits of the deep; its cuttle-fish, decked in all the colors of the rainbow; all its wondrous fauna crowded into the crystal waters of the tropics; or its whales and seals and countless lower animals swarming in its polar seas— how few of all these things we think of when we talk about the ocean!

We pass words that mean big things, just as merchants pass bank-notes of immense value with the same ease that they handle small coin, never thinking of their prodigious significance. I have alluded to this ease with which we use words that denote stupendous things, to excuse what may seem criminal levity in men, when they talk with comparative indifference of the great things revealed to us in this Word of God. Thus the text speaks of "everlasting life" and the way to get it. Perhaps some of you are already disappointed as you think I am going to preach only about everlasting life. If so, I am not surprised. I do not think it strange that you, with your vague and dreamy notions of eternal life, should be more interested in the life that now is, than in that shadowy life which is to come. But while I make this concession to your spiritual stupidity, I warn you that this indifference is madness and ruin.

Let me, then, try to expand your conceptions of what the Bible means by "everlasting life."

1. Eternal life is said to be the "gift of God"—the best thing that God with His infinite resources can confer upon man. You put a locked casket in my hands and tell me a merchant-prince has sent it to me; but I am not to open it for ten years; that it contains, in his judgment, the richest present that he, with all his wealth, can bestow upon me; that he has searched the world for it, and spent an immense sum in procuring it for me. Would I not be a fool if I should throw it away or despise it? Just such a gift is everlasting life. "God so loved the world that," at an infinite sacrifice, "He gave His only begotten Son, that whosoever believeth on Him should not perish, but have everlasting life." God knows what it is worth; and if He thinks it of unspeakable value, is there not enough in this single fact to lead you to think it worth striving for?

2. But eternal life is the opposite of eternal death. Ah! if you could form any conception of what it is to be damned, to be shut up forever in the same dungeon with thieves, murderers, adulterers, blasphemers,—the foul, the impure, the obscene,—to range wildly around the vast caverns of hell, and meet no friends, see no smile of love, hear no voice of joy; to be haunted by the sighing and wailing of anguished spirits; to roam at large with raging lusts unsatisfied; to feel the intolerable pangs of conscience; to be actively engaged in hating God and cursing Him; to be making giant strides in malignity, depravity, and despair, and daily increasing in capacity for sin and suffering, till the woe of the soul is vaster than the wreck of a world; —oh! I say, to escape from all this even by annihilation, would be worth unspeakable effort. If eternal life were nothing but the escape from such a destiny, it would be a gift worthy of God.

3. But eternal life is no such negative thing as a mere escape from doom. David says: "In Thy presence is fullness of joy, and at Thy right hand are pleasures for evermore." In what does the fullness of joy of a rational, moral spirit consist?

(1.) Man is an intellectual being; and he cannot be happy without acquiring knowledge. And what he wants is certain knowledge. Hence it is that the "exact sciences," as they are called, have such a charm. Whatever else may turn out to be false, the mathematician knows that his deductions are everlastingly true. The sun may burn up, the stars may fall; but amidst the wreck of matter and the crash of worlds it will remain true that "the square of the hypothenuse is equal to the sum of the squares of the other sides."

Now, in the world beyond the grave, every step we shall take into the territory of knowledge will be a permanent conquest, an everlasting possession. And the soul will exult and revel in the certitude of its acquisitions.

This is eternal life, says our Saviour, to know the true God, and Jesus Christ. But we can know God only mediately, through His works of creation, providence, and redemption, through the experience of His gracious work in our hearts, through Christ, who is the image of His person, and the fullness of the Godhead bodily. If the heavens are telling His glory to us even now, what visions of that glory shall we see, when, new-fledged with immortal pinions, we shall flit from star to star, unimpeded in the study of the Divine astronomy!

If all history is a revelation of God's attributes, what splendid discoveries shall we make of them, when the veil is torn off from all that is now dark, and the promise shall be fulfilled, "Thou shalt know hereafter!" Again, if

> "God, in the person of His Son,
> Has all His mightiest works outdone;"

if, with all our researches, we have not been able to master the sublime Theology, what treasures of knowledge shall we amass, when the conflict of ages shall be adjusted, and we shall know Him even as we are known by Him!

This is eternal life, to know God,—to know Him in the miracles of creation, in the opened mysteries of providence, and in the comprehended marvels of Redemption.

(2.) Man is essentially an active being. His eternal life must consist in doing something. But work here is painful and repulsive. It is necessary, but it does not bring unmixed good. Activity must be spontaneous in order to be a source of happiness. Let me illustrate:

Look at a little boy in learning to walk; see his first efforts to keep from falling on the hard floor. He is doing the hardest kind of unpleasant work.

But look at him a few years later on the play-ground. He walks, he runs, he leaps, he wrestles. The boy is happy now and he laughs in the gladness of his heart. That which was work is now play.

So it will be with us in the eternal world. The restless spirit cannot be idle, but its activity will involve no weariness. The faculties, trained and disciplined in God's nursery here, will leap to joyous activity and free-play in the pleasure-grounds beyond the stars. Oh! how the soul will plume its immortal pinions, and like the footless fowl of Indian fable, career amidst the fields of ether, poising itself upon unwearied wing, and finding in its very activity its own end, and aim, and joy.

(3.) Man is a social being. Hence he seeks intercourse with others by a law of his nature. But even when the companionship is most congenial, protracted intercourse clogs his appetite, and his weary intellect and jaded affections demand repose. But in the intercourse of the unseen world there will be no satiety and no weariness. How exhilarating the prospect of constant intercourse with spirits whom, blooming in immortal vigor, "age cannot wither, nor custom stale their infinite variety!"

(4.) Man is a moral being, capable of sin and capable of holiness. Now since God, who is supremely holy, is supremely happy, it is clear that man's highest bliss, who is made in the image of God, must lie in his being holy as God is holy. Hence David cries out, "I shall be satisfied, when I awake with Thy likeness."

(5.) Once more: Man is essentially a progressive being. By the very constitution of his nature, he must grow in all his powers and capacities forever. He must go on from strength to strength. Imagination shrinks abashed in the effort to scale the heights to which the soul may climb; and language is powerless to recount the possible achievements of a human spirit in its progress toward an ever-receding goal. Life in the immortal world shall be none other than this—to rise higher and higher toward that height which we can never climb, leaving below us a depth which there is no line to fathom, while around us stretches an expanse measureless as eternity.

Oh! this eternal life is a mighty, blessed, glorious thing. It is the gift of God and worthy of such a great and glorious giver; it is life given back from a dark and dreadful apostasy, the antithesis of eternal death; it is life the inspiration of which is boundless knowledge; it is life which is activity without weariness, the joyous play of invigorated powers; it is life in the august society of the great and good of all ages; it is life supremely blissful, because supremely holy; it is life in all the opulence and glory of never-ending growth and expansion. Oh! is not life like this worthy of the aspiration of immortal spirits like yours? Now, what must you do that you may inherit eternal life? Listen, while I tell you.

Let us, in imagination, ascend Mount Hor, near whose base are encamped the hosts of Israel. The wide extended plain of the Arabah stretches out before us to the border of Edom. It is dotted all over with the tents of sleeping Israel. The day is just dawning; and as the eastern belt of the mountains begins to glow with the first rays of the morning sun, the Hebrew children stir in their tents, and go out to collect the manna, which lies like hoar-frost on the ground. But their soul "loatheth this light bread"; and the want of water adding thirst to their sufferings, they begin to speak against God and against Moses, saying, "Wherefore have ye brought us up out of Egypt to die in the wilderness?" Suddenly a cry is heard. It is echoed and re-echoed throughout the vast encampment. "The serpents! the serpents!" The air is filled with flying, fiery reptiles, whose sting brings anguish and sudden death. They creep from the fissures in the earth; they dart out from the clefts of the rocks; they crawl to the pallet where the infant is sleeping; they coil around the limbs of stalwart men; they pierce the bosoms of helpless women, and leave the death-wound behind. The poor people are hopeless and helpless. They cannot destroy the serpents, for they are innumerable; they have no antidote for the strange poison; they despair, they die. They cry to Moses for help. He intercedes for them with God. God commands him to erect upon a pole, so that all may see it, the image of the fiery serpent carved out of brass; and the command is issued to all the people, " Look upon this brazen serpent and live." "And it came to pass that if a serpent had bitten any man, when he beheld the serpent of brass, he lived."

Upon what easy terms these poor distressed Hebrews saved their lives! They had only to lift their dying eyes and fix them on this image; and this they might do without money and without price, and without moving from the spot where they were standing. *Looking* was all they could do. The cure was immediate. They did not merely begin to get better; the moment they looked they were well. Nobody could explain how this was. Those who were bitten did not wait that they might understand before they looked, how looking could save them. They looked first and at once. And if they did not understand how it was, afterward, they knew that they were well.

Now Christ himself declares that in the same way, by looking at Him, you may have eternal life. He it is that has prescribed the simple condition of believing on Him. " As Moses lifted up the serpent in the wilderness, even so must the Son of Man be lifted up, that whosoever believeth on Him ";—observe it is " believeth," instead of looketh. You see that believing is equivalent to that eager, longing look, which the dying Israelite would cast toward the brazen serpent. Have you never seen the eloquence of a look far exceed the power of speech? Have you never seen the dying man, too weak for words, tell his heart's desire, without words, in a look? Have you never been overcome by a wistful look of your little boy, when he looked and looked, but was afraid to say a word lest you should answer "no"? Well now, believing on the Lord Jesus Christ is just that look of desire, as the soul sees Jesus Christ set forth in the Gospel. "If you can remember how you felt as a little child, while you timidly plead by a look, when you dared not *utter* your wish, and you perceive that your present desire for salvation is like that,— then this is 'believing.' "

Now why should you say, "How can this simple act of faith save my soul?" The efficacy of the act depends on God's appointment. Can you not believe that a thing is, without knowing how it is?

Let me then hold up before your eyes the antitype of the brazen serpent. If any of you are mourning over your guilt and are full of anguish, raise your believing eyes to Him who is lifted up in this assembly, and one look will enable you to dry your eyes forever. You who may be groping in darkness, look there to be enlightened. You who are weak, look and be strong. You who are polluted, look and be pure. You who are hardhearted, look at Him hanging on the tree, and be melted into contrition and love.

You who are agonized with doubts as to whether you are a child of God, look and gain a firmer assurance of your adoption. Whatever your infirmities or sorrows, or sins, from every part of this Hall, oh! look to Him who is lifted up in the midst of this congregation.

As the serpent was lifted up in the centre of the camp, so Christ has been lifted up in the centre of the world, that all eyes from east and west, from north and south, might fix on Him. There He hangs, and every lacerated vein bleeds balm for the healing of the nations.

And when in your terror or in your agony you cry out, "What must I do to be saved?" from the top of the bloody cross, hear the echo, "Be saved," "Look unto me, and be ye saved, all ye ends of the earth." While millions of eyes are turned thither from all regions of the globe, and millions of souls are healed by a look, how like that wondrous scene in the wilderness! And while ten thousand eyes glisten with tears of joy as they look and are saved, "How shall you escape if you neglect so great salvation?" Oh! remember, it is life eternal that is staked on this simple act of believing, and death, eternal death, that hangs on your refusal.

And though you may weary of hearing this oft-repeated, familiar story, yet I will follow you with it till you take the final plunge into the gulf of despair. So that the last sound you shall hear from my lips while on this side of perdition shall be, " Behold, behold the Lamb of God, which taketh away, which taketh *away*, the sin of the world."

X.

GRACE REIGNING.

"For sin shall not have dominion over you; for ye are not under the law, but under grace."—ROMANS vi. 14.

LAW is a rule of action prescribed by a supreme power commanding what is right, and prohibiting what is wrong, with a penalty annexed for its violation.

The law referred to in the text is the moral law of God. "It is a shallow attempt to fritter away the meaning of Scripture to say that by 'law' here, Paul means only the ceremonial law." * "To be under law means to be under its authority, and under its constraining influence. The Apostle means to say we are under neither. We are not only free from its objective authority, but from its subjective influence." †

The assertion of the Apostle, then, is that believers are not under that law which is summarily comprehended in the Ten Commandments.

A very startling statement! It seems to countenance the heresy of John Agricola, who in the middle of the sixteenth century originated the doctrine known as *Antinomianism*. He taught that the law is of no use or obligation under the Gospel dispensation; that good works do not promote our salvation, nor do bad ones hinder it; that repentance is not to be preached from the Decalogue, but only from the Gospel. The Antinomian sect sprang up in England during the protectorate of Cromwell, and extended the system of libertinism much farther than Agricola did. Some of them maintained that if they should commit any kind of sin, it would do them no hurt, nor in the least affect

---

* Plumer. † Hodge *in loco*.

their eternal state:—that it is one of the distinguishing characteristics of the elect that they cannot do anything displeasing to God. Of course such an interpretation is monstrous, especially as the Apostle in this very connection is unfolding the doctrine of sanctification.

The subject of the relation of believers to the moral law has been the theme of much discussion. The reason of this is, that the New Testament seems to contradict itself. Thus we find our Lord saying, "Think not that I am come to destroy the Law or the Prophets: I am not come to destroy, but to fulfil. For, verily, I say unto you, Till heaven and earth pass, one jot or one tittle shall in no wise pass from the law, till all be fulfilled. Whosoever, therefore, shall break one of these least commandments, and shall teach men so, he shall be called the least in the kingdom of heaven: but whosoever shall do and teach them, the same shall be called great in the kingdom of heaven." Stronger language could not be used to assert the abiding force and obligation of the law. So, too, we find the Apostles always enforcing the duties prescribed by the law. Thus the Apostle James exhorts the disciples "not to speak evil of the law or to judge it, but to fulfil it." The Apostle Paul says, he himself is "under the law to Christ"; and he presses on his converts at Rome and in Galatia the exercise of love, on the ground of its being "the fulfilling of the law." Yet, this same Apostle, in writing to Timothy, says, that "the law is not made for a righteous man (that is, for the justified believer), but for the lawless and disobedient, for the ungodly and for sinners," etc. (1 Tim. i. 9). And in the Epistle to the Romans (chap. vii. 6), "Now we are delivered from the law, that being dead wherein we were held, that we should serve in newness of spirit and not in the oldness of the letter." Then the text, "Ye are not under the law, but under grace." There must be some way of reconciling statements so apparently contradictory. Their perfect harmony, I hope to make apparent in this discourse.

In what respect, then, can it be said that believers are free from the Moral Law?

I answer:

1. *Believers are not under the law as to the ground of their condemnation or justification before God.* It is not to the law, but to Christ, that they are indebted for pardon and life; and receiving these from Him as His gift of grace, they cannot be brought by the law into condemnation and death. The reason is that Christ has, by His own pure and spotless obedience, done what the law in the hands of fallen humanity could not do. He has brought in the everlasting righteousness, which by its infinite worth has merited eternal life for as many as believe on Him. "There is, *therefore*, now no condemnation to them that are in Christ Jesus." "Whosoever believeth upon Him, is justified from all things from which ye could not be justified by the law of Moses" (Rom. viii. 1; Acts xiii. 39). Or in the stronger and more comprehensive language of Christ himself, "He that heareth my word and believeth on Him that sent me, hath everlasting life, and shall not come into condemnation, but is passed from death unto life" (John v. 24).

It is sometimes said that we, as distinguished from the saints under the old dispensation, are delivered from the law as a covenant of works, and there is an implied contrast between our condition and theirs. This language is adapted to mislead; for it seems to imply that as the law certainly formed the basis of a covenant with the Old Testament Church, its being so formed made it something else than simply a rule of life, and warranted the Israelite to look to it in the first instance, at least, for life and blessing. This, however, was not the purpose for which the law was given as a covenant among the Jews. Deliverance from the law, as a rule of condemnation or of justification, marks no essential distinction between the case of believers under the Old, and that of believers under the New Testament dispensation. That is, it was just as true of Abraham and of David that they were not under the law, but under grace, as it is true of believers now. Strictly speaking, the Church never was under the law as a covenant. It was only a mistake of the carnal members of the Church to suppose so. We are just as much under the law now, as was any member of the Jewish Church,—no less, no more. He was not under the law in the sense that by doing the works of the law he could have been justified; neither are we. He was, and we, alike, are naturally under law to God; and as transgressors of law liable to punishment. But through the grace of God in Christ, we are not so under it, if we have become true believers in Him. We have pardon and acceptance through faith in His blood; and even though in many things offending, and in all coming short, yet while faith abides in us, we cannot come into condemnation. To this effect are all the passages which treat of justification, and declare it to be granted to the ungodly as a free gift of grace in Christ, without the deeds of the law.

2. But this is not the only respect in which believers are free from the law. In this sixth chapter of Romans, the Apostle distinctly teaches that *believers are not under the law as to their walk and conduct.* In this respect also he affirms that we are dead to the law and are not under it, but under grace; " the grace of God's indwelling Spirit, whose quickening energy and pulse of life take the place of the law's outward prescriptions and magisterial authority." The Apostle tells us in other places that the "law is not made for the righteous": that believers "have the Spirit of the Lord, and where the Spirit of the Lord is, there is liberty." Christ says, " If the Son make you free, ye shall be free indeed "; *i. e.*, free from the law as a condemning power, and free from it as a *commanding* power. An old divine has very forcibly expressed it thus: " Our Lord Jesus put Himself under the commanding power of the law, and gave it perfect obedience, to deliver His people from under it. God sent forth His Son, made of a woman, made under the law, to redeem them that are under the law. That they then should put their necks under that yoke again cannot but be highly dishonoring to this crucified Christ, who disarmed the law of its thunders, defaced the obligation of it as a covenant; and, as it were, grinded the two stones upon which it was wrought to powder."

I know this will strike some of you as new doctrine. It is, however, no newer than Augustine, and Luther, and Calvin. But you will ask, " Is not this dangerous doctrine? Where now is the safeguard against sin? May we not do as we list, oblivious of any distinction between holiness and sin, or even denying its existence as regards the children of God, on the ground that where no law is, there is no transgression?" The Apostle's reply is, "God forbid"; so far from it, freedom from the law has for its sole aim deliverance from "sin's dominion" and "fruit unto holiness." Let me state the doctrine in the language of one of the ablest divines of the Free Church of Scotland. "The truth fully stated is simply this: When the believer receives Christ as the Lord, his Righteousness, he is not only justified by grace, but he comes into a state of grace, or gets grace into his heart as a living, reigning, governing principle of life. What, however, is this grace, but the Spirit of life in Christ Jesus? And this Spirit is emphatically the Holy Spirit: holiness is the very element of His being and the essential law of His working. Every desire He breathes, every feeling He awakens, every action He disposes and enables us to perform, is according to godliness. And if we are only sufficiently possessed of this Spirit, and yield ourselves to His direction and control, we no longer need the restraint and discipline of the law: *we are free from it, because we are superior to it.* Quickened and led by the Spirit, we of ourselves love and do the things which the law requires."

Does not nature itself teach substantially the same lesson in its line of things? The child, so long as he is a child, must be subject to the law of his parents: his safety and well-being depend on his being so; he must on every side be hemmed in, checked, and stimulated by that law of his parents; otherwise mischief and destruction will infallibly overtake him. But as he ripens toward manhood, he becomes freed from the law, because he no longer needs such external discipline and restraint. He is a law to himself, putting away childish things, and of his own accord acting as the parental authority, had he still been subject to it, would have required and enforced him to do. In a word, the mind has become his, from which the parental law proceeded, and he has consequently become independent of its outward prescriptions. And what is it to be under the grace of God's Spirit, but to have the mind of God—the mind of Him who gave the law simply as a revelation of what was in His heart respecting the holiness of His people? So that the more they have of the one, the less obviously they need the other; and only require to be complete in the grace of the Spirit in order to be rendered wholly independent of the bonds and restrictions of the law.

Or think again of the relation in which a good man stands with respect to the laws of his country. In one sense, indeed, he is under them; but in another and higher sense, he is not—he is above them, and moves along his course freely and without constraint as if they existed not. For what is their proper object but to prevent, under severe penalties, the commission of crime? Crime, however, is already the object of his abhorrence; he needs no penalties to keep him from it. He would never harm the person or property of his neighbor, though there were not a single enactment on the statute-book. His own love of good and hatred of evil keep him in the path of rectitude, and not the fines, imprisonment, or tortures, which the law hangs around the path of the criminal. The law was not made for *him*.

Precisely so is it with the man who is under grace. The law considered as an outward discipline, placing him under a yoke of manifold commands and prohibitions, has for him ceased to exist. But it has ceased in this respect, only by taking possession of him in another. It is now within his heart. It is "the law of the Spirit of life in his inner man"; emphatically, therefore, "the law of liberty": his delight is to do it, and it were better for him not to live, than to live otherwise than the tenor of the law requires. We see in Jesus the perfect exemplar of this free-will service to heaven. For while He was made under the law, He was so replenished with the Spirit, that He fulfilled it as if He fulfilled it not; it was His very meat to do the will of Him who sent Him; and not more certainly did the law enjoin, than He in His inmost soul loved righteousness and hated iniquity. Such, also, in a measure, will ever be the case with the devout believer on Jesus—in the same measure in which he has received of the Master's Spirit. Does the law command him to bear no false witness against his neighbor? He is already so renewed in the spirit of his mind, as to speak the truth in his heart and be ready to swear to his own hurt. Does the law demand through all its precepts supreme love to God and brotherly love to men? Why should this need to be demanded as a matter of law from him who has the Eternal Spirit of Love bearing sway within, and may therefore be said to live in and breathe an atmosphere of love? Like Paul, he can say with king-like freedom, "I can do all things through Christ strengthening me": even in chains, I am free: I choose what God chooses for me: His will in doing or suffering, I embrace as my own; for I have Him working in me both to will and to do of His good pleasure.

It is to this freedom from the law as a command that the prophet Jeremiah refers, "After those days, saith the Lord, I will put my law in their inward parts and write it in their hearts, and will be their God and they shall be my people; and they shall teach no more every man his neighbor, and every man his brother, saying, *Know the Lord;* for I will forgive their iniquity, and their sin I will remember no more" (Jer. xxxi. 34). To the same intent is the promise of God by the prophet Ezekiel, "And I will put my Spirit within you, and cause you to walk in my statutes, and ye shall keep my judgments and do them."

When the Apostle says, "Ye are not under the law," he does not teach that the law is abolished. He merely says that, through grace, believers are not under it. In one place he exhorts believers to "fulfil the law of Christ." Conformity to the law's requirements is held forth and inculcated as the very perfection of Christian excellence. For it is not as if there were two,— the law and the Spirit—contending authorities or forces drawing in separate, distinct lines. On the contrary, they are essentially and thoroughly agreed—emanations, both of them, of the unchanging holiness of Godhead—the one in its outward form and character, the other its inward spring and living pulse. What the one requires, the other prompts and qualifies to perform. And as the law at first came as an handmaid to the previously existing "Covenant of Grace," so does it still remain in the hand of the Spirit to aid Him in carrying out the objects for which He condescends to dwell and act in the bosoms of men. The law of the Ten Commandments and the law of the Spirit of life in Christ, both say, "Do this." But here is the difference; the one says, "Do this, and live"; the other says, "Live and do this." The one says, "Do this *for* life"; the other says, "Do this *from* life." *

If all this is true, the question arises, of what use is the law to those who are really under the Spirit? I answer: the law would be of no use, if the work of spiritual renovation were perfected in us. But since imperfection still cleaves to the child of God, the outward discipline of the law cannot be dispensed with.

There are three different respects in which, although free from the law, we need the law. Here again, I quote in part from Dr. Fairbairn.

1. "We need the law to *keep* us under grace. The law was not only our schoolmaster to *bring* us in the first instance to Christ; but it is now our guardian to *keep* us to Christ, by continually forcing upon us the conviction that we must in every respect be the debtors to grace and grace alone. And just in proportion to the clearness with which we discern the breadth and spirituality of the law, and our utter inability to meet its demands, does it serve this end of driving us for peace and consolation to Christ alone."

2. "The law is useful to restrain us from the commission of sins, either through the power of some lingering lust, or through ignorance that they are sins. 'By the law is the knowledge of sin.' It is true that in the subject of grace there can be no habitual inclination to live in sin; for he is 'God's workmanship in Christ Jesus, created in Him unto good works'; he 'delights in the law of God after the inward man; but there is a law in his members (*i.e.*, in his carnal nature), warring against the law of his mind'; and the moral law with its discipline comes in to supply the imperfections of the spirit and to curb the remaining tendencies to sin."

3. "The third use of the law is to hold up before the mind a clear representation of the holiness which believers should ever

---

* "Marrow on Modern Divinity," p. 174.

be striving to attain. The law stands before them with its revelation of holiness, like a faithful and resplendent mirror in which they may see without danger of delusion or mistake the perfect image of that excellence which they should ever be exhibiting. 'We are free,—we have the Spirit, and are not subject to bondage.' True, but free, only to act as the servants of Christ:— free, but not to introduce anything we please into the service of God; free, but to worship Him only in spirit and in truth; free, but not to withhold from Him that proportion of our annual income which He has expected from His Church in all ages; free, but not to observe one day in ten, instead of one in seven as a day of sacred rest. If you are really filled with His Spirit, the love of God must have been so breathed into your soul as of necessity to make it your delight to do whatever you can for His glory, and to engage in the services which bring you into nearest fellowship with heaven. And the law is of use to tell you what to do, in order to do this. It tells you what you cannot know by the mere illumination of the Spirit; but what the sanctifying power of the Spirit inclines you to do as soon as you learn from the law that this is the will of God."

Now, perhaps, you are able to see the difference between the law as a command with a penalty attached to its infraction, and the law as a rule, or as a guide to Christian conduct. The whole moral law as a command is abolished for every believer; and the whole moral law in all its spirituality is in full force as a rule. It is said of Luther, that when this truth first dawned on his mind, it gave him such relief from the pangs of his tortured conscience, "he considered himself as standing at the gate of Paradise." A very homely illustration may aid you to grasp this distinction more firmly. The law as a command is like the rails on a railroad, which force the carriage to keep a certain direction on penalty of disaster if it flies the track; the law as a rule is like a finger-board at the fork of a turnpike, pointing out the right direction, which will be spontaneously followed by the traveller who desires to reach his home.

This doctrine is of the highest importance, and serves to distinguish those who are trying to keep the law from a servile fear of God's judgments, and those who, not being under a bondage of fear, find it "their meat and drink to do the will of their Father in heaven."

If all believers could apprehend the truth which I have this day endeavored to set plainly before you, the whole complexion of the Church would be changed. It is because so many only half believe the doctrine that they go downcast and mourning over their religious condition. Show me a line in the New Testament that encourages a Christian to entertain for a moment a feeling of sadness, or doubt, or despondency. The whole tone of New Testament Christian experience is that of jubilant triumph. Its language is, "Rejoice, and again I say, rejoice." "Ah!" some of you say, "this is addressed to those who can find something in their high attainments for which to rejoice." I say, No such thing; it is addressed to any man who has received Jesus as his Saviour, before he has made attainments of any sort. It was appropriate to the thief on the cross, to the jailer of Philippi, to the poor publican as he returned from the temple justified rather than the good Pharisee who had made high attainments in piety. I say, it is addressed to any one of you who has faith in Christ only like a grain of mustard-seed. Well may you rejoice; for you are not in the realm of the law; you are in the kingdom of grace. Why do the laws of China give you no concern? Because you owe no allegiance at Pekin. In like manner, the moral law ought to inspire you with no dread. You owe no allegiance to Sinai. You are in the kingdom of grace, and your allegiance is due to Mount Zion. "For ye are not come to the mount that might be touched and that burned with fire, nor unto blackness, and darkness, and tempest, and the sound of a trumpet, and the voice of words: but ye are come unto Mount Zion, and unto the city of the living God, the heavenly Jerusalem, and to an innumerable company of angels, to the general assembly and church of the first-born which are written in heaven, to God the judge of all, and to the spirits of just men made perfect, and to Jesus the Mediator of the New Covenant, and to the blood of sprinkling that speaketh better things than that of Abel." This is the glorious kingdom of grace—a kingdom which has no law and no penalties—a kingdom in which the very name of punishment is excluded from its vocabulary, because obedience is spontaneous and love to Christ the constraining impulse. Love being the law, His yoke is easy and His burden light.

Now, you see the force of the Apostle's reasoning: "Sin shall not have dominion over you; *for* ye are not under the law, but under grace." A strange reason to the minds of those who do not understand the doctrine. "You shall cease to sin, because the law commanding you not to sin is, for you, abolished and destroyed"!!! The very law which you supposed was ordained to deter you from sin is ground to powder. The tables of stone are broken a second time; and yet, says the Apostle, ye shall not sin against them. Wonderful paradox of Divine grace! And yet as easily explained, as it is superlatively wonderful. For the same Spirit of grace, by whose instrumentality alone you have been constrained and enabled to receive Christ and thus have been transferred from the domain of law into the domain of grace,—this same Spirit writes the law anew in your heart, and makes you a law unto yourself; and thus by His quickening and sanctifying power constantly operating in you, generates spontaneous obedience to the will of Christ which is in perfect accord with the abolished law.

What need now to remind you to keep the Sabbath holy, when a day in His courts is better than a thousand, and you had rather be a doorkeeper in the house of God than dwell in the tents of wickedness? What need now to enjoin upon you to "have no other gods before Him," when the language of your inmost soul is: "Whom have I in heaven but Thee? and there is none upon earth that I desire besides Thee"? What need now to remind you that the second Commandment is like unto the first, "Thou shalt love thy neighbor as thyself," when ye have heard from Christ His new commandment, "that ye love one another"? What need now to tell you that God has always expected at least a tenth of His people's income to be devoted to Him when you "thus judge that if one died for all, then all died; and that He died for all that they which live should not henceforth live unto themselves, but unto Him that died for them"; when the Spirit of Christ that is in you prompts you to sing,

> "Were the whole realm of nature mine,
> That were a present far too small ;
> Love so amazing, so Divine,
> Demands my soul, my life, my all"?

Oh! brethren, if you only apprehended the full meaning of the text, you would be delivered not only from the bondage of fear, but from bondage to the world. What a scene of holy work for Christ this congregation would present! What entire consecration of everything! What holy joy! What a busy employment of all the talents! Not from constraint, but from pure, irrepressible, overflowing love to Him who hath redeemed you from the curse of the law, and introduced you into the free kingdom of grace, and made you not subjects, but "SONS OF GOD."

XI.

TRUE FREEDOM.

"If the Son therefore shall make you free, ye shall be free indeed."—JOHN viii. 36.

THERE is no word, the meaning of which is so little understood, as the word freedom. Thousands are slaves who boast that they are freemen.

In the conversation between our Saviour and the Jews recited in this chapter, they made an empty boast of their descent from Abraham, and seemed proud that they were never in bondage to any man. Forgetting that they had lost their civil liberties, they gloried in the fact that they were not in a state of domestic slavery. Like thousands among us at the present day, they thought that freedom consists in the absence of external restraint—a state of irresponsibility to any authority. Now this opinion carried out to its logical results would make the savage state the perfection of liberty, and consequently the highest form of human existence.

To such an erroneous estimate of the true nature of freedom, the Scriptures justify us in opposing the grand proposition that *true liberty consists in voluntary subjection to legitimate authority.*

A child who is subject to his parent whom he loves and whom he joyfully obeys, is free in the true sense of the term.

A wife who yields a loyal obedience to her husband, is also free.

A subject who yields a voluntary homage to his ruler, whether he be President or King, or Imperial Despot, is free.

In his last discourse to the children of Israel, when all the tribes were gathered at Shechem, Joshua said: "Choose ye this day whom ye will serve." They were free to choose, but they must choose to *serve*, to serve either the gods of the Ammonites or the God of their fathers.

True liberty, I repeat it, consists not in freedom from restraint, but in voluntary subjection to legitimate authority.

This definition is applicable alike to personal liberty and civil liberty, and at your leisure you may subject it to the most rigid criticism, and you will find that it will stand the test at the bar of history, of common sense, and of Scripture.

Without pausing now to justify this definition, I proceed upon the assumption of its soundness. If this definition is correct, if liberty in the creature consists in subjection to lawful authority, then most men are slaves. Even under the mildest form of civil government, men may be, and thousands are, slaves. They may be free from physical restraint; there may be no bodily servitude; but to real freedom they may be entire strangers. This was what our Saviour intimated to the Jews when they claimed that they had never been in bondage. He distinctly denies their proud claim. Passing from the region of the secular, the civil, and political, and rising at once to a view of their spiritual condition, in answer to their indignant demand, "How sayest Thou, Ye shall *be made* free?" Jesus answered them, "Verily, verily, I say unto you, whosoever committeth sin is the slave of sin."

My object in this discourse is to analyze spiritual bondage and spiritual freedom, to show you the elements in each, and to lead you by the contrast to seek the glorious liberty of the children of God.

Liberty, I have said, consists of two essential elements: First, voluntary subjection; second, subjection to legitimate authority. A state or condition in which either of these elements is absent, is a state of bondage. Now this state of bondage is the condition of all who are not the children of God.

In the first place, all such persons are in subjection to sin. Sin rules in them as the dominant master of all their actions. Sin pervades all their purposes. Sin animates all their hopes. Sin gives color to all their desires. Sin leavens all their emotions and affections. Sin directs their whole course of conduct; it gives character to every product of their intellect, their imagination, and their fancy. Every power of their souls is under the dominion of sin. But this subjection is *voluntary*, and one of the elements of slavery would thus seem to be wanting. For no man can say, that when he yields himself up as the servant of sin, any power from without coerces his will. Oh no! it is your boast that you are free agents, and this it is that renders your bondage to sin not only a misfortune, but a crime. But if your servitude to sin is voluntary, how then according to our definition can it be called a condition of slavery?

I answer, in the first place, because the other element in true freedom is wanting. The sinner *is* the voluntary slave of sin, but sin is a *usurper;* you have voluntarily subjected yourselves to an *illegitimate* authority. What right has sin to claim lordship over you who belong to God as your rightful Master? In becoming the servants of sin, you have thrown off your allegiance to *God*, and as He is your only rightful Master, you are slaves.

But in the second place, in a very important sense, your servitude to sin is *involuntary*. That is, it is not engaged in with the full consent of all the powers of your nature. Both reason and conscience protest against it all the time. In the interval between the revels of the passions, reason lifts her voice and tells you, sin is folly and madness. Conscience, with still small voice, distinct but low, utters her protest against this subjection to sin, and declares that it is wrong and ruin. Now the structure of man essentially considered, the original constitution of his soul, and the design and meaning of that constitution, are not to be mistaken. Reason and conscience are his ordained guides; he knows and feels that God ordained them to be his guides, and their utterances are in themselves above everything else. Hence a created mind whose will acts in obedience to conscience and reason, rises to the true ideal of a perfect moral being. This is the highest freedom; it is power, it is glory. The will in any being is truly free and truly strong, when it is thus determined and controlled.

When, then, the will is in subjection to these ordained authorities—these vicegerents of God in the soul, the whole man is in perfect harmony with the original constitution of his nature, and he is free in the highest conceivable sense. But in the unregenerate soul there is a continual schism; for although reason and conscience assert their right to rule supreme, they can put forth no activity out of themselves to control the will. They can only present truth and duty to the mind; they cannot coerce the rebellious will into conformity with their decisions; and sin, or the total depravity of man's nature, gains the mastery, stifles the protests, drowns the voices of these heaven-appointed guides, and the man is thus bound in chains by sin and becomes his slave. In this sense his bondage is a forcible coercion of his nature. If by any spiritual legerdemain the service of sin could be made to appear reasonable and right, the struggle in the soul would cease, and this bondage to sin would lose one of its most bitter elements. But since this is impossible, the service of sin will always be in one sense involuntary, as long as reason and conscience protest against it. It is indeed true that a man may be brought so far under the dominion of sin, that he seems to have yielded up every power of his soul, so that he seems to take delight in his chains; but it is not necessary to prove that his condition is irksome, in order to prove that it is a real slavery.

In the third place, the service of sin is a slavery, because no man can free himself from it at pleasure. This is the most painful and most terrible element in spiritual bondage. To know that in one sense you choose it, and to know at the same time that even if you try, you cannot shake off your chain—this, this is a bondage indeed. Men do resolve again and again, that they will free themselves from this tyrant. But after all their struggles, he retains his hold upon them. How often has this been the case with you, my hearer! Have you not again and again resolved that you would abandon your sinful life and become virtuous and good, and after frequent and protracted effort have you not reached the settled conviction that you are practically unable to free yourself from this galling yoke? Ah! the evil is found, by experience, to lie beyond the reach of the convictions of the reason and the demands of the conscience.

You have realized, as have all who have made similar efforts, that sin has possession of your tastes, inclinations, affections, and desires; that you are slaves to sin, because these elements in your nature are totally depraved and corrupted.

Now, as no amount of direct effort on your part can change your heart, you can never free yourself from this state of slavery any more than the Ethiopian can change his skin or the leopard his spots.

The consciousness of every man authenticates this statement, without any appeal to the Word of God for confirmation.

Here, then, are all the elements of the most abject slavery.

First, subjection; second, involuntary subjection; third, involuntary subjection to a usurper; fourth, a subjection from which you cannot free yourself; and to render it more bitter and degrading still, " involuntary subjection to a usurper, from which you cannot free yourself, and yet voluntary to such an extent as to render the slave morally guilty for remaining a bondman."

This, this is a slavery from which a man may well groan to be free—well might he cry out in the agony of his fruitless struggles for deliverance, Oh, wretched man that I am! who shall deliver me from this body of death?

This would seem to be enough to justify the declaration that most men are slaves; but this is not all. The slavery to sin is only *one* of the chains which bind the sinner.

This subjection to a tyrant and usurper brings the man into a state of bondage to another, but in this case a *legitimate* authority. It brings him directly under a bondage to the law of God. Here the authority is legitimate; but the bondage is wholly *involuntary*. In this case the thraldom is that of a criminal as contrasted with the freedom of a loyal subject. The latter is bound, too, by the law, and as long as he obeys it, he is protected by the strong arm of his sovereign in the enjoyment of life and liberty, and in the pursuit of happiness. He who transgresses that law is bound; but bound by its penalties. He is restrained of his liberty by the prison-walls which the law has provided for those who throw off its allegiance. This is the bondage of him who has become the servant of sin. He has rendered himself obnoxious to the penalties of the law which he was bound to obey, by swearing fealty to another and a hostile power. He is a traitor under arrest awaiting his trial and his doom. He is a captured fugitive, cowering under fear of the lash. He is a prisoner on parole; but not set free—a convict whom justice may spare from immediate punishment, but against whom the law has pronounced the sentence of condemnation.

Now, consider some of the elements of terror in this bondage to the Law of God.

What I wish you to do, is to look steadily at the facts of your condition as bondmen under a violated law.

First. The first fact is that this bondage to the law is a state of actual condemnation to an eternal punishment. You act as if your case were not yet adjudicated, as if sentence had not yet been pronounced against you. But, my hearer, the Scripture declares that you are condemned already. You seem to think that the probation which God gives you is precisely similar to that which He gave to Adam and Eve in the garden of Eden; and that you are free to choose for yourselves, whether you shall be classed among the loyal subjects of your King, or whether you will renounce His authority; whereas, the very truth is, that you are criminals, arrested, tried, convicted, and condemned; and only awaiting the execution of a sentence which has been delayed at the sovereign pleasure of God. You stand as if coolly balancing in your mind, whether or not you will choose to be lost; whereas the very truth is, that you are already lost. You seem to act as if you supposed that you may at any time release yourself from captivity to the law of God, and walk forth to freedom the moment you choose to signify your willingness to renew your oath of allegiance to the Sovereign whose authority you have renounced, whose law you have broken; whereas, if, from this hour forward, you should keep the whole law, you would still be a condemned criminal and justly exposed to Divine wrath. It is because you do not realize this, that you sit here unconcerned about your spiritual condition. Oh! if you unconverted men and women in this assembly could realize that you are *lost sinners,* LOST *sinners,* sinners upon whom the *wrath* of God is actually abiding—oh! terrible words!—the wrath of God! you would be unable to restrain your cries,—you would fill this vaulted roof with wailing and lamentation, and prostrate yourselves in supplication, crying out, God be merciful to us sinners.

And this leads me to speak of another element of terror in this bondage to the law.

It is a bondage from which you cannot redeem *yourselves.* You began life bankrupt, and every hour of your existence has only plunged you deeper into debt. Like those imprisoned for debt, the very condition in which you have been placed has precluded the possibility of your ever liquidating your obligations.

Repentance will not free you from this bondage, any more than the regrets of the spendthrift will deliver him from the debtor's prison. Absolute and complete reformation of life, were this possible, will not release you, any more than the payment of all your future expenses will settle the debts you have heretofore contracted.

Here, then, is another fact of dreadful import in the sinner's bondage to the Law of God—nothing he can do will release him from its dreadful penalties.

Now, men realize these truths with different degrees of distinctness at different times. Hence there is a third element in this bondage to the law which is more or less operative in making it oppressive. In proportion as a man is conscious of his exposure to the penalty of the law and of his inability to satisfy its demands, he is brought under what the Apostle calls a bondage of fear. He lives all his lifetime in servile dread of God's vindictive wrath, or as the Apostle has it, "through fear of death is all his lifetime subject to bondage" (Heb. ii. 15).

This apprehension of the wrath to come is more vivid at one time than at another, but its influence is never wholly absent from the soul. It poisons every cup of pleasure, and dashes every draught with an element of bitterness; it is the thorn that lies half concealed beneath every rose—the sting that envenoms life's happiest hours. It is this fear of death that sits like a nightmare upon your spirits and that casts a dark shadow over your whole pathway through life. It reveals itself on your countenances, and even in your gayest hours the shrewd physiognomist can discern the traces of its presence in the permanent lineaments of your faces. They who thus live in bondage to the law are aptly described by our Saviour as "weary and heavy laden." You often try to shake this burden off; and when absorbed in business or intoxicated with the pleasures of life, you do succeed in forgetting it for a moment; but when released from the struggles of the market and the toils of the counting-room, you sit down to calm reflection; or when suddenly arrested by the death of some one whom God has struck down either in His love or His wrath, this fear of death and of coming judgment casts a shadow upon your souls.

Here, then, are the three prominent features in the sinner's bondage to the law:

(*a.*) Present condemnation and consequent exposure to instant wrath.

(*b.*) Utter inability to redeem himself.

(*c.*) Servile dread of death and its consequences.

Here, then, is a threefold bondage of the unregenerate and unforgiven sinner—a slavery to sin, to the law, and to the fear of death.

Have I not proved the proposition with which I began, that most men are slaves? Let us now contrast with this wretched condition the glorious liberty of the children of God.

From this slavery the Son of God came to set us all free. If the Son therefore shall make you free, ye shall be free indeed, free indeed; *i. e.*, the freedom which the Son gives involves all the elements of true freedom. This freedom is not a condition of irresponsibility, or of exemption from the claims of law; but it consists essentially in a voluntary subjection to the legitimate sovereign of the soul. It is a freedom which is secured by the actual dethronement of the usurper, sin, and the actual redemption of the sinner from his bondage to the law. As our bondage was a twofold bondage to sin and to God's law, the freedom which the Son confers is a twofold enfranchisement.

The first chain which is knocked off by the Son is the chain of the law. Christ *redeems* us from the curse of the law, *i. e.* from its condemnation. Hence, says the Apostle, there is therefore now no condemnation to them that are in Christ Jesus. By nature, we were the children of wrath, but now God has accepted us in the beloved. At the very instant at which we became the children of God, by faith in Christ, we were redeemed by His vicarious atonement from the penalty of the law; we entered at once, on the instant, into a new relation to God; we came under a new dispensation, which is one of grace and pardon. We are no more under the law, but under grace.

The moment we become united to Christ by believing on Him, the penalty of the law, so far as we are concerned, is abrogated and the demands of the law upon us are fully satisfied. As the debts of a wife must be discharged by her husband; and as by her marriage all her maiden obligations are at once transferred to him, so the believer being married to Christ, and having become His bride, becomes a "*femme covert*," and is no longer responsible to the law. Says Luther, "Everything which Christ has becomes the property of the believing soul. Everything the soul has becomes the property of Christ. Christ possesses all blessings and eternal life; these are, therefore, thenceforward the property of the soul. The soul has all its iniquities and sins; these become thenceforward the property of Christ. It is then that a blessed exchange commences. Christ the Almighty and Eternal taking to Himself by the nuptial ring of faith all the sins of the believer, those sins are lost and abolished in him; for no sin dwells before His infinite righteousness. Thus by faith the believer's soul is delivered from sins and clothed with the eternal righteousness of her bridegroom, Christ. Oh, happy union! the rich, the noble, the holy bridegroom takes in marriage his poor, guilty, and despised spouse, delivers her from every evil, and enriches her with the most precious blessings."

By one single blow Christ, the Son, redeems us from captivity to the law, knocks off our chains, opens the prison door, and we become as really free from the guilt of sin as if we had never sinned at all. This was the freedom of which Isaiah spoke when he represents the great deliverer as saying, "The Spirit of the Lord God is upon me, because the Lord hath appointed me to preach good tidings unto the meek, to proclaim liberty to the captives, and the opening of the prison to them that are bound."

This is the first element in the freedom wherewith Christ makes His people free. So far as they are concerned, the penalty of the law is abolished.

My Christian brethren, you have heard all this before. Do you, however, realize the full import of these truths? Do you know that the true children of God are at this moment as free from all liability to punishment as if they had already reached their home in heaven? Now, is not this almost too good to be true? *But it is true.* Hear! oh hear, ye disconsolate believers, hear again the glorious Gospel, the *glorious good news*, which I am commissioned to sound once more in your ears—proclaim it to every weeping Christian whom you may meet. There is *now*, *i. e.*, at the present time, no condemnation to them that are in Christ Jesus. Who shall lay anything to the charge of God's elect? It is God that hath justified them, who is there to condemn them?

Do you believe this, and do you realize this, and yet remain a poor, desponding, downcast mourner? Oh! the thing is impossible. I do not mean that it is impossible for you to mourn, although you are really pardoned. Many a poor child of God does mourn, not because he does not believe this truth, but because it is a point he longs to know,—Am I His, or am I not?

But what I do mean is, that if you realized what it is to be pardoned, if you only knew how full and complete is the transfer of your guilt to Jesus, you would dry your tears forever and never weep any more. If you only knew the full import of the doctrine; if you could only realize that God does not half-way justify a believer, that He pardons him fully and freely for every sin, and regards him as forever redeemed from the law, you would become a joyful, cheerful Christian; you would return to your houses this day with songs and everlasting joy upon your heads.

But the work of our enfranchisement would be only partially accomplished if Christ freed us only from the curse of the law. You remember our bondage is twofold. We were also under the dominion of the usurper, sin. Now, to complete the work, Christ fulfils to believers His promise that " sin shall not have dominion over them." Christ dethrones this tyrant, unseats this usurper by the actual exertion of a supernatural power in the soul. He changes the heart, regenerates the affections, and releases the will from its bondage to Satan and to sin. This regeneration of the soul is a real, miraculous work, wrought in the bosom of every man whom God has justified in the eye of the law.

By striking off the first chain, Christ freed us from the penalty; by a second blow, He frees us from the power of sin. In the first act of justification, He gives us a righteousness *without* us; in the second, He works a holiness *within* us. The former is a cause of which the latter is an effect; our justification is effected by Christ as a Priest, and has sole reference to the guilt of sin; our sanctification is effected by Him as a King, and has respect to the dominion of sin. The former act deprives sin of its damning power; the latter of its reigning power. In the former act, He magnifies the law and makes it honorable; because the law has legitimate authority and cannot be set aside; it must be equitably satisfied. As a priest, He makes atonement to its insulted majesty and buys us out of our captivity. But in the latter act, He comes riding as a victorious king to dethrone sin, the usurper, and to vindicate His rightful dominion in the soul. By sending His Spirit into these hearts, His people, who were once the willing slaves of sin, are made His willing subjects in the day of His power, and He tears them away from the grasp of their former tyrant. They are led by Him as captives; but rejoicing captives, voluntary subjects to their rightful Sovereign, and thus they enter upon the glorious liberty of the children of God. Grace reigns triumphant, and they are free from the power of sin.

This is the triumphant reply which the Apostle gives to all Antinomians, and to those who would charge him with Antinomianism. He declares that those who are justified and thereby freed from the penalty of sin, shall be also freed from the dominion of sin. Shall we continue in sin that grace may abound? God forbid. They who are dead to the guilt of sin shall be powerfully delivered from its predominant influence. They are not now under the law, but under grace; and therefore they shall have that holiness which is not the fruit of the law, but is the result of that liberty wherewith Christ hath made His people free. Christ has now become the absolute master of their hearts, and He promises that He will reign in them by the invincible power of victorious grace.

Being made free from sin, says the Apostle, they become the servants of righteousness (Rom. vi. 18). But you ask, If all this is true, how do you account for the fact, admitted by all, that true believers are liable to sin, and do actually commit grievous sin? To this I reply by an illustration. When a tyrant has been dethroned, the effects of his misrule are visible long after he has ceased to reign. His evil influence is operative for many years after his supremacy has been destroyed.

This, I think, is a fair illustration of the manner in which sin dwells in believers long after their deliverance from its bondage. It dwells in them as a dethroned, but not as a dead tyrant, who is continually warring with the spirit to regain his lost ascendency. But, blessed be God! we have His word and promise that sin shall never regain his dominion. We shall be kept, by the *power of God*, not by our own power, through faith unto salvation.

Having begun a good work in us, He will perform it until the day of Jesus Christ (Phil. i. 6). If the Son therefore shall make you free, ye shall be free indeed.

And now what becomes of the third chain that bound us—the fear of death? Why, that falls off of itself. Oh death, where is now thy sting? The true believer no longer fears this once dreaded enemy. He knows indeed, that for a time he must yield his body to the grave, but there are no terrors now that lie beyond it. His fears have all been conquered by the power of that cross whereon his debt was paid and his sins were slain. Death is now to him the gate to endless joy—the way of nearest approach to the court of the monarch whom he loves. He is no longer a slave, but a son. He obeys because he loves. He renders homage, but it is not servile. He walks a freeman, an heir of God, within the very palace of his King. He is now the brother of the Captain of his salvation. Nay, he is himself a king. His inheritance is incorruptible, undefiled, and fadeth not away. He is an heir of God, a joint heir with Jesus Christ. The Son has made him free, and he is free indeed. Glorious hopes inspire him. He walks the earth erect, and conscious of his noble destiny. All things are his. Paul, Apollos, Cephas, the world, life, death, things present, things to come, all are his, he is Christ's, and Christ is God's.

He rises superior to the ills of this present life; he masters and triumphs over all the evils of his earthly lot. He reckons that the sufferings of this present time are not worthy to be compared with the glory that shall follow. He is free because the love of Christ is his constraining motive. He is happy because he knows that nothing can separate him from God's love. His galling chains have all been broken, and he is now led by the cords of love. This is liberty indeed, the glorious liberty of a willing subject—a full deliverance from his former bondage consistent with justice, satisfactory to God, and therefore satisfactory to the believer's own conscience.

No longer the slave of sin, his accusing, condemning conscience is pacified; his reason is satisfied, and the old schism in his soul is at an end. Being justified, he has peace with God and peace with himself. Being renewed, and sanctified although only partially, he is filled with spiritual joy. Being adopted as a son, he has access to God. He has freedom and enlargement in his communion with God. If the Son therefore shall make you free, ye shall be free indeed. Now there is no happier being on earth than he whom the truth has thus made free.

It would be easy to show, if the time would permit, the historical as well as the logical connection between spiritual and civil freedom. In proportion to the prevalence of these doctrines among a people, will they demand and secure political liberty. No king, no despot, is able to enslave a nation of Christ's freemen. Souls emancipated from sin and Satan are not the materials out of which Russian serfs and Italian lazzaroni can be made. Let men once learn the lesson that the "Son of Man hath power on earth to forgive sins," and that they need no priestly intercessor to come between them and their God, and the figment of a sin-forgiving church, which for centuries held men in civil as well as ecclesiastical bondage, is exploded. It is to the promulgation of the great doctrine of our text, and the great system of theology which is bound up in it, that we owe the civil liberty which we this day enjoy.

I need not remind you that this is the anniversary of the day* on which our fathers rose up in the majesty of insulted nature, to vindicate the rights of man. The political principles in the maintenance of which they shed their blood, and to which they pledged "their lives, their fortunes, and their sacred honor," were the direct outgrowth of their religious convictions—convictions which they inherited from the great leaders of the Reformation. If you would transmit unimpaired to your children the liberties you now enjoy, you must cherish as a sacred legacy the faith of your revolutionary sires. Let it then be inscribed on your banners, and let it mingle with the shouts of a jubilant nation, "If the Son therefore shall make you free, ye shall be free indeed."

---

* Preached in the Music Hall in Cincinnati on Sunday, July 4, 1880.

XII.

LIGHT.

"Ye are the light of the world."—MATTHEW v. 14.

Our Lord is here addressing His disciples and the multitude who had gathered together to listen to His wondrous words of truth and grace. It cannot be that He intended to apply what He says in this and the preceding verse to all His hearers indiscriminately. Many of them were the wicked people, who, afterward, had a hand in His death. Most of those who listened were not the salt of the earth, and were far from being in any sense the light of the world. The transition from the general address to the whole multitude to the special address to His disciples is made at verse eleven, in which He pronounces a benediction upon those who suffer for His sake. Ye who in your poverty have hungered for and obtained righteousness; ye who have been addressed as having, like the prophets before you, the ingratitude, scorn, and persecution of the world as your earthly reward; ye who correspond in character with those whom I have just pronounced "blessed," "ye are the light of the world." In another place Christ says of Himself, "I am the light of the world," and in the Old Testament prophecies He is called the "Sun of Righteousness"; and the aged Simeon, when holding Him an infant in his arms, describes Him as a "light to lighten the Gentiles."

In what senses, then, does Christ compare His disciples to light?

I. Light is the appropriate emblem of *purity*. Of all the works of God, none approaches light in its freedom from everything like impurity. Philosophy tells us that it may be analyzed so as to exhibit in its component rays the colors of the rainbow; but even these are free from all appearance of defilement. We speak of pure, white light. Poetry uses it as the emblem of unapproachable, immaculate innocence. It contracts no stain from the foulness of any medium through which it may pass, nor does it pollute anything upon which it may fall. Even the purest water may be rendered foul and unfit for use; the air of heaven may be tainted with unwholesome vapors; and thus both air and water may become the vehicle of disease and the cause of death; but light emerges from the medium through which it passes as unsullied and inoffensive as when it first gushed forth from the orb in which it originated.

It falls on the petals of the lily, and leaves no stain upon their velvety surface; it falls on the damask of the rose, and it blushes in unsullied beauty; it kisses the fair cheek of the maiden, and her virgin purity is undefiled; it falls on the black cloud, and, lo! it becomes a radiant glory; it falls on the dark, blue mountains, and the far-off heights are clothed in untarnished gold; it falls on the dew-drop, and the green sward is decked with sparkling gems; it falls on the cataract as the dark waters plunge into the abyss, and the white foam reflects it back to the eye of the beholder, unsullied by the contact.

Thus light is a beautiful emblem of that moral purity which contracts no stain from contact with pollution, and which lends its own lustre to whatever comes within the range of its benign influence.

II. Light is used as an emblem of *knowledge*. Ignorance is likened to darkness. As those who are in the dark see not, and consequently know not the objects which surround them; and as those who walk in the light have a clear perception of external objects, the figure is eminently appropriate. Says Isaiah: "To the law and to the testimony; if they speak not according to this word, it is because there is no *light* in them"; *i. e.*, they are destitute of knowledge. So the Psalmist says: "The entrance of Thy words giveth *light*"; *i. e.*, knowledge. So Solomon says: "The commandment is a lamp, the law is *light*"; *i. e.*, the source of knowledge. So Isaiah, speaking of those who obscure the truth by the teaching of error, says that they "put darkness for *light*." Light and understanding were found in Daniel; *i. e.*, he had knowledge and discernment. The knowledge of God is called by the Apostle, "the light of the knowledge of the glory of God." "To walk in the light" is equivalent to knowing the truth; "to have the eyes of the understanding enlightened," is equivalent to having the understanding illuminated with spiritual knowledge.

Now, the appropriateness of this emblem is manifest from the fact that most of our knowledge of the external world comes to us through the agency of light. The ideas which we have of form, though to some extent produced by the sense of touch, are mainly due to the sense of sight. All our ideas of color and of material beauty are derived solely through the instrumentality of light. In the beautiful language of Dr. March, "The pupil of the eye is the portal through which light brings in all the riches and glories of the earth and heavens to adorn the inner chamber of the soul. The mind sits enthroned as a sovereign in its secret place, and this swift-winged messenger comes flying with intelligence from every point in the whole landscape, and from the far-distant orbs of heaven. The mind has only to lift the curtain of the eye, and millions of bright heralds rush in to describe the form and hue and order of everything in the world of vision. Some of the messengers have brought their tidings in an instant, and some have been on the way a million of years to tell me where of old the breath of God blew a million of suns into flame, and sent them forth to sing and shine among the rival spheres of heaven. And as I stand gazing from some giddy height, it is as if all this vast and varied scene were the creation of light itself. Take from me the faculty of vision, or, what would be the same thing, destroy the light, and in place of all that wondrous world of beauty, a blank and pitiless wall of darkness shuts me in on every side."

III. Light is a symbol of *activity*.

Is it possible to conceive of anything more subtle and active than a beam of light as emitted from the sun? Philosophers tell us that light travels at the rate of one hundred and ninety thousand miles in a second. But it is not only the rapidity with which it travels that conveys the idea of its activity, but the fact that its very existence *as light* depends upon its rapid progress from one point to another. If it could be conceived of as pausing in its rapid flight, it would lose its character *as light*. When it falls on a black surface that absorbs it, and thus terminates its passage, it terminates its existence, it ceases to *be* light —it becomes darkness. So, too, a luminous body, like the sun, or a candle, would cease to be *a* light the very moment that the rays which stream forth from it should cease to pulsate through the air. Thus, whether we think of light as an emanation from a luminous orb, or of the orb itself, it suggests the idea of restless, unwearied activity and action.

Follow in imagination a single beam as emitted from the sun. With inconceivable velocity it begins its excursion into the unlimited fields of space. It flies in a right line toward our earth; it touches our atmosphere and is at once refracted, but not delayed in its mission. Turned aside from its direct line of approach, it still hurries on until it reaches its goal. It touches the summit of the hills, and then leaps down to the valley; it glances upon the pale stream, and gilds it "with a heavenly alchemy"; reflected from the flashing waters, it leaps up again with undrooping activity to gladden the eye of man, or to "kiss with golden lip the meadow green."

By a natural transition from light itself as an object of thought to its effects upon nature and upon all living things, it suggests still more vividly the idea of activity, in that it is the cause of all activity in men and animals.

Every morning we see the magic influence of light in waking the drowsy world to life and motion. All is stillness and repose; but the sun pours a tide of glory over nature, and the gloom and horror of the darkness vanish. The early lark begins to carol to the rising day; the squirrel leaps from bough to bough; lowing herds welcome the growing light; the blushing morn peeps through the windows of human habitations, and then the smoke of farm-houses rises on the distant landscapes; the silent sea of still life in the great city begins to heave and roar with the rising waves of toil and traffic; the prattle of children mingles with the clatter of wheels and the cry of busy men. All is activity now, where but an hour before the stillness of mimic death reigned supreme.

Thus light in its source, in itself, or in its effects, is an appropriate emblem of life, energy, action.

IV. Light is a symbol of *unity*.

The discoveries and generalizations of modern science have revealed beyond a shadow of a doubt that all force has its origin, *i. e.* its ultimate origin, in the heat of the sun; and what is true of heat is true of light, which always accompanies the production of heat. Thus, to take a representative case: "I hold in my hand a lock of cotton, which I ignite; it bursts into flame, and yields a definite amount of heat and light. Now, precisely that amount of heat and light was abstracted from the sun in order to form that bit of cotton. This is a type of the whole. Every tree, every combustible substance capable of yielding light grows and flourishes by the grace and bounty of the one central source of light. The very lightning is his transmuted blaze. Every fire that burns, and every flame that glows, every flickering taper dispenses light which originally came from the sun." *

Thus it is literally true that a grand unity exists among all the various forms in which light appears to illuminate the darkness of our world. It is the self-same ethereal essence that, Proteus-like, assumes a million shapes and hues. Hence, we speak of "*the* light" as of a common possession of all ages, races, continents, and generations. The light which God called into being at the beginning by His potent word, is the one unebbing flood of glory that has been bathing the world in radiance since order was evoked from chaos.

Thus light is a symbol of unity.

---

* Tyndall.

V. This, however, does not exhaust the catalogue of conceptions of what it is the emblem.

Light is the symbol of *beneficence* and *benedictions*. It were an endless task to enumerate the myriad blessings to man of which light is the cause and source. It fills our homes with joy and gladness; it reveals to us the smile of love, the tender look of affection, the gushing tear of sympathy; it is the one indispensable instrument of all human activity; it brings us into contact with the whole external world, and makes it available for our wants and comforts. In a perfectly scientific as well as a poetical sense, it is the source and producer of life. To appreciate the blessings which light confers, we have only to picture the effect of its sudden extinction. Where there is no light, there is neither animal nor vegetable life. If the light of the sun should be put out, in less than a week all signs of life would disappear from the globe. The air would be filled with deluges of rain and snow; the ocean, the lakes, the rivers would become as solid as the granite of the mountains; the whole world would become a wilderness of death, "seasonless, herbless, treeless, manless, lifeless."

Lord Byron, in his "Dream of Darkness," has given us a grand and gloomy sketch of the consequences of the supposed extinction of the sun—a conception "terrible above all conception of known calamity, and too oppressive to the imagination to be contemplated with pleasure, even in the faint reflection of poetry."

Hence it is that the presence of light is always employed as a synonym of joy, of happiness, of comfort, of warmth, of peace; and its absence, to call up to the imagination the terrible images of sorrow, gloom, desolation, suffering, affliction, and hopeless despair.

We need not have recourse to the gloomy dream of the poet, which represents the light of heaven extinguished, in order to appreciate the blessings which light confers upon mankind. If the sources of even our artificial light were destroyed, so that no candle or torch could be ignited to banish the darkness from our houses and streets, after the sun had sunk below the horizon, the sum total of human happiness would be immeasurably abridged. Let one or two particulars serve as examples of the whole.

The student could no longer pursue his midnight researches into the realms of knowledge; the lonely watcher by the sick-bed would sit with bowed head, and long for the morning; the streets of the great city would be paced with nervous dread by those whom business or duty should drive from their darkened dwellings; the mariner would dread his approach to the land over a sea upon whose dangerous rocks no Pharos flung its beams of warning; the halls of pleasure would be deserted by their gay votaries; the temples of worship, now open to those who would end their Sabbath with sacred songs and holy prayers, would be closed at early evening; in a word, how dull and empty would be one-half of our working hours, if even the taper lights of our own kindling were irrevocably extinguished! The cry would go up from our whole race to the Giver of every good and perfect gift to restore to us light in our dwellings, that there might be gladness in our hearts. "Light!" "light!" "light!" would be the universal prayer at the hour of evening sacrifice.

This brief survey of the blessings which light diffuses shows us that it is our greatest necessity, and that it is an eminently appropriate symbol of beneficence and benedictions.

Thus we have seen that light is the symbol of *purity*, of *knowledge*, of *activity*, of *unity*, and of *beneficence*.

Although all these ideas are readily suggested by the word light, yet, when our Saviour declares that His followers are the light of the world, the reference was probably to the most obvious and familiar points of correspondence, and not to those which are recondite or latent. Still, we need not, on this account, exclude from our view those points of analogy which might not at first sight have occurred to His hearers. The thought necessarily suggested to the mass of His hearers would be that of communicating knowledge, rectifying error, and dispelling the gloom which is inseparable from a state of spiritual ignorance, implying alienation from the only source of truth and goodness. This office was to be performed, this influence exerted, by the followers of Christ as individuals and as a body. Hence, to the Church, as a whole, or to each individual member of it, the address is appropriate: "Ye are the light of the world."

Now, there are one or two ideas remotely suggested by this figure, which I wish to present:

1. Christians are like lights, because lights do not shine for their own sake alone. The very end for which a lamp is lighted is that it may give light to others. "Light, in order to be valuable, must be seen. The illuminating influence of Christ's disciples is a nullity, without actual diffusion on their part and actual perception of it on the part of others. To claim the character, without acting in accordance with it, is as foolish, says our Saviour, as to build a tower upon a hill and then expect it to be unseen. If, then, Christians are lights, they must, from the very nature of the case, shine, *i. e.* they must be the source of divine and saving knowledge to the world; they must not do anything to defeat the very end of their existence by concealing or withholding what they have received, not only for themselves, but for the benefit of others."*

2. A second idea suggested by comparing Christians to a light is, that, as the candle or lamp in the process of giving light is itself consumed, so the true disciple consumes himself in the act of conferring blessings upon the world. The practical bearing of this thought is of immense importance. It brings home to every one of you, my brethren, the question: Why has God called me out of the world and introduced me into the kingdom of His dear Son? Why has my lot been cast here in this city, this centre from which stream forth such stupendous influences, for good or for evil, upon our whole land? Did He send His grace into my heart and convert me, that I only might be saved from hell; and did His design stop there? Am I to lock myself up in my safe retreat from the storm of divine wrath, and look out calmly through the casement of my fortress, and do nothing to save those who are perishing all around me? Must I make no sacrifices for the sake of others? Must I permit the Gospel and

---

* A. Alexander.

its saving ordinances to be dispensed with a niggardly hand, when, by effort and self-denial on my part, it may be made the power of God unto the salvation of the hundreds who come as temporary sojourners in the pleasant places where the lines have fallen to me? I hear you answer, "No, no; let me be consumed, let me live without luxury, let me eat the bitter herbs of poverty; but let me not withhold the bread of life from the hungry souls that are perishing for lack of knowledge. Let the oil in my lamp be all consumed as an offering upon the altar of my God. Let me make my light to shine, though it be exhausted in contributing its feeble blaze to the grand illumination of the world."

3. A third remark I wish to make, is that the illuminating influence of the Church as a whole is very much impaired by the failure to shine of any of its members, even the most humble and obscure. In order to bring this idea prominently before your minds, I present a very homely and familiar illustration. There are certain parts of many large public halls or churches, under the galleries, where it is always too dark to read the Word of God or to see the hymn-book at a night service. The little dim lamps that are hung at long intervals along the galleries are utterly insufficient for the purpose of illuminating the house. They represent those dimly-burning Christians who give *some light*, it is true, but not enough to illuminate the circle in which God has hung them up to give light to all around. Now, to carry out the illustration, suppose that on some unpropitious night, even one of these should go out, or fail to be lighted, do you not see that all who sit in that part of the house will be in comparative darkness? Of what avail is it to them that the people or the choir bask in a flood of light? Their seats are not within the bright circle; and, although they see the light afar off, it does not serve to illuminate *them*. Just so it is with many who call themselves Christians. They are the centres of little circles of friends, and acquaintances, and relatives, who, having had their lot cast among them, are dependent upon them, and them alone, for all the light they can ever get—the light of a godly example; the light of a holy conversation; the light of

devout and prayerful daily habits; the light of patient submission to the will of God; the light of holy resignation to the ills of life. Now it avails them nothing that these lights shine in other dwellings and upon other circles of society. They see these lights afar off, but they do not walk in their salutary beams; they sit in darkness and shadow, because those whom God has hung up to give them their share of the blessed light of life fail to shine upon them.

4. Although thoughts crowd upon me in this connection, I will detain you by only one more remark. Our Saviour says: "Ye are the light of the world"; not, ye *ought* to be the light of the world; *i. e.*, if ye are my disciples, ye do give light. Here then, beloved, is the test and criterion of your discipleship. Ye give the world light. If ye are His disciples, ye shine; for light must shine. If ye are His disciples, ye are characterized by the purity of which light is the symbol; ye are the source and fountain of spiritual knowledge to those who are ignorant; ye are active as the light that glances from the hill-top to the lake; ye are pervaded by the spirit of unity with all God's dear people; your light is the same light as theirs, because drawn from the same inexhaustible fountain of light; ye are the cause of blessings and benedictions to others; ye are shining not to be seen simply, but that others may see by your light; ye are shining not for your own sake, like the phosphorescent glow-worm, but ye are consuming yourselves for the good of others. If ye are His disciples, your light shines; it is not obscured by being hid under a bushel; it is not, it cannot be dimly burning, so as only to render darkness visible; ye burn, ye glow, ye shine; ye pour the bright, white light all around you. Oh! when Christians shall all be burning and shining lights, how the world will glow with the grand illumination! You have noticed the lighting of the streets in a large city; how, when the first lamp is lit, it is plainly seen and disperses in part the surrounding darkness; but when the second, third, fourth, and all the lamps are lighted, light meets light, ray blends with ray, until the whole place is illuminated. Thus it is with the spread of Christian light. The light of life shining from one believer joins and blends with that

of another; the light of one neighborhood with that of an adjoining one, the light of nation with nation, until the whole world shall become filled with the light of the glorious Gospel of the blessed God. Beloved, prove your discipleship by being in your sphere and in your generation " the light of the world."

XIII.

PREPARING AN ARK.

"By faith Noah, being warned of God of things not seen as yet, moved with fear, prepared an ark to the saving of his house; by the which he condemned the world, and became heir of the righteousness which is by faith."—HEB. xi. 7.

LAMECH, the tenth in descent from Adam, was a devout man, and his heart was sad on account of the curse that seemed to rest on the earth. The birth of a son, which took place 600 years before the Deluge, broke like a cheering ray upon his dark spirit. He called his name Noah, which signifies rest, saying, "This shall comfort us for our work and labor of our hands because of the ground which Jehovah hath cursed." After this joyous event in the home of Lamech, 500 years roll away before we hear anything of Noah himself, and then all that is said of him is that he begat three sons, Shem, Ham, and Japheth. We are authorized, however, to believe that during the whole of these five centuries his conduct realized the hopes of his father, for we are told that Noah "found favor in the eyes of the Lord"; that he was "a just man and perfect in his generations," and that he "walked with God." By the command of God, and under the direction of infinite wisdom, he built an ark, by which himself and family escaped the ruin of the universal deluge, which had been predicted to him 120 years before it came. Without dwelling upon the biography of Noah, which is familiar to you all, I wish to use the words of the Apostle in reference to Noah's faith in "things not seen as yet," to set before you some of those "things not seen as yet," which await every man; and to invite you to the exercise of the same wise foresight by which Noah "saved his house," "condemned the world," and "became heir of the righteousness which is by faith."

I remark that the "things not seen as yet," are the greatest and most momentous things in human history.

Most of us live very commonplace and uneventful lives. We are born into the world, and our advent occasions no stir, except in the immediate circle of our own family; we grow up, are educated, take our places in society, eat, drink, sleep, die, and the world moves on, unconscious that we have lived or that we have ceased to live. If there is anything striking or important in our history, it must be in the future, among the "things not seen as yet." Every man feels this to be so, for every man is looking forward to the future as containing for him all the interest of his existence. I think it may be affirmed as a general truth that the great things for mankind, which are not as yet seen, are the greatest things in their history. Some men, even in this short life, have experienced truly wonderful things; their histories have been eventful, and well-nigh marvellous; their biographies have surpassed the creations of romance. Yet what they have seen will not bear comparison with the things which are coming to them, but which are "not seen as yet." Death—introduction into the world of spirits—conscious contact with the Judge of quick and dead—resurrection from the sleep of centuries—all the events of individual life, not merely through an age or a millennium, but through interminable cycles; all these things are "not seen as yet," but they await every one of us. They are in the march of coming events, and they will break in upon our horizon in due time. He who controls human affairs has appointed the very hour of their advent, and, like the laws of nature and the stars of heaven, they will keep their time. When destiny strikes their hour, they will be with us.

Let me enumerate some of the "things not seen as yet" which ought to exercise a controlling influence over every thoughtful man.

The results of present labors are among the "things not seen as yet." Much of the effort which each one is now making seems a useless expenditure of strength. How much mental toil, how much of painful brain-work seems utterly fruitless! This is especially true of labor in the moral vineyard. The apparent hopelessness of achieving any great result is constantly exemplified in the labors of the preacher of the Gospel. Sabbath after Sabbath he presents to men the fruit of his diligent study of the Word of God; and he looks in vain for any result flowing from that which has cost him a world of toil. The same remark applies to the work of the teacher in the Sabbath-school. Week succeeds week, and, so far as he can see, his careful instructions produce no visible effect upon the thoughtless girls or boys who are the objects of his most earnest solicitation and constant prayers.

The same thing is true of the anxious parent whose only desire for his children is that they may grow up to be Christians. He cannot see that they are any more thoughtful or religiously inclined, notwithstanding his daily and hourly solicitude and labor on their behalf.

The same thing is especially true of the student who spends his time and energy in the schools in the acquisition of elementary knowledge. He often says: "Of what practical value will a knowledge of Greek roots and mathematical formulas be to me in the stirring business of life?" And he is often tempted to despair; and is on the point of relaxing effort, because the way seems so long from his present abstract study to any practical result. Now in regard to all these forms of activity the results are "things not seen as yet." But it is in accordance with a law of the constitution of things that every effort thus put forth must one day produce its result. The seed sown must one day germinate. Nothing is really lost. God has ordained an inseparable connection between labor and its ultimate reward. And in His Word He exhorts us not to become "weary in well doing, for in due season we shall reap if we faint not." We are told that "he that goeth forth and weepeth, bearing precious seed, shall doubtless come again with rejoicing, bringing his sheaves with him."

Now the real difference that we observe in the lives of men—some attaining grand results, and some utterly failing to achieve anything great or useful—is in large measure to be attributed to the influence which unseen things have had over them in the earlier part of their career.

Here is a man of varied acquirements and large influence. His opinions are eagerly sought for on every question of practical interest. His words are weighty and powerful. He is a recognized force in the Church, or in the State, or in society. He carries with him a moral momentum, so that, when he moves, masses of men move with him. Gray-headed men, his seniors in age, pay him profound respect, and defer to his superior wisdom. Somehow or other, this man has acquired a strange mastery over his fellows. Young men gaze at him, envying the proud position he occupies. His competitors for public influence ascribe his ascendency to accident or to the capriciousness of the popular mind; and they often wonder that their own fancied superiority is disallowed. Now how is this phenomenon to be explained? May not the explanation be sought in his early history? in the patient discipline to which he subjected himself in youth? Many a night has he spent in arduous study, in laying up stores of knowledge, in training his mental powers; many a stern self-denial has he practiced; many a time has he had the strength of character to forego tasting of the cup of pleasure; many a time has he stopped his ears to the siren song of the charmer, in order that he might waste no time while preparing for the great business of life. Little by little his store of useful knowledge has been acquired. By slow and painful effort his muscles have been hardened, and his nerves strung for loftier and more illustrious exertions. The great destiny which he has reached at last, was a thing "not seen as yet"; but he had faith in the future, he had faith in the well-known laws of human success, and in his preparation for life he was content to "labor and to wait." He knew that he was laying foundations deep and strong; and, although he could not foresee the exact proportions of the structure which was to arise upon them, he was well assured of the great truth, that he who would build up a great and sublime destiny, must, in the beginning, be willing to dig deep, and base his foundation on the rock. The things "not seen as yet" presented themselves in dim and hazy outline before his imagination, and exercised the same power over him that the actual reality now has over others.

In the same spirit the minister of the Gospel labors in his appropriate field and in fulfilling the duties of his calling. He cannot see any of the fruits of his labors. For years he goes in and out before his people, and, to all appearance, his preaching makes no mark and leaves no sign. Men come and go; they listen and then seem to forget; they turn aside for a moment from their business or their pleasure, seem for a moment to be impressed by the solemn message he delivers, and then they rush back again to the world, and become immersed in their business or infatuated in the pursuit of vanities. He often is forced to cry out, "Who hath believed our report, and to whom is the arm of the Lord revealed?" All day long he stretches out his hands to a thoughtless and giddy populace that seem bent on rushing to destruction. Now, what sustains him in his apparently hopeless work?—His faith in "things not seen as yet." He knows that God's Word cannot return unto him void. "As the rain cometh down and the snow from heaven and returneth not thither, but watereth the earth and maketh it bring forth and bud, that it may give seed to the sower and bread to the eater, so shall God's Word be that goeth forth out of his mouth."

Truth has a wonderful germinating power. It may lie hidden in the soil of the mind for many years, and may seem to be dead or hopelessly buried, and yet it will come to life and take root and bring forth an abundant harvest. One great doctrine imbedded in the mind of a congregation may slowly produce results in quickening spiritual life, in stimulating Christian zeal and activity, in strengthening God's people for suffering, and for doing His will, which the superficial and thoughtless hearer of the Word did not dream of, as he turned coldly away while it was taught or defended in the hearing of the great congregation. Hence the minister who seeks for lasting influence over the minds of his hearers disregards the popular clamor for what is called popular preaching, and endeavors to ground his hearers in the great doctrines of the Gospel, content to wait for the far-off results which he knows must accrue at last in the deeper and more intelligent piety of his people. He has faith in "things not seen as yet."

There is another class of laborers to whom it is especially important to have faith in "things not seen as yet." I refer to those who are engaged in the work of teaching in our Sabbath-schools. There is a tendency in the Church to esteem lightly the influence of the Sunday-school on our children. Many parents seem indifferent as to whether their children go to or stay away from this nursery of the Church. Yet, it is one of the most important instrumentalities which God has ever employed for the conversion of the young. Now the teacher in the Sunday-school is constantly exposed to the temptation of utter discouragement. The children in his class are full of levity and thoughtlessness; the most solemn truths seem to produce no impression on their minds or hearts. The instruction seems thrown away. Not so, however. In after-years those truths will appear in their consciousness. The line upon line and the precept upon precept have produced an abiding impression upon their character, and have insensibly controlled their conduct all along. They have been training for usefulness in the Church and in society, at the very time that their humble and perhaps obscure teacher has been lamenting his own lack of skill in imparting religious knowledge. Amid so many discouragements as he continually encounters, no man, no young woman, needs to be more earnestly exhorted to have "faith in things not seen as yet," than the modest, unostentatious Sabbath-school teacher.

These general views of the influence of unseen future things on the labors of men are not without value.

Let me now direct your minds to a closer analysis of the text. Noah, being warned of God of things not seen as yet, by faith prepared an ark to the saving of his house, and condemned the world thereby.

The unseen thing of which God warned Noah was His determination to destroy by a flood the inhabitants of the earth, on account of their wickedness. We learn that Noah spent 120 years in preparing for this catastrophe: that one great object which animated him in all his labors was the salvation of his family from the impending calamity; and that, by his conduct, he condemned the world—*i. e.*, he condemned it by his doctrine, by his obedience, by his example, and by his faith in them all. And Noah is held up to us for our imitation.

But as God has promised that He will not again destroy the world with a flood, it is pertinent to inquire how we can imitate him? What are the calamities of which God has warned us, for which we ought to spend all our years in preparation? The example of Noah is specially held up for the imitation of Christian parents. He " prepared an ark to the saving of his house." It was not solely on his own account that he was moved with fear. His sons and their wives were the objects of his tenderest solicitude. Now, there are calamities much more dreadful than a flood of waters impending over all our families, which ought to move us with fear. Each one of your sons and daughters is a sinner; each one of them must die; each one of them must meet God in judgment, and render a final account for the deeds done here in the body. The solemn questions, then, that I present to you to-day are: Are you " preparing an ark for the saving of your house"? Are you training up your children with worldly views and expectations? Are you impressing them with the sentiment that success in life, or the accumulation of wealth, or prosperous settlements by marriage, or a brilliant social career, is the chief end to be aimed at? Do you by your current conversation and example lead them to think that you regard religion a matter of secondary importance as compared with these objects of worldly interest? Is the study of the Word of God and of the great doctrines of our faith superseded by their exclusive attention to the study of their school books, and by their cultivation of the elegant accomplishments that will fit them to shine in society? Have you relaxed the reins of authority over them, so that they do as they please, go where they please, choose such associates as they please, and indulge themselves without check or restraint? If any one of these suppositions is true, then let me assure you, you are not preparing an ark for the saving of your house. And yet this is the chief end which every parent ought to have in view. It is for this that God spares your life, that you may save your children. You have lived long enough for your own good. You have exhausted all the joy of life; and now the only pleasure you can have is in your offspring. And as the salvation of Noah's house was dependent upon him, so the salvation of your families is in your hands. God holds you responsible to prepare an ark for their saving.

There are three instruments which God has placed in the hands of every parent by means of which he may "prepare an ark" for the saving of his house, and these are precept, parental authority, and example.

Under the first of these heads may be ranged the whole work of religious instruction; the careful indoctrination of your children in the truths of the Gospel, their learning of the lessons for the Sunday-school, their committing to memory the catechism, and all that invisible teaching which is involved in the reiteration of good principles at the table, at the fireside, and in the conversations that are held in their presence by the father and mother of the family.

But mere precept without the exercise of parental authority and discipline is not enough. Suppose you teach your sons that profanity is a sin, and yet permit them to associate with profane companions; or that drunkenness and licentiousness are wrong, and yet suffer them to wander about the streets at night without your knowing where they are, or what den of infamy they frequent, how can you expect them to heed your formal lessons on virtue? Suppose you teach your daughters that worldliness is a sin, and yet yield to their desire to dress in fine clothes and to attend balls and dancing parties, and theatres, and other worldly places of amusement, how can you expect them to be other than frivolous, and worldly, and vain? You have often felt a sort of pitying contempt for that old man Eli, who was so weakly indulgent to his sons; whom, although "they made themselves vile, he restrained not." But if you do not exercise your parental authority in governing your children, how are you any better than he? I hold that as long as a boy or a girl is under the paternal roof, it is the father's solemn duty to control them absolutely; to see that they are always at home as soon as the gas is lighted in the house, and to compel them to observe all the rules of a well-regulated Christian family. I hold that no man has a right to engage in any business which will take him away from his family at night, or at least that will prevent his having an oversight of his sons and daughters. Are there not a sufficient number of examples of boys reared on the streets at night to warn parents of the "things not seen as yet" that await their sons if their rightful authority over them is relaxed?

But precept enforced by parental authority is not enough to secure the desired result. "I do not undervalue a strong and decided government in families. No family can be rightly trained without it. But there is a kind of virtue, my brethren, which is not in the rod—the virtue of a truly sanctified life. A reign of brute force is much more easily maintained than a reign whose power is righteousness and love. There are many who talk of the rod as the orthodox symbol of parental duty, who might really as well be heathens as Christians; who only storm about their houses with heathenish ferocity; who lecture, and castigate, and threaten, and bruise, and who call this family government. They even dare to speak of this as 'the nurture of the Lord.' By no such summary process can you dispatch your duties to your children. You are not to be a savage to them, but a father and a Christian. Your real aim and study must be to infuse into them a new life, and to this end the life of God must perpetually reign in you. Gathered round you as a family, they are all to be so many motives, strong as the love you bear them, to make you Christlike in your spirit. It must be seen and felt by them that religion is the first thing with you. And it must be first, not in words and talk, but visibly first in your love—that which fixes your aims, feeds your enjoyments, sanctifies your pleasures, supports your trials, satisfies your wants, contents your ambition, beautifies and blesses your character. No mock piety, no sanctimony of phrase or longfacedness on Sundays will suffice. You must live in the light of God, and hold such a spirit in exercise as you wish to see translated into your children. You must take them into your feelings as a loving and joyous element, and beget, if by the grace of God you may, the spirit of your own heart in theirs. This is Christian education: this is the 'nurture of the Lord.' Ah! how dismal is the contrast of a half worldly piety, proposing money as the one good thing of life, stimulating ambition for place and show, provoking ill-nature by petulance and falsehood, having now and then a religious fit, and when it is on, weeping, and exhorting the family to undo all that the life has taught them to do; and then, when the passions have burnt out their fire, dropping down again to sleep in the cinders, only hoping still that the family will sometime be converted. When will men learn that families are inevitably ruined by such training as this?"

I have said that in order to make your children Christians, they must see that religion is the first thing with you. Now let me descend to particulars, and show you in what way many of you are teaching your children that religion is the very last thing with you.

Among the most important of the means of grace which God has established in His providence is a weekly meeting for prayer. Those who are "preparing an ark for the saving of their house" are always there. They account it their most precious means of grace. Numbers of you whom I now address are never there, and numbers only occasionally. Now, those who only occasionally come are just as unspiritual as those who never come at all. A duty which may be omitted at the suggestion of caprice or of disinclination, ceases to be regarded as a duty at all. Now, whatever the pretext with which you soothe your conscience in regard to this omission of duty, the real reason is, you do not want to be there. You have no delight in prayer; you have no confidence in the efficacy of prayer, and it is a weariness and disgust to you. I am not now speaking of what you yourselves lose, but of the baneful influence which this conduct has upon your children. It says to them in language louder than words, every time they hear the bell summon you to the house of prayer, and see you complacently sitting down in your parlors entertaining company, or playing upon the piano, or reading a book or newspaper—it says to them, "Your father, your mother, is indifferent to religion; they have no confidence in prayer, no delight in it." The children know the hollowness of the excuse that you "never go out at night," or that you have "no one to go with you," and such like subterfuges. They know that you do go out at night when you want to go, and that whenever you want an escort you can get one. They know that there is no family altar in your house, and no secret prayer; they know that they are living in a godless, Christless home, and that for the saving of that house there is no ark preparing; and therefore they grow up skeptical, like their parents, and utterly incredulous as to the "things not seen as yet." No wonder your children are not converted when you, in whom they confide, are teaching them every day by your conduct, that religion is a delusion and the Gospel a lie.

Or perhaps your excuse is that you have an ungodly husband, and that you stay at home to make home attractive to him. Did it ever occur to you that you might prepare an ark for the saving of that husband, if you would unite with the people of God in praying for his conversion, and if you showed him by your faithful attendance upon the ordinances of the sanctuary that you do not think it a vain thing to serve God? How many a wife has fortified her husband in impiety by stifling her own convictions of duty, and neglecting the very means of grace which might have been instrumental in saving him!

But there is another neglect that seems to me more amazing still. It is the neglect of those who do attend all the means of grace to bring their children with them. The reason which is rendered for this failure in duty is that the children are studying their lessons at the hour of prayer. The lesson ought to be studied at some other time. Everything ought to be made to bend to the performance of this duty. But your accepting and giving this as a valid reason is a direct admission to your children that the attainment of secular knowledge is first in your esteem, and religion second and comparatively unimportant. The consequence is that they grow up with a depreciatory esteem of this important means of grace; and when their school-days are past, they are never seen at a prayer-meeting. Who are the members of this church who never darken the doors of the lecture-room? Those whose parents never brought them there, when they were children. No wonder your children are not converted. You systematically train them to stay away from the means of grace. If I had to choose between the loss of education for my children and the formation of irregular habits of attendance on the sanctuary and at the prayer-meeting, I should say, let them never be educated, let them lose all human knowledge: but let me prepare an ark for the saving of my house in the habits of a godly and pious family, trained in the nurture and admonition of the Lord. It seems to me that unconverted members of the church ought seriously to consider what effect they are producing on their children. "Probably, you do not wish them to grow up irreligious like yourselves; few parents have the hardihood to desire that the fear of God and the salutary restraints of religion should be removed from their children. Possibly, you exert yourselves in a degree to give them religious counsel and instruction. But alas! how difficult it is for you to convince them by words of the value of what you practically reject yourselves. What are they daily deriving from you, but that which you yourselves reveal in your prayerless home and at your thankless table? Is it a spirit of duty and Christian love, a faith that has its home and rest in other worlds, or is it the carnal spirit of gain, indifference to God, deadness to Christ, and love of the world, pride, ambition, and all that is earthly, nothing that is heavenly? Do not imagine that you were done corrupting them when they were born. Their character is yet to be born, and in you is to have its parentage. Your spirit is to pass into them." And then you are to meet them in the future world, when the things not seen as yet shall have become realities, and you are to see how much of blessing or of sorrow they will impute to you. You are to share their unknown future, and to look upon yourselves as father and mother to their destiny. "Loving these children, as most assuredly you do, can you think that you are fulfilling the office that your love requires? Go home to your Christless house, look upon them all, as they gather round you, and ask it of your love faithfully to say whether it is well between you. And if no other argument can draw you to God, let these dear, living arguments come into your soul and prevail there."

Let me then exhort each one who hears me to-day to go home resolved to begin from this hour to build an ark for the saving of his house. What a revolution it would produce in many of the households in this church! How all your habits would have to be changed! And be assured you cannot do it without what will seem to you an herculean effort. Remember that Noah did not think it too much to labor for 120 years amid the scoffs and jeers of all his contemporaries, to build an ark for the saving of his house. You will have to encounter the same obloquy and ridicule. The world will call you a Puritan and a fanatic; but oh! if you save your house, what of that? Your children, so long unused to restraint and discipline, will chafe at first under the new restrictions and burdens; but what of that, if you only save your house? Oh! what a change in the aspect of the church if parents would only believe what God has said about things not seen as yet, and should begin to build arks for the saving of their house. What blessed and delightful meetings for prayer! What a precious revival of true religion would begin among God's people! What conversions of the unconverted members of the church! What a stir would be heard among the dry bones! How would the impenitent be aroused to a sense of their danger, when on every side they should see the signs and hear the sounds of fathers and mothers engaged in building an ark for the saving of their house! Then might they begin to believe that you have faith in things not seen as yet, and that you are in earnest when you tell them you are preparing to flee from the wrath to come. Oh, that God would baptize us all with the baptism of the Holy Ghost and with fire! "Come from the four winds, O breath, and breathe upon these slain that they may live."

XIV.

THE SABBATH.

"The Sabbath was made for man, and not man for the Sabbath."—MARK ii. 27.

THE Pharisees had accused our Lord's disciples of Sabbath-breaking, because to satisfy their hunger they on the Sabbath day had plucked ears of corn, rubbed them in their hands and eaten them.

He defended their conduct, affirming that they had not broken even the strict law of Moses.

To what did He refer when He spoke of the Sabbath? Evidently to the fourth commandment, which is, "Remember the Sabbath day to keep it holy, etc." He does not intimate that He, as Lord of the Sabbath, abolished the fourth commandment. But He declares the true end for which the law was enacted. It was made for the welfare of man as man—not for the Jew, but for *man*.

There is no propriety in speaking of the Jewish Sabbath. It is a day that was observed for centuries before the age of Abraham.

The fourth commandment relates to a day of rest which God appointed from the beginning of human history—a day sanctified by Him in the garden of Eden before the fall of man (Gen. ii. 3); a day honored by Cain and Abel when they brought forth their offerings to the Lord (Gen. iv. 3); a day recognized by Noah in the ark (Gen. vii. 10, 12); a day which was observed by Jacob in the marriage festivities accompanying his marriage to Leah (Gen. xxix. 28); and by Joseph in Egypt during the solemnities attending the burial of Jacob (Gen. l. 10).

The fourth commandment was not the original enactment of a

law, but the republication of one that had fallen into disuse during Israel's bondage in Egypt. In a condition of slavery among a heathen people, the Israelites had not been permitted to observe this day of rest. Hence, when Moses in Deuteronomy repeats the law to the people, he enforces the duty of so observing it that the man-servant and maid-servant may also rest, by reminding the Israelite of his own enforced violation of the Sabbath when he was a slave (Deut. v. 15). Hence the language, "Remember"; *i. e.*, " cease to forget," call to mind the forgotten precept, which, now that you are free, you can obey.

That the Sabbath was an original institute, or ordained from the beginning, is made certain by the fact that traces of its recognition are found among nearly all the nations of antiquity. The Egyptians, Phœnicians, Assyrians, Arabians, and Greeks divided time into periods of seven days, showing that they had derived from ancient traditions the idea of a seventh day as a boundary line between the other days of the week. Hesiod, the oldest Greek poet, Homer, Linus, Callimachus, Solon the great, Aulus Gellius, Lucian, and Lampridius, all make mention of the seventh as a sacred day. Josephus says, "There is neither any city of the Greeks, nor barbarians, nor any nation whatever to whom our custom of resting on the seventh day is not come."

But the most conclusive proof of the existence of a primeval Sabbath is found in the recent "Assyrian Discoveries" of George Smith. He says, "In the year 1869, I discovered among other things a curious religious calendar of the Assyrians, in which every month is divided into four weeks, and the seventh days are marked out as days on which no work should be undertaken." Lines 14, 17, and 18 of the Fifth "Creation Tablet" exhumed by Smith, are thus translated by Fox Talbot: " On each month, without fail, God made days of sacred assemblies, He designated the seventh to be a holy day, and commanded to abstain from all business."

Hence, Canon Tristram, before the English Congress, says: "Amid the controversies on the origin and meaning of the Sabbath, we now know that it was no Mosaic invention, nor exclusive Semitic observance, not even an ordinance delivered to

Abraham to separate his family from surrounding idolatry; but a primeval tradition, recognized, be it noted, by the Hamitic contemporaries of Nimrod, as instituted from the creation: We have thus another definite result, that evidence is afforded that the Sabbath was recognized as a Divine institution before the separation of the Hamitic and Semitic families of man, and that the obligation of its observance was acknowledged by both families." *

I quote these testimonies, simply to show that the Sabbath was not introduced by Moses, and that the abolition of the Jewish economy cannot affect the general question.

Moses was commanded by God to republish the moral law. The fourth commandment stands or falls with the other nine. It was one of the "ten words" graven by the finger of God on two tablets of stone. It was, so to speak, bound up in the same volume with the rest of the moral law.

There was a broad line drawn between the moral and the ceremonial law. The latter, written by Moses, was put in a book and laid outside of the sacred "ark of the covenant." The former, graven by the finger of God, was put inside of the ark to show symbolically that it was inseparable from the covenant of obedience which Christ came to fulfil. If the law of the Sabbath were to be relaxed by the coming of Christ, it would not have been thus shut up in the ark with the rest of the moral law.

It is sometimes said that the decision of the Sabbath question must be sought outside of the Bible. But who would accord any validity to a moral decision not enforced by a *Thus saith the Lord?*

It is also said that, while the other commandments are repeated in the New Testament, the fourth is not repeated. But what more positive reaffirmation of the "ten words" as a whole can any one demand than, "Think not that I am come to destroy the law and the prophets; I am not come to destroy, but to fulfil." "Till heaven and earth pass, one jot or one tittle shall in no wise pass till all be fulfilled."

---

* The Creation Tablets were found by Mr. Geo. Smith on the supposed site of the ancient Nineveh, on the bank of the Tigris.

Now, what is the fourth commandment? "Remember the Sabbath day to keep it holy. Six days shalt thou labor and do all thy work; but the seventh day is the Sabbath of the Lord thy God; in it thou shalt not do any work."

There are two elements in it. One is precept, the other is prohibition. It is with the latter that I am at present dealing—the prohibition of all work.

In the text our Lord says this day of rest was ordained for the welfare of all mankind. I am now only to prove that the highest interests of all men demand a stated day of sacred rest out of the seven days of the week.

First. As a mere *animal*, it is not for the good of man that he work continuously without a seventh day of absolute rest.

In the year 1832 the British House of Commons appointed a committee to investigate this subject. Dr. John R. Farre, an eminent physician, testified as follows:

"As a day of rest I look upon the Sabbath as a day of compensation for the inadequate restorative power of the body under continued labor and excitement. The ordinary exertions of a man run down the circulation, and the first general law of nature is the alternating of day and night, that repose may succeed action. But although the night apparently equalizes the circulation, yet it does not sufficiently restore the balance for the attainment of long life. Hence one day in seven, by the bounty of Providence, is thrown in as a day of compensation to perfect by its repose the animal system."

The law of the Sabbath is "written in man's members" and in the whole animal creation. The wayfarer who rests one day in seven, gets along faster and farther on his journey than he who presses on during seven days. The army which rests on Sunday marches farther in the long run than the army which does not. The team which rests does not become jaded by the whole trip. Droves of sheep, hogs, and cattle are found by actual experiment to travel farther and keep fatter by resting one day in seven. A flouring-mill in England was actually found to have ground 50,000 more bushels per annum after it kept the Sabbath than before when it broke it. "The men having been permitted to wash and dress themselves, rest from business, and go to church with their families, were more healthy, moral, punctual, and diligent. They lost less time in drinking, dissipation, and quarrels. They were more clear-headed and whole-hearted, knew better how to do things, and were more disposed to do them in the right way."

An experiment was once made in England upon two thousand laboring men in one establishment. For years they had worked seven days in the week, and were paid double wages for Sunday work. They were neither healthy nor moral. The policy was changed, and the consequence was they did more work in six days and in a better manner than they had done in seven. The superintendent said this was owing to two causes: viz., the demoralization of the people under the first system, and their exhaustion of bodily strength. These are all well-attested facts, which it is not wise for either employers or employés to disregard.

Let us examine God's Sabbath law. *Thou shalt not do any work.* This clearly prohibits every one from pursuing his ordinary vocation. If obeyed, it would close every store, arrest work in every flour-mill, foundry, tan-yard, wharf-boat, steamboat, railroad, printing-office, ice factory, distillery, post-office, etc., in the land. *Nor thy son, nor thy daughter,* imposes on parents the duty of restraining their children from the violation of the Sabbath. *Nor thy man-servant,* forbids employers imposing any but works of necessity upon hired laborers. *Nor thy maid-servant,* prohibits unnecessary domestic employment. *Nor thy cattle.* Doth God care for oxen? Yes, even the beast of burden must rest. *Nor thy stranger that is within thy gates.* Even the casual visitor that is in your house must conform to the rules of a well-regulated Christian household.

Of course there are many practical difficulties to be encountered in regard to the strict observance of the Sabbath by some of the classes in this enumeration; but none of these difficulties are really insurmountable, and none of them impair the right of every laborer to demand from his employer a day of rest.

How many thousands of the sons of toil would be gladdened by the announcement that all the great corporations upon which they depend for employment and subsistence, had determined that henceforth no work should be done for them on Sunday. What an army of machinists and brakemen and engineers and conductors and other laborers, would be released from toil to go with their families to the house of God, if all railroads would keep God's commandments! How many maid-servants would anticipate with delight the glad Sunday on which no elaborate dinners were to be prepared for their luxurious masters and mistresses, who go to church while they are sweltering in hot kitchens! How many clerks in small corner groceries, shops, and cigar-stores would hail with joy one day of absolute rest! And would the aggregate sales of those who engage in these minor industries be lessened one single cent? Would not the wants they supply be the same whether met on Sunday or provided for on the Saturday previous? Why is it that men who cannot, like the rich merchant, go out of the city to the sea-side or the mountains for rest, will voluntarily deprive themselves and their families of these fifty-two God-ordained weekly vacations, amounting in all to nearly two months of the year?

Secondly. Man is not only an animal, but he is a spiritual being, with a soul that needs spiritual culture and preparation for the great future that lies beyond the grave. I am not now discussing the question as to how every man should employ the day of rest. I am pleading for the workingmen and workingwomen of our city, that they be so released from work as to be permitted to spend the Sabbath in the way ordained by God for the culture of their spiritual nature. The Sabbath was ordained for man's welfare, not only as a dull plodder in the treadmill of industry, but as a probationer for immortality and as a candidate for a home beyond the stars. Give him a day of rest, in order that he may have a chance to make it a day of holy rest. Let not the tyranny of capital cheat him out of a vigorous, joyous, physical life, and at the same time frustrate his preparation for a glorious spiritual life, when he shall have laid down the tools of his drudgery forever.

I come now to a question which has given some thoughtful persons unnecessary trouble. The anti-Sabbatarian says, "However strong the plea you make for the seventh day, this does not prove that the first day of the week, or the Lord's Day, as you call it, should be kept sacred."

I answer: First. There is no doubt that the Apostle Paul, in Colossians ii. 17, states that the seventh day is no longer our Sabbath. What day, then, is it? Some day must be substituted. The moral law is not abolished. What day more likely or appropriate than that which commemorates Christ's entering into His rest, as God did after the creation, on the seventh?

The day may be changed without vitiating the essence of the command to rest one day in seven. No other day than Sunday has a shadow of claim. It must be this or none. It cannot be none, for then the moral law would be abolished; therefore it must be this. The change in the day involves no change in the essence of the Sabbath. The fourth command does not make the *seventh* day holy, but it makes the *rest-day* holy—for this is the meaning of the word Sabbath. "Remember the *rest-day* to keep it holy." "Wherefore the Lord blessed the rest-day and hallowed it."

Secondly. The fact is indisputable that inspired Apostles and their associates, immediately after the resurrection of Christ, avow that they are no longer bound to the seventh day, and at once observe the Lord's Day as a religious festival. Now couple this with the fact that they knew that they, with all the rest of the world, were commanded to keep a Sabbath, and the inference is irresistible that the authority by which they observed the Lord's Day was from God, though they do not say so.

In the same direction is the testimony of the Christian fathers —Justin Martyr, Tertullian, Irenæus, Origen, Cyprian, Clement of Alexandria, and the author of the Epistle of Barnabas. Eusebius says, "All things which it was a duty to do on the Sabbath, these we have transferred to the Lord's Day as more appropriately belonging to it, because it has the precedence, and is first in rank and more honorable than the Jewish Sabbath."

And it is a striking coincidence that as Moses, the first law-giver of enfranchised Israel, was commanded to republish the obsolete law of the Sabbath, so Constantine, the first Christian emperor, legalized the Lord's Day by an edict applicable to pagans as well as Christians.

It is sometimes flippantly said by those who have not gone to the roots of things, that the State has no concern with the Sabbath, and hence has no right to enact laws in regard to Sunday. If by this is meant that the State has no right to enforce the observance of Sunday as an ordinance of Christ's spiritual kingdom, granted. Such observance must be secured by the powerful persuasions of the pulpit, and by the godly training of Christian families. But if it be meant that the State has nothing to do with the enforcement of the original institute of God, before man needed redemption, then this is merely a disguised denial of the doctrine that the State derives all its authority from God. Christians who advocate this view of the relation of the State to the Sabbath know not what they are doing. They are striking at the very foundation of all government, and are playing into the hands of those atheistical enemies of Christianity, who know that if they abolish the Sabbath they will abolish Christianity, but who do not seem to know that if they succeed in this, they will also destroy all the foundations of free institutions.

Since the State itself is an ordinance of God for the good of man, it is charged with the duty of enforcing outward conformity to the law of God. And the same argument which denies the right of the State to legislate on a day of rest, would prove that it has no right to legislate on murder, theft, adultery, or any other violations of the moral law. The argument is self-destructive, because it proves too much. If, as I have shown, the law of the Sabbath was primeval, given before man needed redemption, adapted to secure his welfare as an animal, and as a spiritual being, it is clear that it is binding on the entire race—on Hindoos, Jews, Mohammedans, and Christians, and that it is the duty of the State to conserve the interests and welfare of all its citizens in this regard. If the State recognized its high functions as the minister of God, it would arrest every railway train, tie up every steamboat, stop every mail, shut up every barber-shop and grocery, silence the clangor of every machine-shop and printing-press—not in the interest of religion, be it observed, but in the interest of *rest* for the men and women who are employed in the service of those who create the demand for their labor. It would close every saloon and beer-garden in the city—not in the interest of temperance, be it observed, but in the interest of *rest*, because dissipation is inconsistent with rest. It would close all theatres and other places of amusement; it would arrest all base-ball clubs and brass bands and performances at public gardens—not because it is the function of the State to decide upon the morality of certain questionable amusements, but because these exciting amusements are inconsistent with that rest of soul and body for which a day of rest was ordained, and because the pleasure-seeker has no right for his own amusement to create a demand for the labor of those who pander to his tastes, and thus defraud them of a day of *rest*.

The votaries of pleasure are fond of quoting my text, "The Sabbath was made for man, etc.," as if it teaches that the Sabbath was made for man to do as he pleases with it. Precisely similar would be the reasoning, "Woman is made for man, therefore communism is allowable; and the law of marriage is a tyranny"; or, "Property was made for man, therefore agrarianism is right." To say that God's Sabbath was made for man that it might be used for amusements, which, like some in this city, would have brought the blush to the cheek of a citizen of ancient Pompeii, is a contradiction in terms.

The gradual encroachments made ever since the war, upon the poor man's day of rest, ought to startle the community as soon as attention is directed to them, and ought to arouse them as one man to the work of stemming the tide that threatens to drown the whole people in utter godlessness. One trade after another has been forced to succumb to the rapacity and greed of capital, and to the demands of the lovers of pleasure. Unless these demands and these encroachments are resisted, all the bone and muscle of society will be forced into the chain-gang, and doomed to unending toil, with no opportunity for the spiritual culture of themselves or of their children.

In the year 1834 a graceful writer for *Blackwood* invented a thrilling tale of a political prisoner immured in a dungeon, whose portals never opened twice on a living captive. Its roof, floor, and sides were made of massive iron plates, the joints of which were skilfully concealed. High above his head there ran a range of seven grated windows which admitted light and air.

On the morning after the first night of his captivity, he counted the windows; and could he have been mistaken? Now, there were only six; on the next morning he counted only five; on the next, but four; on the next, but three; on the next, but two; on the next, only one.

Ah! there was no mistake now. His dungeon was getting smaller every day. But surely his remorseless tormentor would relent and leave him this last window through which the light of heaven might pour.

But as the almost noiseless walls began to contract, the horrible truth flashes upon him. "Yes," he exclaimed, looking round his dungeon, and shuddering as he spoke; "Yes, it must be so, I see it now; I feel the maddening truth like scorching flames upon my brain. Yes, yes, this is to be my fate! Yon roof will descend; these walls will hem me round; I shall be shut up and at last crushed in an iron shroud."

It is for this "last window in the prison of the sons of toil" that I am pleading to-day. They remember the years of childhood, when every day was a day of light and gladness. They remember how "shades of the prison house began to close around the growing boy"; and as years advanced, how cares increased and burdens multiplied, and the world grew very dark, and life seemed hardly worth living.

Oh! let not their only day of sunshine on which God's holy light may pour in upon their souls be clouded too. Let not the last window of a holy Sabbath be closed, if you would not have them crushed beneath the ponderous roof and between the collapsing sides of a pitiless, Godless *Iron shroud*.

XV.
WHAT IS LIFE?

"Man shall not live by bread alone."—MATT. iv. 4.

The whole significance of the text to you depends upon what you understand by the word *Life*. For there are many who would readily admit the truth of the text who lead a life which denies it.

What, then, do you understand by life? What is it *to live?*

Observe that the text concedes that man does live by bread, but denies that "bread alone" is the means of life. And it is because men lose sight of this important qualification in the concession that they fall into the snare of the devil.

It is right to labor for the support of the body. Bread is essential, and it can only be had by incessant labor. The primal curse imposed upon man the irksome necessity. "In the sweat of thy face shalt thou eat thy bread." "He that laboreth," says Solomon, "laboreth for himself, for his mouth requireth it of him." Of course, then, I freely admit that men must take thought for what they shall eat. But it is just at the point of this concession that the tempter persuades them that this is all that is essential to life.

Let us trace a few of the practical results of the abnegation of the doctrine of the text.

I. The first necessary consequence of this theoretical sensualism is the inordinate desire of accumulation, so rife in the church and the world. If life, in the sense held by the men of whom I speak, is of paramount importance, then the inference is immediate that men ought to be laying up treasures to maintain it against an evil day. That such a view of life leads to covetousness, is distinctly stated by our Lord in the caution He gave to the man who begged Him to interfere in the division of an estate: "Take heed and beware of covetousness; for a man's life consisteth not in the abundance of the things he possesseth." Now, that many men entertain the view of life which our Saviour condemns, is evident from the fact that one of the most popular maxims of worldly prudence is this: "Make all you can, and keep all you make."

It is true that a man may practice this maxim and remain an honest man; but the transition is very easy from covetousness, to dubious views respecting the distinction between legitimate and illegitimate modes of acquiring wealth. By the ardent pursuit of wealth as a good in itself, the moral sensibilities are impaired and the conscience blunted; and hence you will find the man who began life with this maxim as his motto, at a later period expressing the conviction that a man is entitled to all he *can* make, and, in practice, giving a very liberal interpretation to the word "can," making it cover transactions of doubtful honesty, and justifying all the tricks of trade. It is true that what is called high commercial integrity is found to coexist with an inordinate desire for wealth; but that is produced by the constraints of selfishness, and not by virtuous principles. Many a man is honest in performance merely because "honesty is the best policy," who is a thorough knave at heart, his honesty being nourished in the soil of intense self-love. No man can be inordinately covetous and be at heart an honest man.

Another result of this theoretical sensualism is the utter destitution of all real benevolence. When this habit of heart is fixed, it intrenches itself behind two favorite maxims of worldly prudence—one, secretly whispered within the heart in order to fortify it against all the claims of charity, which reads thus: "A penny saved is a penny earned"; the other, which is flouted defiantly in the face of any one who begs a pittance for a distant philanthropy, embodied thus: "Charity begins at home." It is impossible for the man who loves money for its own sake, or on account of its power to provide him bread, to be a truly benevolent man.

Another result of this false view of life is a scoffing skepticism in regard to the existence of those virtues in others, in which the man is conscious of his own deficiency. Men judge others by themselves. They rarely accord to others virtues which they do not themselves possess. Especially is this true of those who have formed no conceptions of a higher life than their own, and have never experienced the inherent pleasure of elevated, virtuous affections. Whenever, therefore, they are called upon to forecast the probable conduct of others, or to interpret their actions, they always apply their own little standard of measure. As the result of their study of human nature, such men will enlighten you with profound proverbs like these: "Touch a man's pocket and you touch his heart," "Every man has his price." What a melancholy aspect must human nature wear in the eyes of a man who believes that these proverbs are universally true! How thoroughly pervaded by the essence of sensualism must that man be who can thus ignore the possibility of virtue's ever rising superior to the miserable creed of those who believe that man *doth* live by bread alone.

Still another result of this wretched creed is an inveterate utilitarianism in all its forms. *Cui bono?* "What is the good of it?" is the query it propounds to every scheme of public enterprise, to every endeavor to refine the public taste or improve the general condition of the community. Not, what good to the public? But, what good to me? Indeed, it often propounds the same question to every endeavor to enlist it in the work of its own culture and improvement. The man pervaded by this spirit ignores his own mind and soul. He has no desire for the intellectual culture either of himself or his family. The world of knowledge and the world of beauty in nature and in art are to him like the veiled Isis. He never knows, nor does he care to know, the secrets they conceal. He would not, if he could, drain one of their hundred breasts. He maintains with stolid obstinacy the dead level of his grovelling spirit, and walks the treadmill circle of the unlettered hind who "glorieth in the goad and whose talk is always of bullocks." Now, from such a position there is but one step to a loss of all principle and to the basest sordidness of character. The man who is industrious in order to make his living is doing the right thing; but, if he goes beyond, and makes money itself the end of his labor; if he is bent, not only on competence, but accumulation; if he is making haste to be rich for the sake of being rich, he has already fallen into the snare of the devil. Let a man once lose the practical distinction between making money to live and living to make money; let him once yield himself to the dominion of the "almighty dollar," and his moral character is ruined. He will soon come to regard wealth and goodness as synonymous, and his spirit will soon be the abject slave of Mammon. If, now, at this point, the lust of the flesh is brought into collision with principle by any great temptation, the man will almost surely discard the last vestige of his integrity, even at the risk of the loss of reputation; and he will certainly do this if he has hope of concealment. In this way I account for the sad defection from honesty so common among old men—men whose integrity had stood proof against a thousand previous temptations. We may lay it down as a truth established by the widest induction, that when the naked alternative of bread or principle is presented to him who holds that man can "live by bread alone," he will sacrifice principle for bread. There have been many conspicuous examples illustrating the power of the opposite principle in enabling men to overcome the temptations based upon an appeal to their bodily necessities. I shall mention only one, which for moral sublimity has hardly a parallel in history—an example which is especially pertinent, because the precise alternative presented was the sacrifice of principle on the one hand, and the sacrifice, not of luxuries, but of daily bread, on the other.

You have all heard of the Free Church of Scotland; but perhaps you do not all remember that this Church owes its present existence to the heroic assertion by her ministry, in the ears of all mankind, that "man doth not live by bread alone."

A brief statement, abridged from Hanna's "Life of Chalmers," will put you in possession of the prominent facts.

Previous to the year 1843, the Church of Scotland was connected with the State, and "established" by law. Her ministers derived their support from endowments. On this ground, the civil courts claimed jurisdiction over her spiritual affairs. Her ministers resisted what they considered an invasion of *their* jurisdiction. After much negotiation the British Parliament decided in favor of the ruling of the civil courts. The issue was now distinctly made up; and the question was whether a church that for years had been peacefully united with the State should renounce her principles, or, refusing to do this, her ministers should become outcasts and beggars. Men of the world hooted at the idea that those poor ministers would think of abandoning their comfortable manses and adequate incomes for the sake of a mere spiritual abstraction. Even such a man as Dr. Cumming, of London, himself a Scotchman, assured the government that the Church would yield rather than starve. One of the most sagacious statesmen in Edinburgh said, " Mark my words: not forty of them will go out."

The next meeting of the General Assembly was the first occasion on which events would determine how far these prophecies were founded in wisdom.

The day of trial came at last. Edinburgh was crowded with visitors from every village and hamlet in Scotland who came to see the issue. The church of St. Andrew's, where the Assembly was to convene, was filled with spectators at 4 o'clock in the morning, who knew that they must wait nine hours in their seats before the session would begin. As the day advanced, business was almost entirely suspended throughout the great city. Crowds gathered in the streets, all faces wearing a grave and earnest cast. No wonder Presbyterian Scotland was thus deeply thoughtful and anxious. The honor of the National Church and her very existence as a spiritual organization were at stake. She was to decide that day whether she would sacrifice her conscience or her bread. Her ministry were about to be called on to say whether or not thenceforward she should be as sounding brass and tinkling cymbal, a hissing and a byword to all passers-by. As hour after hour elapsed, the strained feeling of the multitude who occupied every inch of sitting and standing ground in St. Andrew's was beginning to relax. At last, however, the rapid entrance of a large body of ministers into the space railed off for the members, told that the Assembly was about to convene. Dr. Welsh, the moderator, entered and took the chair. Soon afterward his Grace, the Lord High Commissioner, was announced; and the whole assemblage received him standing. Solemn prayer was then offered. The members having resumed their seats, Dr. Welsh rose. By the eager pressure forward, the "Hush! Hush!" that burst from so many lips, the anxiety to hear threatened to defeat itself. The disturbance lasted but a moment.

"Fathers and brethren," said Dr. Welsh, and now every syllable fell upon the ear amidst the breathless stillness that prevailed, "according to the usual form of procedure, this is the time for making up the roll. But, in consequence of certain proceedings of her Majesty's government affecting our rights and privileges, I must protest against our proceeding further. The reasons which have led me to this conclusion are fully set forth in the document I hold in my hand, which, with the permission of the house, I will proceed to read."

He then read The Protest against the encroachments of the Civil Court, which, after reciting the wrongs inflicted on the Church, closes with the announcement that the signers of that paper, then and there, renounce their livings and deliver up the keys of all the churches and manses to the government, because of its interference with the conscience of the ministry and the supreme spiritual authority of Christ in His Church. Having read the protest, Dr. Welsh laid it upon the table, turned, bowed respectfully to the Lord High Commissioner, left the platform, and proceeded down the aisle to the door of the church. Dr. Chalmers, in his nervous way, seized his hat and followed; all the great leaders—Campbell, Gordon, McDonald, McFarlan—of course, went out with them. This was the critical moment. It was easy enough for such men as Chalmers to give up their government patronage; for they were great lights in literature as well as theology, and they were the idols of the nation. But would the obscure village pastors, who must the next day leave their manses and go forth houseless—would they dare to renounce the Establishment?

The whole body rose to their feet. Man after man, row after row, moved down the aisle, until the benches, lately so crowded, showed scarcely an occupant. A vast multitude thronged George Street outside, and crowded in upon the church doors. And when they saw the forms of their most venerated clergymen emerging from the church, they sent up a shout of stern but sacred joy that shook the very walls of the ancient city. No wonder that the stern old Presbyterians were filled with a frenzy of enthusiasm. They were standing under the shadow of edifices, every tower and turret of which was radiant with historic glory. They were treading on soil that had mingled with the ashes and drunk the blood of Presbyterian martyrs.

The church from which the procession emerged was the very one in which John Knox "first opened his mouth in public to the glory of God." In sight was the cathedral where he preached in defiance of the Bishop of St. Andrew's attended by his file of loaded muskets. Near by was the church of St. Giles, whose rafters once rang with the voice of Knox thundering against the "idolatrous Jezebel," Mary. A little beyond, but in full view of many, stood the old Grayfriars, upon a level stone in whose graveyard a whole nation, 200 years before, had signed the National Covenant of resistance to Charles I., Archbishop Laud, and Episcopacy. They were standing on the very spot where Patrick Hamilton, the protomartyr of the Scottish Reformation, died at the stake, as only one of God's heroes can die. They were treading over the tablet under which once lay the remains, and on which were cut the initials " J. K.," of the intrepid Presbyterian " who never feared the face of man."

With all these glorious memories recalled by these architectural surroundings thronging their minds, no wonder that their bosoms glowed with a holy joy when they beheld a visible demonstration that the heroism of their Calvinistic ancestors had descended to their sons, and that God's truth is immortal.

There was no design on the part of the seceding clergymen to form into a procession ; but they were forced into it by the narrowness of the lane opened for them through the heart of the crowd. As they marched three abreast, they were in full view of tens of thousands of men and women who had come from all parts of Scotland to see if they would dare to do the deed. "Some smiled in mockery. Some gazed in stupid wonder. The vast majority looked on in silent admiration; while here and there, as the daughter or wife of some outgoing minister caught sight of a father's or a husband's form, accomplishing an act which was to leave his family homeless, warm tear-drops formed which, as if half ashamed of them, the hand of faith was in haste to wipe away."

Elsewhere in the city, Lord Jeffrey, a nobleman "who cared for none of these things," was sitting in his quiet chamber reading. Some one burst in upon him exclaiming, "Well, what do you think of it? More than four hundred of them have actually gone out." He dashed his book to the floor and sprang to his feet, shouting, "I am proud of my country; there is not another land on earth where such a deed could have been done."

Such is a brief history of the Exodus of the Free Church of Scotland. She marched forth homeless into the wilderness, despising the fleshpots of the Establishment, her banner inscribed with the historic legend of the ancient Church of Israel, "Man shall not live by bread alone, but by every word which proceedeth out of the mouth of God." In a wonderful dispensation of Providence, she has been fed with the heavenly manna, and with meat that her oppressors knew not of. And she stands this day the light and glory of that land—strong in her resources, strong in her faith, and only purified by the fiery ordeal through which she was called to pass. The Lord has given her grace, and the Lord has given her glory. He "has withheld no good thing from her, because she walked uprightly."

My hearers, you may never be called to such a conspicuous display of the conflicts which must go on in your souls between principle and bread: but if you would triumph in your little struggles with temptation, you will be victorious only as you imitate her example in believing that the life of a man "consisteth not in the abundance of the things he possesseth." Perhaps I have dwelt too long on this division of the subject, but I could not refrain from warning my younger hearers against the gross and sensual views of life which characterize the practical philosophy of our times, and I would raise my voice to rescue you from the fate of those miserable old men whom you see all around you, who have emasculated their souls and squandered their lives in laying up for themselves—what?—only riches, wretchedness, and spiritual ruin.

II. But there is another mistake in regard to life which, although nobler in origin than that just discussed, is none the less a mistake fatal to the true life of the soul—the error of supposing that the life of a man consists in the cultivation of his intellect.

Says Dr. Chalmers: "The pleasures of the intellect, though calm, are intense, insomuch that a life of deep philosophy is a life of deep emotion. Even in the remotest abstraction of contemplative truth there is a glory and a transcendental pleasure that the world knoweth not." When, in addition to the pleasure the intellectual man derives from the acquisition of knowledge, he considers the practical power it gives him to benefit his race, the really beneficial influence he may exercise through its instrumentality, it is not surprising that he should come at last to think that life consists in the accumulation of knowledge, and in the exercise of the intellect. Intimately connected with the satisfaction which flows from the culture of the understanding, are the pleasures of taste. The universe not only teems with truth, but it is profusely garnished with all the elements of beauty. . . . . Now, the man who sees and feels this in Nature, must know that he is living a far more exalted life than the mere man of business who walks through the world unconscious that he is moving about in a palace fit for the abode of angels. It is not surprising that he should at last believe that that which so exalts his being above the grosser pleasures of the senses, is indeed the very wine of life drawn from the fountain of immortality. And there can be no doubt that the man of cultivated taste does live an infinitely higher life than the mere sensualist, and is effectually fortified against the indulgence of the baser appetites. Perhaps there is no class of intellectual men who realize more deeply than the lovers of the beautiful the truth that "man does not live by bread alone."

Now add to this the universal homage paid even by the sensual and sordid to intellectual culture, the unconscious and instinctive tribute which rudeness renders to refinement, the undisputed supremacy which the educated mind maintains over the mere working mind of a community; and it is still less surprising that many should think the solution of the problem, "What is it to live?" is to be found in the culture of the intellect, and the refinement of the taste.

Although the number who really take this higher view of life may be small, still there are some here to-day. It may not be amiss to assure any and all such that the merely intellectual man has not solved the problem, "What is life?" He has, indeed, reached the truth that man does not live by bread alone; but he has grasped only a part of the truth, when he thinks that the activity of the mind makes up the complement of life. "Man liveth by every word that proceedeth out of the mouth of God."

It is true that the universe is a revelation of God, and every floweret is an expression of divine thought; but he who has studied nature with the eye merely of a savant or an artist, for the sake of satisfying the cravings of his intellect or his taste only, has stopped short of the goal. Like the impotent astrologers at the court of Belshazzar, he beholds the handwriting of God, but he knows not the interpretation thereof. I may go even further, and admit that mere knowledge may lead a man from the contemplation of Nature to the recognition of God, and to a sentimental worship of the Great Architect; and still he may be totally ignorant of the higher life of the soul. For in this connection we must never forget that the highest intellectual development may coexist with an utter destitution of holiness. The history of the human intellect affords many examples of gigantic intellectual powers, large and varied attainment, coupled with moral depravity and spiritual blindness. And this brings me to the last division of this discourse.

III. Life, in its highest acceptation, must comprehend, as an essential and as a predominant element, the spiritual life of the soul. Here I must say, do not understand me as depreciating intellectual life, or as intimating that it does not enter largely into spiritual life. When invited to the contemplation of intellect in its sublimest offices; when I see the highest displays of its glory; when I consider its lofty aspirations, its exalted and exalting sentiments, its generous sympathies, its splendid imaginations, its ethereal and blissful activity, its searching, lucid, and commanding reason, and its inborn thirst for truth, I glory in the consciousness of being a man, and that I may enjoy the immunities of intellectual life. But I cannot forget that the Word of God declares that a man may be intellectually alive and yet dead—dead in sin, devoid of all true spiritual life. I cannot forget that the Scriptures teach that the chief end of our present life is holiness now and happiness to come; labor in the present for reward in the future; moral discipline now for perfection hereafter. Intellectual activity here has therefore little value, except so far as it contributes to the nourishment of spiritual life in this world, and the attainment of eternal life in the world to come. No attentive reader of the Bible can fail to observe that the Scriptures everywhere speak of a divine life in the soul as something actual, and as entirely distinct from the ordinary activity of the mental faculties. Such expressions as these: "Your life is hid with Christ in God"; "The life which I now live in the flesh, I live by the faith of the Son of God"; "To be spiritually-minded is life"; "The life of Jesus made manifest in our mortal flesh"; all show that there is a state of the soul attainable in this mortal life, which is called "Spiritual Life." At the same time it is very difficult to form a clear conception of what it is. But the following statement is true, though not exhaustive :

1. The divine life as it may exist in the human soul is a supernatural condition produced and maintained by the direct personal agency of the Spirit of God. It is a real, vital change in its modes of being—a change and state as real as any of the phenomena of external nature; a change as real as would be a transition from physical or natural death to physical or natural life.

2. This spiritual life may be most comprehensively described as consisting in the personal acquaintance of the soul with a personal God, in personal union with Jesus Christ, and in personal communion with the Father and the Son through the Spirit of God actually dwelling in the soul as in a temple.

3. The presence of this spiritual life in the soul is manifested principally in the acts of the affections and the will rather than by any achievements of the intellect, although it undoubtedly imparts energy and gives complexion to all the exercises of the understanding. But since its most direct influence is upon the moral constitution, we detect its workings mainly in those acts which are the exponents of character.

4. Another characteristic of the divine life is that into whatever soul it enters, it enters to inaugurate a conflict between the principle of holiness and that of sin. That bosom is at once an arena where the spirit warreth against the flesh and the flesh against the spirit. And as the result of this struggle there accrues to the soul what the Scriptures call spiritual strength, or what we call strength of principle—a strength to do, a strength to suffer, a strength to resist evil. For this the Apostle made intercession in behalf of the Ephesians, when he prayed continually that they might be " strengthened with all might by the Spirit in the inner man."

5. Another striking peculiarity of the spiritual life is that, for the most part, it is hidden : often unknown to the world around. The kingdom of God is often set up in many a heart " without observation." In this respect it differs from other life. It is hidden, because the animating principle, the vital operative element is not in itself, but in another. It is a life grafted into another life. " Your life is hid with Christ in God."

It is hidden, in that in its results upon individual minds it is directly the reverse of the natural life. This seeks notoriety ; that, retirement from the market-place ; this seeks companionship with man ; that, with God. There may be, doubtless there are, within these walls some who, all unknown to the mass of the church, have been for years growing up into the perfect proportions of a lofty spiritual stature ; humble men and obscure women who, could we see them as they appear in the eye of God, would tower up above us all in the moral sublimity and grandeur of "the fulness of the measure of the stature of men in Christ Jesus"; and yet we know them not. They have been moving in their noiseless walk through life, accomplishing a ministry of doing and suffering, humbly and patiently doing the work and bearing the burdens which God has appointed them. Perhaps they are the sons and daughters of poverty; perhaps unlearned; perhaps regarded by the rich and prosperous as the offscouring of the earth. Perhaps they cannot even give utterance in fit language to their devotion to Christ; and yet, if called to do, or suffer, or die for Him, they would write new days in the calendar of Christian heroism, and leave names to be added to the catalogue of those "of whom the world was not worthy."

6. Still another characteristic of the spiritual life is that, when it is weakest in its own estimation, then it is strongest in its might. In this connection let me call your attention to the contrast between intellectual and spiritual strength. Read the description of Mr. Webster just before he was to make his celebrated reply to Mr. Hayne, in the Senate of the United States. It is said of him, "He perceived and felt equal to the destinies of the moment. The very greatness of the hazard exhilarated him. His spirits rose with the occasion. He awaited the time of onset with a stern, impatient joy. He felt like the warhorse who paweth in the valley and rejoiceth in his strength; who goeth on to meet the armed man, who sayeth among the trumpets, Ha! ha! and who smelleth the battle afar off, the thunder of the captains and the shouting."

We feel that this is a fitting description of gigantic intellect reposing confidently upon its own resources. But in the domain of spiritual life, "man is never so weak as when he casts off his burden and stands upright and unincumbered in the strength of his own will; never so strong, as when bowed down in his feebleness, tottering under the whole load that God has laid upon him, he comes humbly to the throne of grace to cast his care upon God who careth for him."

Such are some of the characteristics of the spiritual life, and it is manifest that it requires for its sustentation something different from either knowledge or bread. It must have "meat to eat that the world knows not of." It must derive its aliment direct from heaven.

This was the life that Christ came to give to men. "He that hath the Son of Man hath this life." And this life can be perpetuated, as it is originated, only by a vital union with the Son of God. "For the bread of God is He which cometh down from heaven and giveth life unto the world; and he that eateth this bread shall live forever." Happy is he who, sated with the bread that perisheth, but still unsatisfied, has turned away from the beggarly elements of this world, and cries out in conscious emptiness, "Lord, evermore give me this bread."

"This spiritual life is a real, blessed, glorious, mighty thing. It is a life begotten of Love, incarnate, redeeming, crucified Love. It is life given back from an awful perdition—the life of a soul reunited to God after a dark apostasy. It is life from God and in God, as the stream contains the waters of a fountain. By it we are made 'partakers of the divine nature.' It is life in all the opulence, freshness, and glory of the divine ideal ' when man was made a living soul.'" It is the very beginning and portal of Eternal Life.

Now, this spiritual life is within the reach of every one who truly desires it. But, in order to obtain it, you must be born again; you must be made new creatures in Christ Jesus. In order to eat of the hidden manna, you must receive the "white stone on which is written a name that no man knoweth, save he that receiveth it." You can never feed on the heavenly bread, or drink with relish from the living fountain, until you are endued with a life from on high.

In this discourse I have brought into vivid contrast, sensual, intellectual, and spiritual life; and, now that the picture is finished, I beg you to compare the wretched pigmy who lives by bread alone, with that man who lives by every word which proceedeth out of the mouth of God, and decide which of these portraits shall be yours. If, when your mortal career is about to close, and you are entering upon the long career of your immortality, you would not be a miserable dwarf among the lofty intelligences of another sphere; if you would not enter into eternity a poor starveling, a spirit emaciated for want of food; if when stepping into the Great Future you would meet not strangers, but friends, in the noble and august society of heaven; if you would receive the congratulations of wise and great beings—the holy welcome offered by warm and noble hearts,—then go and write it in your ledgers, write it in your counting-rooms, write it in your workshops, write it on the door-posts of your houses, write it on the fleshly tablets of your hearts,—" Man doth not live by bread alone." For as you sow in your daily life, you shall likewise reap. "He that soweth to the flesh shall of the flesh reap corruption; but he that soweth to the Spirit shall of the Spirit reap Life, *Life Eternal.*"

XVI.

FRAGMENTS.

"Gather up the fragments that remain, that nothing be lost."—JOHN vi. 12.

OUR Lord having been absent from Capernaum, which was on the northwest side of the Sea of Galilee, returned thither, and as soon as His presence was known, crowds thronged around Him. But He had been engaged in arduous labors and needed rest. He therefore took the twelve disciples, and entering a boat, they rowed northeast six miles to the eastern side of the lake beyond the mouth of the Jordan, to the plain of Batiha, under the shadow of Bethsaida, where He might rest in the quiet glens that opened up from the lake. But the people seeing the direction He took, ran around the head of the lake; and, as they went, crowds joined them; and by the time He had reached the shore, the whole plain was swarming with men, women, and children. The sick and helpless had come, or had been brought in the arms of friends. Passing through the crowd, healing by a word or by a touch all who asked Him, He ascended the hillside, and gathering the multitude into a compact mass, He spoke unto them the words of God.

The day was far spent; but the people would not go away. The disciples urged Him to send them away, that they might buy bread in the adjacent villages. He told them to feed the people themselves. He was not willing to dismiss them hungry, lest they should faint by the way. The disciples were amazed;— How could they feed them? Two hundred dollars' worth of bread, in our money, would not be enough to give every one a small piece; and they had only five barley loaves and two small fishes. He said, "Make them sit down."

It was the month Nisan, the season of flowers. The hillside was covered with a carpet of grass. The long shadows from the western hills were projected across the lake. The heat of the sun was abating. The disciples arranged the multitude in companies of fifty and a hundred. He took the five barley loaves and the two small fishes and began distributing food to His disciples; and they, to the multitude. "And they did all eat and were filled." But there was more than enough. Then said Jesus, "Gather up the fragments that remain, that nothing be lost." And they took up twelve baskets full—a great deal more than they had at first.

You can form some conception of the magnitude of this miracle by remembering how the vast crowd that filled this hall last Sabbath impressed you with the idea of numbers. It is easy to talk of 5,000 men, but when you see them sitting in regular companies of fifty and one hundred, you get an idea of what a vast concourse of people means. Think how much bread and fish it would require to satisfy the hunger of this famished multitude. Christ fed them all by the exercise of His omnipotent power. But what was the meaning of this command? What a singular combination of lavish expenditure and frugal economy! Was it necessary that He, who had only an hour before exhibited His ability to provide for thousands, should husband the broken morsels remaining after the bountiful supply? Or rather, was it not because He wished to teach a great moral lesson in connection with this miracle of beneficence and power?

What, then, is the lesson which we are to learn from this example of Divine economy? The great principle which our Lord intended to inculcate, is contained in the following proposition, *That which is valuable as a whole, is valuable in its minutest parts.*

We see the principle illustrated in Nature, through which lavish profusion and boundless expenditure seem to run riot. The falling leaves of autumn, though scattered all over the earth, are not really lost. They have their resurrection in the budding glories of the spring-time, which by their decay they have nourished. We ourselves may be feeding on the bones of extinct races of men and beasts long since perished, whose ashes fructify the soil from which spring our harvests of golden grain. The cautious jeweller, who works in the precious metals, understands the principle when he gathers the minutest filings of gold that fall from his vise, and treasures them against the day when he shall fashion them into a trinket, to adorn the bosom of beauty, or melts them down into ingots from which to shape the plain gold ring which is to be the emblem of wedded love.

The law of the land forbids the "sweating of coin"; because although each piece of gold or silver loses a mere fragment of value by the process, yet the aggregate result of the petty peculation proves that what is valuable as a whole is valuable in its minutest parts.

Go to the national mint, and you will find the floor covered with a perforated carpet through which the minutest particles of gold-dust gradually filter, and they are gathered at the last, to be coined into the money of the realm.

Now let us consider the principle in its application to us. What are some of the things valuable as a whole, the minutest parts of which we are prone to undervalue?

First. *Money.* All value money in the mass. The more of it men have, the more they set store by it. But what is money? It is in the last analysis, the representative of *labor*. However acquired by any one, whether as an inheritance from a father, or obtained by industry, every cent represents one drop of that sweat of the face by which man earns his bread. Money is the representative of toil. It is not found, it is not stumbled upon by accident or luck; it is wrought out of the travail of body, and brain, and soul. It represents the entire travail of the human race. For whether it exists in the form of gold or silver coin, or bank-stock, or real estate,—all property which may be represented in dollars and cents is the representative of labor rewarded by God's providence.

Now everybody values *money.* I need not exhort you to a love of it. Alas! it is the crying sin of our age, and of every age; a sin as old as the time of the Apostle, who said the love of money is the root of all evil. It is not against the sin of covetousness that I now lift up my voice. I am trying to impress on you the truth that, much as you value money in the aggregate, there is not one of you who places the proper estimate upon its smaller parts. Now, as all you have comes from God, He holds you responsible for the manner in which you dispose of the smallest portion of His gifts. Too many feel that as they have made their money by their own exertions, they have a right to spend it as they please, or to throw it away. Not so. Who gave the strength of arm, the health, the skill, the foresight, the dexterity, by means of which you make money? Who sent favorable seasons upon the growing grain? Who wafted the precious cargoes by prosperous gales? Who warded off tempest and fire from the packed warehouses? God. And as the result of this fostering care and Divine superintendence, you have become prosperous and comfortable in your worldly estate. Now what right have you, as God's steward, to throw away any portion of what He has committed to you? You say you *do* lay up every year for your family; you do give a portion to the benevolent enterprises of the day; you do help support your church. Ah! how much more might you do, if you would only save the pennies and the dimes that you throw away in useless and sometimes sinful indulgences.

The rich man does this continually. He knows that he ought to make some return to God for all His benefits, and in looking at his abundance he sometimes recognizes God as the Giver, and *says* he *is* thankful. Few men are willing to bear the character so aptly described by the sacred poet:

> " That man may last but never lives,
> Who much receives, but nothing gives,—
> Whom none may love, whom none may thank,
> Creation's blot, creation's blank!"

Yet there are multitudes to whom these lines apply. They intend to do something for God and for the good of men; but day after day passes away without the performance of their good intentions. The tide of selfish expenditure flows on without abatement, and the end of the year comes without their having executed one of their benevolent intentions. No widow's heart sings for joy at the mention of their names, no eye grows brighter when men think of them; the blessing of none ready to perish greets their ears. Oh! had they only reflected as they squandered dimes and pennies, that whatever is valuable as a whole is valuable in its parts,—and gathered up the fragments from their overflowing purses, they might all the year through have been reaping the blessing of him "who considereth the poor," whom "the Lord will deliver in time of trouble."

It is very agreeable to the poor to hear the rich upbraided for their want of liberality, and they sit by complacently and enjoy the castigation. But I charge the same sin upon the poor. Of how many acts of sinful waste are they also guilty! How often do they plead their poverty as an excuse for withholding gifts which they might bestow, had they only gathered up the fragments of their limited supply—fragments which have been cast into the ocean of waste and utter unfruitfulness! Ah! this charge of *waste* is one to which rich and poor alike must plead guilty.

Second. *Time* is a gift of God, for the use of which we are all responsible.

Life is the time in which to serve God and prepare for eternity. All value life supremely. "All that a man hath will he give for his life." And so short is it, that men are constantly complaining of its brevity. Yet, how much of it they waste! Such is the constitution of things that it is broken up into fragments. Few have the opportunity of continuous labor. So imperious are the demands of the body, that little remains for doing the great work of life—the preparation of the soul for its high destiny. Take out of life the time for working, eating, sleeping, and recreation, and what remains but the fragments of scattered days? And these fragments cannot be gathered together. They can only be utilized as they occur. They are the merchant's half hour after dinner, the mechanic's evening after supper, the housekeeper's interval of waiting for the good man to come home, the mother's respite from nursing the baby after it has folded its little hands to sleep. How favorable these intervals for solemn self-inspection, for reading a short lesson in the Bible, for silent communion with the great Father, for brief colloquy with Jesus, for cherishing the presence of the Holy Spirit! What opportunities for increasing knowledge, cultivating the mind, and garnering up treasures from pages "rich with the spoils of time"! To some men and women of leisure, time is such a burden that they tax their ingenuity to devise methods for "killing it." Yet they value life as a whole supremely.

This strange perversity in human nature is aptly illustrated in the following story:

A felon, condemned to death, was respited on the following condition: He was confined in a well-lighted cell, supplied with well-seasoned food, and doomed to perish at last for want of water. A concealed tank, of dimensions unknown to him, was placed in the adjacent cell, and a faucet from it passed through the wall into his apartment. It contained all the water he would ever have to drink. When it should be exhausted he must die of thirst. You may imagine his feelings when he learned that the length of his respite was measured by this fixed but unknown supply. How timidly he drew the first cupful! How cautiously he turned the spigot! How sparing his first indulgences! How long he endured the pangs of thirst before he would venture on a second draught! But as day succeeded day, the stream ran strong and full. At length familiarity banished his early fears. He indulges in more generous draughts. He goes oftener to quench his thirst. He laughs at his former timidity. He riots in excess. He drinks as if some tempting fiend were urging him to defy his doom, when lo! to his horror and amazement, the last drop trickles from the spout. Too late now to curse the madness and delirium of his reckless and ill-timed profusion. How priceless now the wasted draughts of yesterday! He dies of thirst because there was nothing more to drink.

Thus, thus it is with your life. You know not how short or how long it may be; but you do know that your days are numbered, and that every day brings you nearer the end. You cannot, like this poor convict, by self-denial husband your store. The onward sweep of your life is like the wave of the ocean rolling without one moment's pause until it break on the shore.

But though much of the past is lost, all is not lost; then gather up the fragments that remain, that nothing more be lost. O Lord! "so teach us to number our days, that we may apply our hearts unto wisdom."

Third. A third talent which God has given to every human being is *Influence*—the power of affecting the character and destiny of others. Some say, and perhaps believe, that they have no influence. But as every atom in our globe helps to preserve the balance of the solar system; as the mote which sparkles in the sunbeam stretches out its attracting power to the distant star, so every one is a centre of influence that is streaming forth like the viewless magnetic current of the loadstone. The very worm at your feet, or the serpent that crosses your path, produces some change in your conduct or purpose. And can it be that you, with the power of speech and "discourse of reason," are a mere cipher in the jostling crowd that hear your words and see your actions? Let no one say that he is so insignificant as to be powerless to influence the character and destiny of others. And what makes the responsibility so solemn is that our involuntary influence is often more potent than our conscious efforts to mould others to our will. One look of mild reproach drove Peter to penitence and tears. A tone of sympathy has often cheered a heart bowed down with grief. A word spoken in season has served to arrest the mad career of one hastening to ruin. A single smile has been to a darkened heart like a bar of sunshine in a closed room. A single wanton leer has lured to crime and shame. A single idle word or irreverent jest may be the seed of a harvest of sin and blasphemy. You cannot divest yourself of an immortality of influence. Like the fabled shirt of Nessus, it cleaves to you with the tenacity of your being. You may take the wings of the morning and fly to the uttermost part of the sea, yet you will leave your footprints on the shore. You may sail out upon a shoreless ocean, yet you will leave a wake behind you that will surely be followed by many a pursuing bark.

Observe, I am not speaking of your direct, but of your indirect and involuntary influence upon your fellows. How few regard the isolated impulses they impart to others! How few are so circumspect as to trivial actions and unguarded words, as to make them distil like dews brushed from the wings of angels as they pass! Oh! gather up these fragments, that nothing be lost.

There is one class of my hearers to whom I now make special appeal. I refer to you women who are here to-day. As a general fact to which there are rare exceptions, the influence of woman is limited to that circle in which she is confined alike by the laws of Nature and the Word of God. The office of wife and mother, to which God has ordained her, is more potential for good or evil than any other she may aspire to fill, through a perverted ambition or mistaken sense of duty. In rare emergencies, when "men have ceased," God has raised up a Deborah to save His people, or a Joan of Arc to revive the sinking spirits of desponding patriots, and inspire heroes with new-born enthusiasm; but to the vast majority God has dedicated the home and the fireside as their appropriate sphere. And by leading a true and beautiful life, she can refine, elevate, and spiritualize all within her reach, so that she can do more to regenerate the world than all the reformers that ever agitated, or the statesmen that ever legislated. To her, God has given the work of training and moulding immortal spirits at the very dawn of their being. And this she does, not by formal precept or didactic lesson, but by her silent example and the outgoing contagion of her inner life. They see her looks, hear her vehement expression of passion, note the undisguised gush of feeling, thrill in sympathy with her bursts of emotion, glow with her joy, and tremble with her fear. She can cause flowers of truth, beauty, and spirituality to spring up in her footsteps, till the earth smiles with a celestial loveliness; or she can transform it into an arid waste covered with the blight of all evil passion and swept by the bitter blast of everlasting death. Is this a trivial mission? Has she no worthy work to do? Is the sphere God has given her so narrow that she must step outside of it to intrude upon the hustings, the platform, or the pulpit? Like the chaste Diana she may be hidden behind the veil of clouds, but even then her sway will be as imperial and resistless as the lunar reign in the world of waters. Some one has said, " Let me write the ballads of a nation, and anybody may write their laws." I say, let me train the young women of this nation, and I shall sit upon a throne of power that will eclipse the empire of Sesostris, of Alexander, or of Cæsar. I call upon you, mothers, and you, young women, who one day will sit as queens in the empire of your home, not only to use your more potent energies for the glory of God and the good of society, but to "gather up the fragments that remain, that nothing be lost."

And may God give to all grace so to use their money, their time, and their influence, that at the last, when the awards of eternity shall be made, each of you may hear the applauding word, "Well done, good and faithful servant; thou hast been faithful over a few things; I will make thee ruler over many things; enter thou into the joy of thy Lord."

XVII.

THE GLORY OF GOD.

"Whether therefore ye eat, or drink, or whatsoever ye do, do all to the glory of God."—1 Cor. x. 31.

The doctrine which underlies this text is that the manifestation of the Divine glory is the end of creation.

Keep in mind the distinction between God's essential and His manifested excellence. In His essential glory there can be no increase or diminution. But it is not at all inconsistent with His immutability that His manifested glory should be every day growing more splendid and more refulgent.

I. Now, the Bible doctrine is that the ultimate end which God had in the creation of the universe was the display of His manifested glory. The proofs of this proposition are innumerable and overwhelming.

It is a necessary deduction from the conception of the God as *Absolute*. If absolute, He must be the sole end of all His acts; if absolute, He is self-determined. Every motive which quickens His activity must originate in His self-sufficient pleasure.

It is impossible to believe that God could seek any other than the highest end in the creation of man. But the highest conceivable end is the glory of the infinite and absolute Being. We may conceive of many subordinate ends that He may have had in view, but we can conceive of no supreme end short of Himself, without derogating from His perfect excellence. Since God is the greatest being in the universe, since in comparison with Him heaven, earth, angels, and men are as a drop to the bucket or as a bubble to the ocean, the manifestation of His excellence and the gratification of His infinite goodness must be for Him the highest motive for all His works. The glory of the infinite God deserves from Him the highest regard. "It became Him" to prefer this to all other ends, as really as it becomes Him to prefer an archangel to a butterfly. He did not create this world simply or chiefly to gratify His benevolence by conferring happiness on the creatures of His hand; but the chief end of all this expenditure of power and wisdom was that His power, wisdom, holiness, justice, goodness, and truth might, as it were, shine upon one mirror, and be reflected back to Himself and blaze out upon the eyes of an intelligent, admiring universe.

That the glory of God is the end of creation, is proved further by the fact that this is the end which the course of His providence is actually accomplishing—the end toward which all things are irresistibly tending.

Look back through the centuries, and you will see that every successive cycle has evolved some new display of the Divine glory. You read of nations rising and falling, of empires growing and decaying, yet in their rise or fall, their growth or decay, disclosing His power and will as the moving force in their varying fortunes and shifting destinies. Behind the great panorama of history He Himself stands concealed; and from one generation to another He veils His far-reaching designs; but by him who will with a reverent spirit study the march of events through the ages, the hand of God will be discerned, "working all things after the counsel of His own will, whereby for His own glory He hath foreordained whatsoever cometh to pass."

The whole career of the Church from the calling of Abraham, through all its vicissitudes down to this moment, has been an unbroken exhibition of some one or other of the Divine attributes. All the great tragedies of Divine retribution—such as the Flood; the destruction of Sodom and Gomorrah; the overthrow of Pharaoh and his host; the extermination of the idolatrous nations of Canaan; the demolition of Babylon and Tyre; the desolation of the Holy City; and the decline and fall of empires, of which we read in secular history—are disclosures of the attributes of God's justice—a partial manifestation of His glory, it is true, nevertheless real flashes from the Godhead gleaming out over the tide of time.

Or, descend from this high point of view and consider the history of the individual men and women whose names have survived the wrecks of time, and you will see that the Divine glory has in some measure been enhanced, either directly or indirectly, by their lives or by their deaths. For in the moral world men may either become saints or fiends; but whether saint or fiend, whether blessing or cursing, whether loving or hating God, they either give praise or occasion for praise. For "He maketh even the wrath of man to praise Him."

The same thing may be said of the realm of human thought. Every step of progress in civilization and knowledge, every advance in the arts, every utilization of the forces of nature is an occasion of "glory to God who hath given such power unto men." Every true science is, in fact, a psalm of praise. Geology in curious research rewriting the history of our globe, and filling up the details of that chasm which the inspired penman had left between that elder beginning, in which God created the heavens and the earth, and that morning and evening of the day on which man became a living soul; Astronomy resolving the problems of the skies, and, as it were, summoning the "morning stars to sing again together"—all arts and all the sciences gather together to fling their many crowns at the foot of Him who is "God over all, blessed forever."

Thus reasoning from the conception of God, from the course of His providence, and from what our own eyes see around us, we are forced to the conclusion that His own glory was the end He sought in the creation of the universe.

But the decisive argument which really settles the question, is drawn from the Bible itself. We find in the book of Revelation the same doctrine that we have been reading in the books of Nature and Providence. The Scriptures reiterate the doctrine in various forms.

It is said of the universe as a whole. Thus, "of Him, and through Him, and to Him are all things." "For Thy pleasure they are and were created." "All things were created by Him and for Him." "The Lord hath made all things for Himself."

The glory of God is declared to have been the final cause of the work of redemption. It is true that the Scriptures give prominence to the doctrine that the work of redemption originated in the everlasting love of God for the world. Such passages as "God so loved the world that He gave His only begotten Son, that whosoever believeth in Him might not perish," etc., and many others of like import, teach that God had regard to the happiness of His people in devising and executing the work of redemption. But who does not see that the expression of His infinite love to men in the gift of His Son, the gratification of His yearnings to His fallen creatures in their rescue from perdition, and, above all, the illustration of His mercy, which could not otherwise have been displayed to the universe, constitute important elements of the glory which accrues to God in the salvation of men. Hence, on that illustrious night which preceded the day of the world's redemption, angels, when they proclaimed it, sang, "Glory to God in the highest." Christ, when about to achieve and consummate it, prayed, "Father, glorify Thy name." Believers are said by the Apostle to be "predestinated to the adoption of children to the praise of the glory of His grace." The graces, the joys, and the hopes of believers are declared to be produced in them, in order "to make known the riches of His glory." The fruits of righteousness are wrought in them "by Jesus Christ to the glory and praise of God." All the myriads of redeemed saints are saved, as the Apostle says, "that He might make known the riches of His glory in the vessels of mercy which He had afore prepared unto glory." And the theme of triumphant song which shall ever gush from the choirs of the saints in heaven, will be, "Unto Him be glory."

The glory of God is said to have been the end for which particular providential events were decreed and accomplished.

For example, the choice of the Israelites as a peculiar people was that they might be to Him "for a name, and a praise, and a glory" among the nations. For this end were all His dealings with His chosen people, that He might "be glorified in His servant Israel."

Paul declares that it was for this cause he was commissioned to preach the Gospel among the Gentiles; "to the intent that now unto principalities and powers in heavenly places might be made known by the Church the manifold wisdom of God."

There is an emphasis in the inquiry of Joshua that sinks deep into the heart of every godly man, " O Lord, when Israel turneth their backs before their enemies, and the Canaanites cut off our name from the earth, what wilt Thou do unto Thy great name?" And there is deep doctrinal significance in the prayer of Jeremiah, when, pleading for his backslidden countrymen, he says, "Do not abhor us; for Thy name's sake, do not disgrace the throne of Thy glory."

Now a very specious objection is sometimes urged against this doctrine, that it exhibits God in the light of a purely selfish being, controlled by a motive unworthy of Him. But in the first place, if we can form a conception of no higher end in the universe, how can it be unworthy of God to seek this end? Would it not be unworthy of God to seek any other as the chief end of His working?

In the second place, the objection is based on the assumption, that what it may be wrong for us to do or desire, would be wrong in God, which is practically dragging God down to a level with man, making Him such a one as ourselves. A creature is nothing compared with God, and therefore for a creature to seek his own glory is to disregard God's glory. But to whom is God beholden? Whose glory but His own can He seek? Since He is Himself the greatest and most glorious of all beings, He is the only end worthy for Himself to seek.

And in the third place, in reply to this objection, it may be said that it is only by the manifestation of the Divine glory that the highest happiness of the universe can be secured. The glory of God and the good of the universe cannot be separated. When the glorious Being whose name is Love, acts for His own glory, He acts for the good of His creatures. Thus briefly do I dispose of this objection.

II. I come now to the second great lesson of the text, viz.: That every man is bound by the will of God to *select* the promotion of His glory as the governing motive of his life. This is the motive which God demands shall control all rational creatures in all their actions—in the choice of a profession or vocation, in the pursuit of knowledge, in the acquisition of wealth—in short, in the whole conduct of life.

Just here let me define what I mean by a governing motive. A governing motive is one which, while it does not exclude subordinate motives, and which, while it may be temporarily sunk in consciousness, nevertheless does exclude all other motives inconsistent with itself, or motives which would frustrate its operation. When, therefore, I say that the glory of God should be the governing motive of our conduct, I mean that the desire for its promotion and enhancement should be the chief principle of action, that it should pervade and leaven all the rest, modify them, conform them to itself, tinge them with its own hue, resist and expel all that are inconsistent with itself; just as the majestic Mississippi rolling on to the Gulf receives all its tributaries into its bosom, hurries their waters on with resistless sweep, tinges them with its own color, and, though temporarily diverted from its channel and sometimes whirled in vast eddies along the shore, and sometimes impeded by winds and reversing storms, still moves onward and down to the great meeting of the waters.

Now the question recurs, Why are you bound to select the glory of God as the governing motive of your life?

I answer:

1. Because God is the greatest being in the universe. This by itself would be sufficient reason to our minds, if our affections were not polluted by sin. But it accords with our moral judgment of what is right. It is an instinct of our natures to acknowledge that a being superior to ourselves has a claim upon us simply on account of superiority. If we could realize the greatness and majesty of God, we should feel it to be as really a law of our reason to render Him glory, as we feel it to be a moral obligation to love what is lovely, or an æsthetical necessity to admire the beautiful.

We know, too, that it is *our* duty, because angels and all holy beings joyfully recognize this as their first and most imperative duty. They spend day and night praising Him, saying, "Holy, holy, holy, Lord God Almighty, which was, and is, and is to come. Thou art worthy, O Lord, to receive glory, and honor, and power; for Thou hast created all things, and for Thy pleasure they are and were created."

Now while all holy beings select the glory of God as their supreme end, shall man, the pigmy insect of a moment, turn his back on God, and thus say he would rather glorify himself? When we contemplate such a picture our feeling of resentment is swallowed up in contempt for the littleness and meanness of the creature himself. Yet this was the essence of human apostasy, which was a falling out of God into man's little self. It was the "loving and serving the creature more than the Creator."

Now while most men are supremely selfish, yet we meet occasionally a few choice spirits, inspired with nobler impulses—men who do live out of themselves—the noble men of nature, "wrought within a finer mould, and tempered with a purer flame"; but alas! though so generous in their sympathies, so elevated in character, one thing is wanting—they are not religious; and comparing them with Christians whose opportunities for generous culture and elevated social intercourse have been very limited, you ask, "Can it be that these narrow Christians are more fully discharging their duties to God than those whole-souled men you have just described?" Yes, it is even so. For those elevated and noble men (who does not love them?) might be all that they are, and do all that they do, even if there were no God. God is not in all, nor in any of their thoughts. They do nothing with a view to His glory; yet they, as much as any, are bound to "glorify God in their bodies and spirits which are His."

2. This general obligation to glorify God arising out of His supreme excellence and grandeur is enhanced by the relations you sustain to Him. (*a*) You are His creatures. "He hath made us, and not we ourselves"; therefore, says the Psalmist, "let us fall down and worship before the Lord our Maker."

(*b*) He is your preserver. He keeps your souls alive. "In Him we live, and move, and have our being." If for one instant He should turn away from you, you would sink and die, and to-morrow would be the tenants of the grave. (*c*) Then again, you are the recipients of constant blessings from His hands. He maintains in you the light of reason. He furnishes the air you breathe, the light by which you see, the food that nourishes, the water that refreshes, and the raiment that warms you. He spares the friends who cherish and comfort you, and the wife and children who make your home an earthly paradise. "It is of the Lord's mercies that we are not consumed, because His compassions fail not." Now, how base it is to live on God's bounty, and yet despise the claims of the Divine glory upon you! How mean it is to presume upon His forbearance, because the bread is given and the water sure! How strange the complacency of those who can "smile and smile," and yet be guilty of such ingratitude to the "Giver of every good and perfect gift!" (*d*) But all these blessings, great as they are, are obscured in the view of redemption, just as the stars pale before the glories of the rising sun. Redemption! Redemption! is far more than all else besides. For although God is the greatest and best of all beings in the universe, and on this account worthy of undivided homage, man disallowed His rightful claims upon his obedience, love, and worship. Although He made man, and preserves and blesses him every day, he has fallen into an abyss of sin so deep that he could never hope to regain his footing on the height from which he fell; although God created him that he might "glorify God and enjoy Him forever"; although He stamped His own image upon him that he might always bear in himself a symbol of the Divine glory to remind him of the end for which he was created; in spite of this, "he has sinned and come short of the glory of God"; and here on this earth, where God had a right to be most honored, has He been most *dis*honored: and for four thousand years generation after generation have persisted in dishonoring His name and violating His law. And He has borne with it all, and forborne to glorify His justice in the quick destruction of the entire race.

Now why? Why this wonderful forbearance and long-suffering of our God? Here is the explanation. It was in order that here on the greatest scene of His dishonor, here on this earth, where man had sought to dim the splendor of His glory, He might be more conspicuously glorified in the salvation of man, "to the praise of the glory of His grace." And this office of glorifying Him He committed to His dear Son. Hence, as the work of man's redemption was about to be consummated, Christ claims that He has fully discharged His office; "I have glorified Thee on earth, I have finished the work which Thou gavest me to do."

And thus, "It was on the very spot where man was most dishonoring God that man's representative was most glorifying Him. Where man was exhibiting the most appalling wickedness, there man's surety and substitute was giving the most signal display of God's mercy; where man, breaking loose from all restraint, was abandoning himself to open rebellion and to defiance of God's law, there his atonement was becoming 'obedient even unto death'; where the wildest passions that ever stirred the human breast were raging uncontrolled, there, in our name and nature, was One giving the most moving display of a tenderness that could not be ruffled, and of a love that could not be quenched." "Where sin abounded, there did grace much more abound."

Christ, our redeemer and representative, is lifted high upon a cross, that He might become a spectacle; and in the view of all men, in the view of principalities and powers and the wondering angelic hosts, and in view of God the Father and God the Holy Ghost, glorify God the Father, Son, and Holy Ghost, wherein He had been most dishonored. Thus, created for His glory, we sinned against His glory, and were lying under condemnation for His glory, and now we are redeemed for His glory, that we might be "to the praise of the glory of His grace." Oh, what tongue can body forth in fit language the glory of this, the grandest display of the Divine character. We are now no longer our own, for we are bought, bought back, bought back with a price, in order that we may glorify God with our redeemed bodies and redeemed spirits, "which are His." No wonder that in a burst of sacred enthusiasm and holy power, the devout Heber should exclaim:

> "Salvation! Oh! salvation!
> The joyful sound proclaim,
> Till earth's remotest nation
> Has learned Messiah's name."

No wonder that, despairing to proclaim the glad tidings of salvation fast enough to reach the perishing myriads for whom it was provided, and impatient to make known "what is the riches of the glory of this mystery which hath been hid from ages and generations," he should apostrophize the unconscious elements themselves and cry out:

> "Waft, waft, ye winds, the story,
> And you, ye waters, roll,
> Till, like a sea of glory,
> It spreads from pole to pole."

And no wonder that the everlasting song of the redeemed before the eternal throne shall be, "Unto Him that loved us, and washed us from our sins in His own blood, and hath made us kings and priests unto God and His Father—to Him be glory and dominion forever and ever. Amen."

Now, although wicked men may think that they are not bound to glorify God for the work of redemption, it will always seem right to all holy beings that God should make the demand upon them; and in the event of their final rejection of the great salvation, that He should glorify Himself in their damnation, to the praise of the glory of His righteousness and justice.

But how strange is it that Christians should choose to do anything else than live for His glory!

When I see those "who profess and call themselves Christians" apparently totally immersed in the world and in the accumulation of money, or when I see them expending immortal energies in puny efforts to enhance their own reputations and win the applause of men, I cannot help asking: Are these the men who "thus judge that if One died for all, then all died, and that He died for all, that they which live should not henceforth live unto themselves, but unto Him that died for them and rose again?" Yet, men and brethren, I know, and you ought to be told, that you are self-deceived, unless you make God your chief end. This is not a duty that simply flows out of redemption, this is redemption itself. For redemption consists in our being bought back in order to the glorifying of God.

III. And this leads me to the last reason why you should select the glory of God as your chief end, viz.: The consequences to yourselves. It is your highest duty to be holy. But to glorify God constitutes the highest phase of moral excellence. This is the last, as it is the first step in spiritual life. It is the point at which the babe in Christ feels the first impulses of the Divine Spirit, and it is the goal toward which the Seraphim and Cherubim are ever striving. But holiness and happiness are inseparable. Happiness consists in fulfilling the end of our being and in abiding by the law of our constitution. And in glorifying God we accomplish the chief end of man, and therefore must enjoy God forever. We shall "behold His glory, even the glory which the Son had with the Father before the world was," and our souls shall be "filled with all the fullness of God."

If the great doctrine which I have thus unfolded could become a power in the lives of men, it would revolutionize the aspect of society. The merchant, the farmer, the mechanic, the artisan, the student, the artist, the poet, the philosopher, the man of science, then would show forth God's praise in the vocation of their lives.

Then all thought, and all objects of thought, would become "holiness to the Lord." Men would not then regard God's house as the only appropriate place for worship, but all their work would be worship, and all the arts and sciences would be liturgies of praise. Then the telescope of the astronomer, the laboratory of the chemist, the pencil of the painter, the chisel of the sculptor, the pen of the poet, the hammer of the carpenter and of the blacksmith, would be dedicated to a diviner use; then should we mingle our voices with the sound of instruments vocal under the touch of consecrated art, and

> "Praise Him with the psaltery and harp,
> Praise Him with the timbrel and the dance,
> Praise Him with stringed instruments and organs,
> Praise Him with high-sounding cymbals."

Then should "every thing that hath breath praise the Lord."

Then, too, nature would seem to all to have acquired a new significance: and the traveller, as he stands at the foot of Alpine glaciers, or wanders through green forests, or gazes on cataracts that fill the hills with hollow thunder, questioning for whom and by whom all these things were made:

> "God! let the torrents answer like the shout of nations,
> And let the ice plains echo, God!
> God! sing, ye meadow streams, with gladsome voice;
> Ye pine-groves, with your soft and soul-like sounds:
> And they too have a voice, yon piles of snow,
> And in their perilous fall shall thunder, God!
> Ye living flowers that skirt the eternal frost,
> Ye wild goats sporting 'round the eagle's nest,
> Ye eagles, playmates of the mountain storm;
> Ye lightnings, the dread arrows of the clouds,
> Ye signs and wonders of the elements,
> Utter forth God! and fill the hills with praise."

XVIII.

THE WORLD AND THE SOUL.

"What shall it profit a man, if he shall gain the whole world, and lose his own soul? or what shall a man give in exchange for his soul?"—MARK viii. 36, 37.

VALUES are variable. What a man prizes very highly at one time may seem to him utterly worthless at another. Robinson Crusoe on his desolate island hoards every grain of gunpowder saved from the wreck, while he despises bags of gold as useless dross.

In making an estimate of the value of any commodity, there are certain general considerations which influence the judgment; of these I mention three:

1. The intrinsic value of the object.
2. Its distance in time or place.
3. Our personal interest in it.

It is not necessary to prove by argument or illustration that the intrinsic worth of an object must have a controlling influence in our estimate of its value.

That distance modifies estimates of value is plainly illustrated by the profligate spendthrift who mortgages his reversionary rights in order to get from the wily usurer the means of present enjoyment.

Personal interest, too, in any object may give it extraordinary value in our eyes, while all the world besides regard it as worthless. The lock of hair cut from the pale brow of a wife or a sister, while she lay in that cold trance which severed her forever from your embrace, has for you a value which money cannot measure. The difficulty of putting a correct estimate upon many objects of desire is great, even when we have a standard of comparison. So many elements come into the calculation, that even after careful deliberation, we are liable to wide mistakes. But when we come to an estimate of comparative values in a case where there is no standard of comparison, and where the objects differ wholly in kind, the danger of forming incorrect judgments is immensely enhanced.

It is to precisely such a comparison of values that the text calls your attention. "What shall it profit a man if he shall gain the whole world and lose his own soul? or what shall a man give in exchange for his soul?"

This question is addressed to each one who hears it. As if you were standing in the great mart of the universe, the solemn question is ringing in your ears, "What now will you take for your soul?" Calculate its value. Will you take a part of the world, or, if not, will you take the whole world? Or if there are any who have bartered away their souls, what will you give in exchange to buy them back? These are the questions I propound for you to settle this night.

But as there is no standard of comparison between things so different in kind, as there is no coin that passes current between the natural and the spiritual world, in order to make the estimate aright, we must go to first principles and inquire, What is the world? and what is it worth? What is the soul? and what is it worth? And then we must strike the balance between them.

I. *The World!* What a comprehensive term! designating, as it does, everything that ministers to the intellectual or sensual appetites! The world! What a splendid array of dazzling objects is suggested by this single word! *Wealth, fame, pleasure, power!* Wealth, with its long train of glittering attendants; fame, whose temple with gilded dome and crystal walls blazes in the delusive glare that shines on all things this side of eternity; power, with its magic rod of empire, before which thousands kneel in servile homage; pleasure, the very mention of whose name awakes a thousand echoes from the halls of mirth, recalls the song of beauty, the laugh of youth, the rhythm of the dance;

and, to some of you, the noise of the midnight revel or the suppressed whispers of darker scenes of guilt and shame.

Such, under the comprehensive categories of wealth, fame, power, and pleasure, is the world. Whatever ministers to the gratification of our intellectual, emotional, or animal nature, belongs to the sphere of this vast whole.

Now, the question comes, "What is it worth?" At once I answer, it is worth a great deal. It is worse than folly to try to make anybody believe that it is worth nothing. Do not suppose that I am about to underrate the world. I am willing to concede to it all that the most inveterate worldling claims for it. A rational estimate of the world must lead to the conclusion that it has an *intrinsic* as well as a factitious value. Who can deny that wealth has a real intrinsic value? It insures food, clothing, shelter, bodily comfort; it buys social position, influence, friends; it secures education, books, pictures, statuary, and all the works of art; it enables its possessor to send ten thousand ministers of blessing on errands of mercy, and thus to secure for himself the blessing of him who considers the poor; nay, it enables him to extend his influence beyond the natural into the spiritual world by sending forth the tidings of salvation, "till, like a sea of glory, it spreads from pole to pole." In these and a thousand other ways, wealth may minister to happiness and thus prove itself a real good.

So, too, let no one underrate an honorable fame. A good name among men! how eagerly sought! how highly prized! how justly lamented when lost! It has a real value in the happiness it brings to its possessor, the *prestige* it gives him in the world, the honor with which it crowns his posterity, after he has gone beyond the praise or censure of mankind. An honorable fame, whether acquired on the gory battle-field, or in the debates of the council-chamber, or on the perilous heights of executive power, or in the peaceful walks of letters or science, or in art, or in commerce, or in finance,—is a real, substantial good.

Pleasure, too, performs an important part in making up the sum total of human happiness. Solomon tells us that there is a time to laugh as well as a time to weep; and the fact that God has so constituted our natures that we are susceptible of enjoyment in social intercourse, in the chase, in the excitement of manly games, the free play of bodily vigor revelling in its unconsciousness of weariness or care, proves that there are innocent recreations and legitimate modes of relaxation from the stern work of life.

In addition to all this, I do not deny that in an estimate of the value of the world, we must not forget that it offers all its attractions to its votaries at the *present time*. It does not dismiss them to a distant future, but it presents itself in a tangible form to be enjoyed at once. Now there is no principle more fully endorsed by human experience than that embodied in the homely proverb, "A bird in the hand is worth two in the bush." I would not have you lose sight of this important admission.

But there are two important considerations which may prevent your over-estimating the value of the world, and these I now present to you.

First. However valuable the world may be in the abstract, the value to each *individual* is limited to a very brief period. You are all familiar with the principle recognized in our courts that a life estate is worth much less than a title in "fee simple," as it is called. A lease for a limited term may be bought for a much smaller sum than an absolute title. In all transfers of title, the conditions annexed to the tenure modify the estimate of value.

Now what serves to depreciate the value of the world, is that you can hold it as a life estate, at the very best; that after thirty or forty years, you must vacate the premises under a writ of ejectment. Its wealth, fame, and power must be resigned absolutely and forever at death; its innocent pleasures must lose all their zest, long before you reach mature age, while its sinful pleasures will pall even sooner upon the appetite, and leave a sting behind to render manhood miserable, and old age intolerable, for

> "Rooted stand, in manhood's hour,
> The weeds of vice without their flower."

Second. A second drawback on the value of the world to each individual is his limited capacity for enjoying it.

The very idea of riches is the possession of more than we can possibly use or enjoy. A mere competency is not wealth. However valuable, therefore, it may be in the abstract, the mere *possession* of what we do not and cannot use can confer no real happiness. Thus it is with the world and all it offers. Thus you would find it if the treasures of Golconda were poured into your lap, if the plaudits of nations rang in your ears, if you sat upon the throne of an empire, or if the world were converted into a Mohammedan heaven, and you were lord and master of it all. Solomon tried all these things, and after having drained the full cup to the bottom, he pronounced it vanity and emptiness. Satiety was worse than thirst, because though full, he could not *hold* enough to make him happy.

Here now we are prepared to close our estimate of the world. You see I have not tried to belittle it. I have conceded to it a real, substantial worth, and I simply remind you that our short life and limited capacity for enjoying it diminish its value to the individual man. Splendid, but transient; immeasurably large, but powerless to bestow immeasurable bliss—write this down on one side of the ledger, while we proceed to sum up the values on the other side.

II. *The Soul!* What is it worth? In the former case we had a standard of comparison. Here we have none. There are no balances of human devising which will serve to weigh its value; there is no formula which will eliminate the unknown quantity in the equation of its immortal worth. Still, I do not despair of convincing you that its value far exceeds imagination or comprehension. Our knowledge of immensity may be accurate as far as it goes, although we can never have an adequate conception of the Infinite. There are depths of ocean which have never been sounded. Still, the oftener he casts his lead into its fathomless abysses, the more forcibly is the sailor impressed with the vastness of the watery domain.

With a similar object in view, let me suggest some of the thoughts by which you may reach the conviction of the immeasurable value of the soul.

First. The manifest adaptation of the external world to the gratification of man's spiritual nature argues in favor of the value of the soul. The landscape and the flower might be divested of every element of beauty, and yet all the physical necessities of man be provided for. The ear is filled with music that might lead the soul of silence captive, and the eye is ravished with scenes of surpassing loveliness which awaken emotion and thrill the soul with ecstasy. If these were all destroyed and the world were converted into a dull, monotonous workshop, men's bodies might be as comfortable as before. Therefore, whatever in external nature awakens pleasing emotion or confers intellectual pleasure, is a tribute to the value of the soul.

Second. The instinctive homage which all men pay to the spiritual in man is a proof of its worth. This reveals itself in the tendency to incorporate with the products of the useful arts, the elements of the "fine" or ornamental arts. The rude implements of the farm, the tools of the workshop, the utensils of domestic economy, are made to assume forms of grace and beauty, in order to delight the mind while the hand is at work. This is strikingly exemplified in the art of architecture. A tight barn is just as warm, and is as good a shelter as a brown-stone front. The lofty decorations of our public edifices do not contribute in any way to bodily comfort. But they do address the *soul* in eloquent silence, and awaken elevated thought and holy emotion. Thus, even amidst the sordid or sensual pursuits of men, the soul extorts an acknowledgment of her supremacy and asserts her worth.

Third. Not only do men instinctively acknowledge its value, but they consciously allow its claim to supreme importance. Every instrumentality for the education and culture of the mind, every college and university, nay, every log school-house and every tattered spelling-book, is a witness for the soul testifying to the incalculable value attached by intelligent man to the spiritual part of his nature. And why have we assembled here at this hour? Why on this holy Sabbath has the din of labor been hushed all over our broad land, and why do thousands crowd to hear the Gospel? Why, but because they all, and we all, believe, deny it as many do in their practical life, that the soul is the one great possession and its salvation the one great concern.

Fourth. Again, the value of the soul is evinced in its power to master the body. The story of martyrdom furnishes innumerable proofs of the dominion of the soul over physical pain. Some have believed that *miraculous* fortitude was given to the victims of ancient persecution. What a godlike substance the soul must be which, amidst unutterable agonies of the body, could wreathe its lips with a smile of triumph, and force the shrivelled tongue to exclaim, " This fire is a bed of roses to me ! "

Fifth. This leads me to mention its crowning glory. The soul is immortal. In this aspect, we have a standard of comparison by which to measure its value. The world and all that is in it must one day pass away and be burned up like chaff. " The cloud-capped towers, the gorgeous palaces, the solemn temples, the great globe itself, yea, all which it inherit, shall dissolve, and like this insubstantial pageant faded, leave not a rack behind," while the soul will be living on in immortal freshness and vigor.

Sixth. But the great argument which stamps the soul with the mark of infinite worth is the incontestable fact that, in order to redeem it from a terrible perdition, the Son of God " emptied Himself " of the glory which He had with the Father before the world was, and came into the world to die for sinners. No words can intensify the force of this argument. Here it is in all its simple grandeur—the one great miracle of redeeming love. The Devil and all the horrid crew of hell striving for six thousand years to get possession of human souls, and Heaven stooping to give them immortal life by union with Him, who only hath immortality !

No wonder that the angels who worship around the throne hang over the battlements of the crystal walls, in breathless suspense awaiting the issue of this contest between the Son of God and the powers of darkness. No wonder that " there is joy in the presence of the angels of God over one sinner that repenteth," when every soul thus saved is a trophy of the victory of the " Strong Son of God, immortal Love." The soul of man must be of priceless value when it can enlist the energies of such contestants for its possession.

Now I have answered the question, "What is the worth of the soul?" It is for you to say *what you will take for your soul*.

Satan, who is the loudest bidder in the great mart of souls, is most skilful in adjusting the false lights with which he illuminates the gaudy trickeries of the world, which he offers as the price. The very nearness of the objects magnifies their false attractions, while it is only as with a telescope that I can show you those lights of eternity that illuminate the real value of the soul.

If, therefore, with a weak or inoperative faith you discern eternal realities, you may even now be balancing the question whether the enemy of souls is not offering you a fair price.

Before you consent to make the exchange let me put the question of the text, with another emphasis, "What shall it profit a man if he shall gain the whole world and lose *his own* soul?" With this emphasis it is not a question of intrinsic values, or of relative values in the *abstract*. It is now a question in which your *personal* interest in the exchange ought to determine your conduct. It is not whether you will barter *a* soul for the world, but whether you will exchange *your own* soul; whether you will accept the splendid but transient, the ample but unsatisfying attractions of earth, for heaven lost to you and hell as your portion; whether for a few years of fitful enjoyment and feverish excitement you will forego the heights of glory to which you may aspire, and at last lie down in everlasting burnings.

And now, if there are any here who have already made the terrible bargain, there is one more question in the text that merits their special attention—"What shall a man give in exchange for his soul?" That is, Having sold it, how shall he buy it back? The mere surrender of the world will not effect the repurchase of it now. The Devil is too shrewd a trader to take back a mere bauble for an immortal treasure. What *can* a man give in exchange for his *soul?*

Do you wish to recede from the bitter bargain? Do you desire to find the priceless pearl with which you may redeem your captive spirit? Come with me to the blood-stained cross whereon a ransom was paid for a spirit lost like yours. Come with me to Him who led captivity captive, triumphed over Satan, and despoiled him of his prey.

Know, O lost sinner, that even in your last extremity, when you cannot redeem your own soul, there is One who has paid a ransom for you. Look unto Jesus and you may yet be saved. The voice of Mercy cries, "Deliver him from going down to the pit: for I have *found* a *Ransom*."

XIX.

SPECIAL PROVIDENCE.

"And a certain man drew a bow at a venture, and smote the king of Israel between the joints of the harness."—1 KINGS xxii. 34.

THE narrative from which the text is taken is a very striking one. Ahab, the king of Israel, to whom reference is made, had been commanded by God through His prophet, to destroy utterly Benhadad, the king of Syria. After a bloody battle in which Ahab was successful through direct Divine interposition, and had captured Benhadad, he made a treaty of friendship with the Syrian king, instead of obeying the command which devoted him to utter destruction. A prophet was sent to him with this awful message: "Thus saith the Lord, Because thou hast let go out of thy hand a man whom I appointed to utter destruction, therefore thy life shall go for his life, and thy people for his people." The peace which he concluded with Benhadad gave him an opportunity to repose at home, and to devote himself to the beautifying and extending of his pleasure-grounds, in the neighborhood of his summer palace at Jezreel. In the neighborhood of this summer palace was a beautiful vineyard of Naboth, held by him as an inalienable inheritance from his ancestors. This vineyard Ahab desired to possess, and he proposed to buy it from Naboth at its full value. Naboth refused to alienate it from his family on any terms, and this made Ahab angry; and, like a spoiled child, he pouted and went to bed, refusing to eat food or to see any one. Jezebel, his wife, who was made of sterner stuff, by an infamous criminal prosecution, sustained by the testimony of false witnesses suborned for the purpose, secures the condemnation and execution of Naboth, and then Ahab springs up from his bed with delight, and makes haste to take possession of the property stolen and stained with blood. The blood-guiltiness rests on him, and the prophet Elijah is commanded by God to go to Ahab while he is walking in Naboth's vineyard and say to him: "Hast thou killed and also taken possession? In the place where dogs licked the blood of Naboth, shall dogs lick thy blood, even thine."

Full three years elapse, and these events are almost forgotten. Peace and prosperity smile upon Ahab and his kingdom. But he is disturbed by the reflection that Ramoth-Gilead was still forcibly held by the Syrians, while it really belonged to the kingdom of Israel. He therefore invokes the aid of Jehoshaphat, king of Judah, to help him recover it. After some preliminary consultation of prophets, who are inspired by lying spirits to assure them of success in the enterprise, the king of Israel and the king of Judah lay siege to Ramoth-Gilead. Benhadad, the king of Syria, gave his captains a special order to single out Ahab as the sole object of their attack. He knew that the expedition had originated with Ahab, and hoped that his death would end the war. Although Ahab could have known nothing of this order, yet he had a secret anxiety as to the issue. Micaiah, a true prophet, had predicted disaster, and he well knew that the Syrians, his ancient enemy, would be more anxious to kill *him* than any one else. He therefore requests Jehoshaphat to go into the battle clothed in his own royal apparel, but told him that he would disguise himself. The meaning of what he said was simply this: "*I* have every reason to make myself unrecognizable in this war; but *thou*, against whom the Syrians have no especial hate, mayst go forward in thy proper apparel." As the battle is in progress, Jehoshaphat is pursued and is about to be slain, when he cries out, and is recognized, and "the Lord helped him, and God moved them to depart from him." For when they saw that he was not the king of Israel, in obedience to their instructions they let him alone. So perfect was the disguise of Ahab, that the Syrians could not identify him, and it seemed as if he was about to escape their vengeance, and as if the word of the Lord by the prophet Micaiah was to come to nought. But God, who controls all events, small as well as great, nerved the arm of an unknown and obscure soldier to bend his bow and shoot an aimless arrow among the contending hosts. "A certain man drew a bow at a venture," and the arrow directed by the hand of God found the only vulnerable point in the armor of King Ahab. It was just at the point where the corselet lapped over the skirt of iron plates that protected the legs, that the arrow entered. Had he been in any other position, the arrow could not have found a crevice in which to enter. Had the armor been a little more carefully adjusted, or had the corselet been half an inch longer, the arrow would have glanced harmless through the chariot. Had the horse which drew the chariot been a little more fleet, the arrow would have fallen behind the chariot, or have pierced some other less protected victim. Had the "certain man" delayed one instant to draw "his bow at a venture," the king would have escaped that shaft. Had the king been dressed in his own armor which fitted him, and not in that of another man which did not protect him perfectly, he might have escaped. But you see, all these things had been arranged by God, and three years before, while the warm blood of Naboth was mingling with the waters of the pool of Samaria, God had inspired His prophet to warn the wicked king that his own blood, shed in his chariot, should be washed from it in the waters of that very pool.

The object of this discourse is to use this narrative to illustrate the proposition that God controls all events whether great or small: that, in fact, there is nothing either great or small in His esteem.

Men are prone to measure the importance of any event by a superficial estimate of its visible effects. Thus, an earthquake, or a great conflagration, or a tornado, is accounted an event of such magnitude, that it is deemed not unworthy of the Divine attention. So, too, the great revolutions of which history takes account, are considered proper objects for Divine interference and control. And so, too, many men are ready to admit that the more striking events in their own personal history are not beneath the Divine notice. Their vicissitudes of fortune, the bereavements they suffer, the accidents they experience or their escapes from great perils, the misfortunes that befall them or the auspicious circumstances that may attend their labors—all these things they are very willing to ascribe to the Divine superintendence; but the ordinary events of every-day life they are prone to think are too insignificant in the eyes of the great Ruler to receive from Him a moment's attention, and they continually refer the occurrence of these events to *accidents* or to *chance.*

This is, of course, not a philosophical or rational view of the subject. Those who entertain it have no consistent theory on the subject of Divine Providence. Their views are not those which we find stated in books or assailed in formal treatises on the subject of Divine Providence. But they will be most satisfactorily disposed of by a clear statement of the Scripture doctrine of Providence, which stands opposed to all incorrect views on the subject.

The Catechism defines God's works of Providence to be " His most holy, wise, and powerful preserving and governing all His creatures and all their actions": *i. e.,* He *preserves* all His creatures and *governs* all their actions. Two elements, therefore, are included in Providence—Preservation and Government. By *preservation* is meant that all things out of God owe the continuance of their existence, with all their properties, to the will of God. By *government* is meant intelligent control, with a design or end in view. It is with this second element in Providence that we are at present concerned. It involves the idea of "an end to be attained and the disposition and direction of means for its accomplishment." If God governs the universe He has some *great end* in view. This great final end includes an infinite number of subordinate ends, all of which must be accomplished in order to the attainment of the one great end of the whole.

Now the Scriptures teach that this providential government is—

(1.) *Universal;* that is, that it embraces the whole physical universe, rational and irrational creatures, things great and things small, things ordinary and things extraordinary.

(2.) That it is *powerful;* *i. e.,* that His omnipotence renders the accomplishment of His purposes absolutely certain.

(3.) That it is *wise;* that is, that the end He seeks is in accordance with the highest wisdom; and further, that the means He employs are the very best adapted to the object; and that His control is suited to the nature of the creatures over which it is exercised. He governs the material universe according to fixed laws which He Himself has established; irrational animals by the instincts which He Himself has given them; and rational creatures in accordance with their nature.

(4.) That God's providence is *holy;* that is, there is nothing in the ends proposed, the means adopted, or the agency employed inconsistent with His perfect moral excellence.

This is the whole Scripture doctrine of Providence. But I wish to confine your attention to only one of these propositions: viz., that the providential government of God is *universal;* that is, extending to the whole physical and spiritual universe, creatures rational and irrational, things great and things small, things ordinary and things extraordinary.

1. This doctrine flows from necessity out of the *Scripture idea of God.* As the Scriptures represent God as infinite in wisdom, power, and goodness, and as the Father of Spirits, if we could suppose it possible that there was one spot in the universe where He was not always exercising supervision and control, we should be denying His infiniteness; and if we should suppose that there was one creature in the universe, whether rational or irrational, whether great or small, for whose good He is not concerned, we should be denying His infinite goodness. It flows necessarily out of the idea of God as the *Creator* of all things, *great* and *small.* The force of this argument is very great. If God did not think it beneath His dignity to *create* all things, great and small, alike, it certainly cannot be beneath His dignity to *care* for them all after they were created. Many seem to think that the universe is a machine which God took infinite pains to construct in all its myriad details, but that after He had built it and set it agoing, He lost all interest in it and left it alone to work out its results. This idea is utterly inconsistent with the Scripture conception of God. When an artificer makes a machine, it will remain in existence though he should die the next moment; because the

material on which he works was ready created to his hands, and he only gave it form and figure. But God gives the very *being* as well as the form; and the very being of the thing depends upon His preserving influence. "In Him," says the Apostle, "we live and move and have our being"; so that if God should cease to exist, the universe would burst like a bubble, and vanish out of existence. "And to suppose that anything is too great to be comprehended in His control, or anything so minute as to escape His notice, or that the infinitude of the particulars can distract His attention, is to forget that God is infinite. God is as much present everywhere and with everything as if He were only in one place and had but one object of attention. The very common idea that it is incompatible with the dignity and majesty of the Divine Being to concern Himself about trifles, assumes that God is a *limited being;* and that because *we* can attend to only one thing at a time, it must be so with God." *

2. The doctrine flows from the evidence which the whole universe gives of the operation of mind in every part of it. There is everywhere manifest the intelligent adaptation of means to an end, as well in the organization of the animalculæ as in the order of the heavenly bodies. It would be as unreasonable to assume that the organized forms of the vegetable and animal world are due to the laws of nature as it would be to assume that a printing-press could be constructed which could compose a poem.

3. The doctrine is demanded by the religious nature of man. Our sense of dependence, our instinctive and universal sense of responsibility, and the instincts of our religious nature, which demand intercourse with God—all teach this doctrine. Unless this doctrine is true, our whole nature is a delusion and an imposition upon us. We are created with instincts and aspirations which cannot be satisfied, unless this doctrine of a *universal providence* is the very truth.

4. This doctrine is involved in all the predictions, promises, and threatenings recorded in the Bible. God promises to give health, long life, and prosperous seasons; or He threatens war,

---

* Hodge.

famine, drought, and pestilence. Such promises and threatenings suppose a universal providence, a control over all the creatures of God and all their actions.

5. The Scriptures are very full of this doctrine stated in a variety of forms.

(1.) In regard to God's providential agency in all the operations of nature.

He guides Arcturus in his course; He makes the sun rise, and the grass grow; He gives rain from heaven, and fruitful seasons; He clothes the grass of the field, which to-day is, and to-morrow is cast into the oven; He makes the winds His messengers, and the lightnings are His ministering spirits; earthquakes, tempests, pestilences, are sent and governed by Him; events to us apparently fortuitous, as the flight of an arrow, the falling of a lot, the number of the hairs of our head, the death of a sparrow, are all controlled by the ever-present and omnipotent God.

(2.) In all the animal world.

Job says, "In His hand is the life of every living thing." The Psalmist, "The young lions roar after their prey and seek their meat from God." "They wait upon Him, and He giveth them their meat in due season." "He hears the young ravens when they cry." "Behold the fowls of the air! Your heavenly Father feedeth them." "He giveth to all life and breath and all things."

Now all these statements are not merely poetical representations of the adaptations of nature to the necessities of the animal creation; but they teach that His creatures are constantly dependent on God's interposition and providential care. The multitude of the cattle was assigned as a reason for the preservation of Nineveh from destruction. God is represented as remembering *Noah's* cattle as well as his sons (Gen. viii. 1). And when our Lord put into the mouth of His disciples the petition, "Give us this day our daily bread," He recognized the fact that all living creatures depend on the constant intervention of God for the supply of their daily wants.

(3.) The Bible teaches that the providential government of God extends over nations and communities of men. "He doeth according to His will in the army of heaven and among the inhabitants of the earth. He removeth kings and setteth up kings." "The Most High ruleth in the kingdom of men, and giveth it to whomsoever He will." "O Assyrian, the rod of my anger, and the staff in their hand is my indignation; and I will send him against a hypocritical nation. Howbeit he meaneth not so, neither doth his heart think so"; *i. e.*, Sennacherib, of whom He speaks, did not design to be the instrument of God's justice, but was only bent on the satisfaction of his own ambition and the extension of his empire. "The shields of the earth," *i. e.* human magistrates, "belong unto God." Who would have thought that the forces raised by Cyrus against Babylon to satisfy his own ambition, should be a means to deliver the Israelites and to restore the worship of God in the temple? Yet so it was. God had this end in view, and Isaiah prophesied it three hundred years before Cyrus was born, calling him by his name: "That saith of Cyrus, thou art my shepherd, and shalt perform all my pleasure, even saying that Jerusalem shall be built."

"Shall the axe boast itself against him that heweth therewith, or shall the saw magnify itself against him that shaketh it? as if the rod should shake itself against them that lift it up, or as if the staff should lift up itself as though it were not wood." That is, God uses the nations as a man uses a staff or a rod. They are in His hands, and He employs them to accomplish His purposes. He breaks them in pieces as a potter's vessel, or He exalts them to greatness according to His good pleasure.

(4.) The providence of God extends not only over nations, but also over individuals. The circumstances of every man's birth, life, and death are ordered by God, whether we are born in a heathen or Christian land, in the Church or out of it; whether we are weak or strong, with many or with few talents, rich or poor; whether we are prosperous or afflicted; whether we are to live a longer or a shorter time, are not matters determined by chance or by the unintelligible sequence of events, but by the will of God. "The Lord killeth and the Lord maketh alive; the Lord maketh poor and the Lord maketh rich." "A man's heart deviseth his way, but the Lord directeth his steps." "Promotion cometh neither from the east, nor from the west, nor from the south." "My times are in Thy hands," *i. e.*, the necessities of my life. "God hath made of one blood all the nations of men for to dwell on all the face of the earth, and hath determined the times before appointed" (*i. e.*, the turning-points in history), "and the bounds of their habitation."

From these comprehensive views of the universal and minute superintendence of Divine Providence, there are many inferences and many lessons to be drawn.

(1.) If God is thus immanent in the world and in us, then the most insignificant of our concerns, and the most trivial events of our life, are under His supervision and control. And in this view there is nothing really trivial in all our personal history. For that which can engage the thought and be ordered by the supreme mind and the supreme power of the universe, cannot be a matter of no importance. In our blindness and in our ignorance of the sequences of things, we may account that a matter insignificant in itself, which nevertheless may be fraught with the most stupendous consequences. In many instances in which the veil has been raised by the hand of God, and He has permitted us to inspect the otherwise hidden connection between a cause and its effects, we discern the fact that circumstances, regarded by those who observed them as utterly insignificant, have been links in a mighty chain by which were suspended vast revolutions in human history. A little pebble from the brook, guided by the hand of God, delivers Israel from the Philistines; a dream of Joseph is the occasion of the ultimate settlement of Jacob's family in Egypt, and all the wonderful subsequent history of the Israelites; Pharaoh's daughter comes casually to wash herself in the river, but conducted by the secret influence of God upon her, in order that she might rescue the infant Moses, so as to train him up in the learning of Egypt, that he might become the deliverer of his people; the viper which leaped upon Paul's hand out of a bundle of sticks, was designed by God to further the propagation of the Gospel; the cackling of geese was used by God as a means for saving the Roman capital from a surprise by the Gauls; and as our text relates, a common soldier draws a bow at a venture, and destroys the life of a wicked king.

You cannot tell what event in your life may be fraught with consequences of the most vast importance to you.

(2.) If this is so, how important to seek Divine aid and direction in everything you do, and for every moment of your life. How can you afford to do without the Divine blessing invoked upon every step of your progress? How can you venture to begin the day without commending your way to Him who will order all the events of the day, all of which will be more or less influential in determining your future course, and in fixing your ultimate destiny?

(3.) This view of the universal and minute providential control of God will enable us to understand what are called "special providences." *There are no such things as special providences, if by this is meant that God interferes in human affairs more actively at one time or on one occasion* than another, for the deliverance of His people from impending evil. What are called "special providences" are only instances in which we are permitted to see more plainly than at other times the immediate instrumentalities by which our deliverance from danger or rescue from threatened disaster is effected. An instance in point is recorded in the book of Esther. On the very night before the day that the destruction of Mordecai and the whole Jewish people was to be accomplished, the king could not sleep and commanded the records of the empire to be read, and God had so ordered it that that particular roll should be read to him which recorded the story of Mordecai's services in exposing and defeating a conspiracy against the king. This led to inquiry, and to the subsequent reward of Mordecai, and the deliverance of the Jews from extermination. Now this would be called a "special providence"; but there was nothing more special in it than a thousand other providences in regard to the Jews, the occasions of which were unknown and therefore unrecorded. I saw not long ago an account of a citizen of this county who was about to embark on a steamboat on the Mississippi; but just as he was going aboard of her, he discovered that his purse had been stolen, and he was compelled to return to his hotel and wait until he could telegraph for more money to his friends at home. The steamboat was lost with all on board. He, of course, escaped on account of the loss of his money, which, if the accident had not happened to the boat, he would have regarded a great misfortune. This loss of his purse he regarded a "special providence"; but it was no more a special providence to him than the providence which kept me at home so that I was not near taking passage in the boat, and which kept me out of the reach of pickpockets, so that I lost neither money nor life.

A New York merchant, not long ago, whose home was in the country, was very anxious to be in the city at a certain hour in order to attend to important business; but it was necessary for him to have a certain paper to take with him. Just as he was about to start, the paper which had been lying on the mantel could be found nowhere. It had not been touched by any member of the family, and all of them had been in the apartment, except for a single moment when all had gone out together, leaving only a two-year-old infant in the room. The search for the paper detained him for a minute; and, though he made haste, he was too late for the early train, and returned from the station to have his disappointment changed into bad humor by the discovery that his little boy had climbed up to the mantel-piece, taken the paper, and torn it to pieces. In a little while the telegraph reported the total wrecking of that particular train, and the killing and mangling of nearly all the passengers. He regarded that as a "special providence" to him, forgetting that the same providence had carried him every day for years over that same road without any accident to him or to any one else. In this particular instance God enabled him TO SEE the connection between the trivial event of the loss of a paper and the preservation of his life; but on a thousand occasions before, his life had been preserved by circumstances equally trivial, only he was not permitted to see their causal efficiency.

(4.) But there is another sense in which the doctrine of a special Providence is true and as precious as it is true. This is the doctrine as stated by Paul, "*All things* work together for good to them that love God, to them who are the called according to His purpose." All things are special providences for the good of God's people. In some way that I cannot comprehend, my life is bound up in all the complicated web of His providence. I cannot unravel the intricate windings of that all-comprehending plan; but I know from His Word that I am personally interested in every process and in every atom of the vast universe, which He manages and controls. "The whole material system is a ministry for good to me. The beauty, the poetry, the majesty, and the wonder of creation reflect the nature and echo the voice of God. A Father's tenderness shines down from every star and smiles upon me from every common flower. His wisdom breathes in the golden calm of the summer's day and His power careers in the storm. Interest in us beams in the countenance of Orion on his distant and dazzling throne; and the landscape beneath us, with sloping vales, wooded crests, and gleaming floods, is the face of a friend. This fallen world is made a scene of benignity and benediction, and all is constrained to work for good to us. All the ages are linked together, and men of all time join hands to bless us. For good to those who love God, Egypt reared its pyramids and Nineveh its palaces, Phœnicia traded, Greece speculated, and Rome conquered. For good to them, the Hebrew conceived sublimity, and the subtle Greek wrought to finest temper his perfect tongue. For good to them, Adam fell, Abraham believed, David sung, Isaiah soared, Jerusalem apostatized, Judas played traitor, the Lord wept on Olivet, agonized in Gethsemane, and died on Calvary."

(5.) If the eyes of God's omniscience are always open to behold us, we may well believe that the arms of His goodness are open to embrace us. As the multitude of His concerns does not hinder His intimate knowledge of them, so neither does it hinder His care over them. The Apostle Peter advises us to cast all our care upon Him, for He careth for us. If God has a tender care for sparrows, and has this moment a conscious knowledge of the number of the hairs in your heads, why should you fear to commit to Him your important concerns? Nay more, why should you fear to consult Him and to ask His interposition in what you may consider matters too insignificant to merit His notice? When He says cast *all* your care, He means *all* your cares on Him, for He careth for all your interests and is not offended when you present the most trivial desire in your petitions to Him.

(6.) Lastly. It is perfectly rational to pray to God for anything for which He has encouraged us to pray in His Word. Solomon prayed for wisdom, Hezekiah for restoration to health, Jabez for temporal prosperity, Asa for victory over his enemies in battle, Elijah for rain, David for pardon and sanctification, and God heard all these prayers. God is immanent in the world, intimately and always present with every particle of matter; and this is a presence not of being only, but of knowledge and power. What sort of God would that be who made a universe of matter, and impressed such laws upon it as to put it beyond the reach of His immediate control? "It is by a natural law or physical force that vapor arises from the surface of the ocean and is formed into clouds and condenses and falls in showers upon the earth, yet God so controls the operation of the laws producing these effects, that He sends rain when and where He pleases. The same is true of all the operations of nature and all events in the external world. They are due to the efficiency of physical forces; but those which are combined, adjusted, and made to co-operate with or to counteract each other, in the greatest complexity, are all under the constant guidance of God, and are made to accomplish His purpose. It is perfectly rational, therefore, in a world where blind natural forces are the proximate causes of everything that occurs, to pray for health, for protection, for fruitful seasons, for success in business and in study, for rain, for peace and prosperity, since all these events are determined by the intelligent agency of God."

My brethren, let not a half-fledged science or the baptized infidelity of half-educated teachers, or the speculations of an infidel philosophy, cheat you out of the consolations and support which the Bible gives you, when it tells you that you would be as helpless orphans but for the constant oversight and protection of a heavenly Father, who, having been great enough to create, is powerful to control every pulsation of the vast Cosmos of which you are a part.

XX.

INFLUENCE.

"And that man perished not alone in his iniquity."—JOSHUA xxii. 20.

THE narratives of the Bible are eminently instructive. All history is providence teaching by example; for as Solomon tells us, "The thing that hath been, it is that which shall be, and that which is done is that which shall be done, and there is no new thing under the sun." Every human life is simply the reproduction of the old in the new. Dr. Johnson has said that "the biography of the most unimportant individual on the globe, were it fully written out so that the life should appear just and fully as it was, would overflow with interest and entertainment for all men." Bible history has the advantage over all profane history. The latter presents facts and the deductions which the writer draws from them. The former presents us with facts too, but furnishes us with their providential meaning as revealed by the pen of inspiration.

Hence Scripture narrative always teaches important doctrines. Men who look upon the narratives of the Old Testament as comparatively unimportant, inasmuch as they are so largely made up of brief biographical notices of comparatively obscure individuals, lose sight of this fact. But the Apostle tells us that "whatsoever things were written aforetime, were written for our learning"; "that these things happened for ensamples and are written for our admonition, upon whom the ends of the world are come" (Rom. xv. 4, and 1 Cor. x. 11). Scripture history is a record not only of the actions of men of the olden time, but of God's dealings with them; and while it represents them as actors, it lifts the curtain from the Divine purpose, and shows us the reasons for the providential dispensations it records. The history of the sin and punishment of Achan is eminently instructive in itself, and very suggestive of important truth. In order to present the subject more distinctly, suffer me to recapitulate the main incidents.

Joshua, by Divine command, besieges the city of Jericho. The whole city was devoted to complete destruction—it was to be razed to the ground and utterly obliterated from the earth. Every living thing, man and woman, young and old, oxen, sheep, asses, were all to be destroyed with the edge of the sword, and everything in it was to be burned with fire. Two exceptions to this decree of general devastation were made in favor—

First, of the family of Rahab, the harlot, because she hid the spies that were sent into the city.

Second, of the silver and gold, which were to be saved and consecrated to the treasury of the house of the Lord. The people were strictly forbidden to appropriate the treasure which should be found in the city, but were commanded to bring it all to Joshua to be set apart to a sacred use. In direct disobedience to the Divine command, Achan, a man belonging to the tribe of Judah, appropriates and secretes a magnificent robe, two hundred shekels of silver, and a heavy bar of gold—burying them in the midst of his tent. His sin was two-fold. (1.) He was guilty of direct disobedience to the commands of God. (2.) He was guilty of sacrilege.

The consequences of his sin at once manifested themselves, not in any direct judgment upon him, but in the evidences of God's displeasure against the whole people. For after the conquest of Jericho, Joshua sent men to Ai, an insignificant town in the vicinity. Its means of resistance were so feeble that he did not judge it necessary to detail more than two or three thousand men for its reduction. The assault upon this stronghold resulted in a shameful defeat, and in the loss of thirty-six men. Instead of fighting valiantly, the hearts of the Israelites became as water. Joshua at once inquires the reason of God, and he is informed that this defeat is a judicial consequence of sin on the part of Israel. "*They* have taken of the accursed thing, and dissembled also, and have put it among their stuff. Neither will I be with you any more, except ye destroy the accursed from among you."

The person who had transgressed was to be discovered by an appeal to the religious lot. The sin is very soon fixed by a process of exculpation and elimination upon the tribe of Judah; then upon the family of Zerah, then upon the family of Zabdi, then upon the family of Carmi, and then upon Achan himself.

When there was no longer hope of concealment, he confesses his sin and discloses the place of concealment. Then Joshua and all the people with him took Achan, and the silver, and the garment, and the wedge of gold, and his sons, and his daughters, and his oxen, and his asses, and his sheep, and his tent, and all that he had, and brought them into the valley of Achor, and all Israel stoned him with stones and burned them with fire, after they had stoned them with stones. And they raised over them a great heap of stones unto this day. And the place which was the scene of this terrible retribution, was called *Achor*, that is *trouble*—to be a perpetual remembrance of this man's sin and punishment.

This transaction was intended to make a deep moral impression on the people. For, twenty-four years after its occurrence, we find Joshua alluding to it in an address he makes to the people; and in the words of our text he reminds them, that "that man perished not alone in his iniquity."

Let us now consider the lessons we are to learn from this narrative.

I. One of the most evident inferences we may draw from this story, is that the true design of punishment is *not* to secure the *reformation* of the offender. This is a doctrine of the Bible which modern legislators and judges continually ignore. It is a fact pregnant with instruction, that just so far as this doctrine of the Scripture is lost sight of in the administration of our criminal law, crimes have increased, and the guarantees which society professes to throw around life and property, are rendered null and void. A sickly sentimentality has dared to substitute imprisonment for life for the penalty which the law of God denounces against the murderer. The consequence is, that throughout our whole land the murderer and the assassin stalk abroad. We seem to have lost sight of the fact that crimes against the good order and peace of society demand *punishment*—that *retributive justice* is due to every infraction of law, irrespective of all the pleas for mercy which may be urged in behalf of the criminal. We can never depart with safety from the law which God has established for the government of human society; and the experience of every human society which has invented expedients for releasing the criminal from the penalty which his sin deserves, goes to prove that it is the will of God that every sin shall meet with its just recompense. Why is it that our whole land is full of assassins and murderers? It is because our short-sighted rulers, seeking to be wiser and more merciful than God, have erected the penitentiary as a place of *reformation* for those whom God has declared to be worthy of death. And it cannot be doubted that God is visiting our whole land with a curse, because of the unexpiated crimes which our rulers and judges suffer to stalk abroad unwhipt of justice. The whole course of God's moral administration goes to show that the *reformation* of the criminal is neither the design nor the ordinary result of the infliction of His punishments. The Scriptures everywhere teach that sin is punished because it *deserves* to be punished, and because justice demands it. It is because the wages of sin is punishment, and not because punishment may lead to repentance, that penalties are attached to the infraction of law. The Scriptures teach even more than this. They teach that, while it is promotive of the best interests of society that crime should be punished, even the *good of society* is not the primary end of punishment—in other words, that judicial penalties are not just because they are expedient, but that they are *expedient* because they are *just*. And we may be assured that the evils which now curse our land, will never be remedied until we shall return to a recognition of these Scriptural views of the true design of punishment.

When justice shall resume her rightful sway, and only then, may we hope to sit, each man under his own vine and fig-tree, with none to molest or make us afraid.

II. A second lesson to be learned from the story of Achan is, that the organic constitution of the *family* is such that the sins of parents necessarily involve their children. Attempts have been made by infidels to render the character of God odious to men by representing the punishment of Achan's *whole family* as a wanton act of barbarous revenge. We are not particularly anxious to vindicate the character of God against such miserable cavillers. Three modes of justifying this indiscriminate sacrifice of the whole family have been suggested.

The first is the supposition that the members of his family were accomplices in Achan's sin. This would be a satisfactory mode of accounting for the slaughter of the adult members of his family, but would not explain the visitation of vengeance on the younger members and the innocent cattle which belonged to him.

The second mode of accounting for it is the supposition that they fell as the victims of a popular outbreak. This might do as an explanation, did not the narrative indicate that the punishment was inflicted by authority and with every appearance of calm deliberation.

A third mode of explaining it is that they were punished by Divine authority and according to the law of God's government; that He visits the iniquities of the fathers upon the unoffending children to the third and fourth generation.

No matter which explanation you adopt, the fact illustrates the truth of the principle that such is the organic relation of the members of a family that the evil deeds of one affect all the rest. This truth is every day exemplified before our eyes.

Look at the drunkard as he reels through the streets. May he not do what he will with his own? He says he is a free man, and if he chooses to wreck his body and soul he injures no one but himself. But look at his family. Look at the wretched woman to whom, in earlier days, he plighted his love, and whom he promised to cherish, support, and nourish, now a lonely watcher by the dying embers of a desolate hearth, nursing amidst her tearful vigils the memories of her early love, and weeping over the graves of murdered joys: and look at his famished children crying for bread, and vainly appealing to their besotted father for a morsel to appease the gnawings of their hunger. Or even in those cases in which the family are not reduced to poverty, see how the depraved tastes of the father are transmitted to the children, and his evil example combines with hereditary proclivities to fasten upon them the sins which have destroyed his life, and to cause them to rush into the same courses of excess and crime.

See how the dishonesty or fraud of men conspicuous in official position brings ruin and disgrace on those who had no part in the commission of the sin. See them pointed out by the finger of scorn and even pursued to the seclusion they may seek in distant lands across the seas by the restless footsteps of Rumor, that sleepless hound that tracks the flight of crime to its most secret haunts, and that howls remorselessly at all who may, by domestic association or casual contact, have been tainted with the odor of fraud or corruption.

See how the Infidel and the Scoffer bequeath their skepticism and ungodliness to their children and doom their innocent offspring to grow up like themselves, abhorred by man and abandoned by God.

If it were necessary to enforce these arguments from example, I might give you names familiar to us all—in connection with which each one of those statements is illustrated. Thus our own observation, short and limited as it is, is sufficiently wide to confirm the doctrine of the text, that such is the organic unity of the family that the sins of parents necessarily involve their innocent children in a common ruin.

III. Another general principle taught by this narrative is that the whole body of any civil community is justly held responsible for the sins of the individuals composing it. That part of the history of Achan which illustrates this is God's displeasure against the whole congregation of Israel for the sin of this one man. He subjected their army to an inglorious defeat and visited thirty-six families with sad bereavement. Those thirty-six men who fell at Ai were not partakers of Achan's *sin*, but they were made partakers of his guilt. The sin of the individual was imputed not only to his family, but to the whole nation, and a portion of the penalty was borne by it. There are some who find insuperable difficulties in admitting that Adam's guilt is imputed to his posterity. Let such consider this narrative and see whether the doctrine that God can impute guilt to those who are personally innocent, does not derive support from this instance of God's dealings with His people. Nor is it so hard to understand the principle upon which God thus deals with communities and nations. Every community is made up of individuals, *governed by laws*, to which each voluntarily confesses his allegiance. It is the duty of each member of such a community to obey the law and to promote both the observance of its precept and the execution of its penalties. Now, if every man *does his whole duty in both these particulars*, all infraction of law would cease: there *could be no crime*. But in every community there will be those who violate the laws. Now, if all the rest earnestly and honestly seek to have the laws obeyed, the criminal never could escape detection and punishment. The certainty of punishment would deter even the vicious from the commission of crime; and though occasionally the restraints of fear would be broken through, yet only occasionally would this occur under the impulse of overmastering passion. It is evident that if each member of a community were held to a practical accountability for the sins of his neighbor, crime would be greatly diminished. If, for example, the loss by burglary or by incendiary conflagration were assessed on the inhabitants of a city, is it not clear that when the burglar or incendiary should be grasped by the clutches of justice, the people would see to it that he should not escape condign punishment? If the family of a murdered citizen were by law supported at the expense of the city or village in which the murder was committed, think you that the murderer would be suffered to walk off in the face of the broad day, or that with his single arm he could defy an indignant populace to take him alive? These supposed cases illustrate the truth that it is in the power of every community to restrain and prevent crime by the cultivation of a healthy public opinion, and a prompt and firm administration of public justice. If on account of low views of morality and a perverted sympathy for the criminal, crime is suffered to escape the arrest or the execution of the law, then is that community held responsible in the sight of God and in the sight of mankind for the sins of its individual members. The ancient Egyptians recognized this principle in their penal code. "Whoever had it in his power to save the life of a citizen and neglected to do so was punished as his murderer; and if a person was found murdered, the city within whose bounds the murder had been committed was obliged to embalm the body in the most costly manner, and bestow on it the most sumptuous funeral." And although we do practically ignore it in these modern days of illumination, it is nevertheless true that in God's providential dealings with communities, He holds the community responsible for the sins of its members. You may ask, is this just? I reply, this is not the question. The question is not one of *justice*, but of fact, and a wide observation of the history of civil society will demonstrate beyond the shadow of a doubt that, in the long run, the penalty of unexpiated crime is paid by society at large. And if we are to learn any lesson from the story of Achan it is this, that it is not only natural but right that this should be so.

IV. A more general principle which I derive from this narrative is that the sins of individuals not only involve them in ruin, but inflict irreparable injury on all who may be either directly or indirectly associated with them. This is seen to be true *a priori* by a consideration of the constitution of human society. The law of society is mutual dependence and influence. Cold isolation, though he may seek it, is impossible for man. You may take the wings of the morning and fly to the uttermost part of the sea, but you cannot sever the links that bind you to your fellow-man. God has so united the whole human family by chains of sympathy and influence, that the actions of every man have their influence upon the character and destiny of every other individual of his species. The examples of men conspicuous before the public eye prove this. It is not necessary to be able to trace the influence of the more obscure members of human society, in order to the proof of the general principle. We know the less by the greater.

When a child projects a pebble across a brook, it is not necessary for us to feel the shock or to detect the vibration, in order to believe that the earth is really deflected from its orbit by the minute concussion. It is enough to know that the law of gravitation is universal, pervading the ultimate atoms of matter. So, also, it is not necessary that we should be able to see in every human being a Jeroboam, who caused a whole nation to sin, in order to believe that no individual can be detached and made independent of the rest. It is enough to know the general law of the reciprocal action and mutual relation of all animated beings. But if we could lift the veil which hides the moral world from our view, and selecting some one individual, could disentangle and detach all his relations from their innumerable complications, and could investigate his whole moral history, we should find that "from the very first moment of his existence, his character has gone on daily and hourly, streaming with a more than electric fluid, with a subtle penetrating element of moral influence; that, in whatever society he mingled, he left on their character secret but not imperceptible traces that he had been among them." We should see that every word he uttered or wrote has flashed along the line of a thousand spiritual telegraphs centring in him; that at every point along these lines, new centres of influence were created, and that thus his thought, his sin, has been transmitted in silent but certain effect all around the world, to the uttermost circle of social existence. We should find that the moral forces thus generated, like the forces which pervade the material world, are indestructible, not a particle ever being lost, and that they will go on thrilling through the universe, all being taken up into the general system of cause and effect, and always operating somewhere.

> " As the small pebble stirs the peaceful lake;
> The centre moved, a circle straight succeeds,
> Another still, and still another spreads ;
> Friends, parents, kindred, first it will embrace,
> His country next, and next all human race."

Now this influence exerted by all is both voluntary and involuntary. Sometimes it is exercised with the conscious purpose of producing a result in those with whom the man is in actual contact; and, so far as they are concerned, he may be considered as having control over it. But by far the larger proportion of each man's influence is exerted involuntarily and unconsciously. And whether an action be performed with or without reference to the production of an effect on another, it produces that effect whether you will it or not. Once done, you cannot recall the influence of actions any more than the unfortunate companions of Ulysses could chain the winds when once released from the bag of Æolus. Thus every man is the unconscious and involuntary agent in the moulding of the character of others, remote from his immediate presence. And his involuntary influence is also constantly streaming forth upon all immediately around. Not like the intermittent glow of the fire-fly, which may be quenched at will, but like the phosphorescent putrefactions of the sepulchre that emit a steady light; not like the transient electric shocks of the torpedo, but like the magnetic current of the loadstone, which never grows feebler and which imparts its own polarity to every object within the sphere of its attraction. Such are some of the *a priori* arguments in favor of the proposition suggested by the text. Were it necessary to illustrate by arguments drawn from example, history would furnish us with innumerable instances. But I turn from the proof of the proposition to some of the obvious practical reflections and inferences drawn from it.

What a vast responsibility rests upon each one of you in view of the momentous consequences that flow out of your conduct and character! It is usual to say that it is an awful thing to *die;* but how much more solemn and awful a thing it is to *live*—to live in a world constituted like ours! Do we realize as we ought, that each one of us is by his habits, by his opinions, by his words and by his actions, concerned in shaping the final destiny of all the rest? Do you realize that you are daily tracing lines upon the characters of all around you, which though now invisible, like pencillings with sympathetic ink, will certainly become legible amidst the fires of the last day, and will reveal your handwriting and identify you as the author? It *is* a solemn thing to live, and the longer life shall be, the more solemn it will be to *die*. For when we come to die, we shall not enter upon our final state without the company of those whom we have educated for heaven or hell. The specific doctrine of the text to which I would most seriously direct your attention is that when a man lives a life of sin and at last goes down to hell, he will certainly involve many others in his ruin. If any of you, my beloved hearers, should at last make your bed and lie down in eternal burnings, it will be written as the vindication of the justice of God in your everlasting torment, "That man perished not alone in his iniquity."

I have already alluded to the fact that the sins of the parents involve their children in the temporal calamities which always follow a course of crime. I might go on to show that in most cases they leave a heritage of spiritual ruin to their unfortunate offspring.

Behold the father of a family—himself ungodly, profane, and worldly;—how can his children be any better than he? What he is they will be of necessity, except in some rare instances, in which by an almost miraculous interposition they are snatched as brands from the burning. He may be a man despised by his neighbors, and without social influence, or perhaps unknown to the busy world around him. But there is one circle where he is supreme: it is in the bosom of his family. And when he dies, he will carry a sufficient number with him to justify the mournful epitaph, "That man perished not alone in his iniquity."

But suppose that he has wealth and social position. Suppose that he is surrounded by dependents and admirers, who feel honored by his smile, and who are only too proud to minister to his passions and imitate his vices. How will these adventitious circumstances help to increase the long train of those whom he drags down to a hopeless perdition! In his case, with how much greater emphasis may we repeat it, "That man perished not alone in his iniquity."

But let us shift the scene. Look at that group of young men, as they stand closely huddled together about some favorite haunt of the idle and the profane. What is it that so engrosses their attention? Are they engaged in some interesting discussion on subjects worthy of the attention of the intelligent and the refined? Ah, no! Their frequent idiotic laughter proves that they are full of vain thoughts. Theirs is the mirth of "*fools who are making a mock at sin.*" And who is it that is able to give them such entertainment? Is it one whom they all admire and respect? Is it some lofty genius before whom they all stand as confessed inferiors? And do they defer to his intelligence and wisdom? And is their applause extorted from their genuine admiration of his person and character? Alas! no. He is a *low* and *vulgar buffoon;* a *depraved* and *ignorant dolt;* a *beastly scavenger of all the foul abominations of the brothel;* a *retailer* of *filthy anecdotes* and jests, treasured up in a mind capacious of such things; a poor, pitiful object of contempt to the very men who hang upon his lips, and seem to drink in his slimy feculence *like honey from Hymettus.* And yet this poor fool, who thus prostitutes himself to their amusement, is thought to be so far beneath contempt that he is accounted to have no influence among his fellows. They seem to think that the *leprosy of a beggar cannot* infect the blood of a *high-born gentleman.* But when he shall perish in his iniquity, it will be found at last that this despicable and obscure insignificant sinner, as they are pleased to regard him, has sown the seeds of corruption in the soil of many a congenial heart, and that "*this man, too, perished not alone in his iniquity.*"

In further illustration of the text, let me draw one more picture. Suppose we enter a group of young men collected in some place of resort, for the purpose of enjoying a midnight revel. The moment I enter, I see that there is *one* who is the master spirit,—the acknowledged leader of the rest. He has talents, he has wealth, he is distinguished by a frank and manly bearing. His beaming eye, his noble brow, show that the influence he wields is due to the native intellect and the magnanimous spirit which God had given him. Although really wicked, he bears, like Satan, some traces of the grandeur that would have ennobled him, unfallen.

He has come to the city, he collects friends, congenial spirits who admire the traits of character I have described. But he has been trained by ungodly parents, or he has cast off the instructions of a pious ancestry. Perhaps he has thought it manly to be an infidel, to sneer at the religion of his father, and to scoff at the holy devotion of his mother.

With such endowments and such appliances and such principles, he is the leader of every bacchanalian rout. Proud of his talents, and anxious to maintain his ascendency, he is the tempter of innocent boys, who came hither with the down of purity still fresh upon their ruddy cheeks.

With no fear of God before his eyes, he riots in all excess of sensual pleasure, and spends his nights in the house of her whose ways take hold on hell. Regardless of the happiness or comfort of others, he corrupts those who can be bribed to minister to his lusts, and deflowers the chastity of the poor or of the social inferiors by whom he is surrounded, without one compunctious smiting of conscience. At last, he goes forth into the great world to enter upon a still wider field of influence, without having left one good impression on his late companions. We look upon his paths, and see that the trail of the serpent is over them all. His former associates go forth too. Some partially recover from the effects of the insidious poison he instilled into their souls; but the larger part have themselves gone on from bad to worse; themselves corrupted, and now in turn the corrupters of others. He may live a long or a short life; but at last he dies a miserable man, his talents squandered, his wealth a burden, his body bloated by wine and filled with the sins of his youth. He dies, and goes down to hell. And when he enters the world of woe, he shall be met at the very portals by the lost souls of those who have gone before him. The Apostle says, "Some men's sins go before them to judgment, and some they follow after." His sins have gone before him in the persons of the wretched victims of his perverted wealth and influence; in the innocence that he tempted, in the avarice that gave him the cup of debauchery in exchange for his gold, in the servile lewdness seduced by his bribes into base compliance, and in all the innumerable ministers to his ambition, his vanity, and his lust. And even before his eyes shall have ranged through the long vistas of his gloomy abode, or have glanced fearfully at the unquenchable flames of the lake of liquid fire, he will meet those there who know him and who will accost him as their destroyer. One shall say, "You first taught my innocent feet the way to dens of infamy and pollution, and here am *I* appointed to be your tormentor forever"; and when he turns to flee from these reproaches, another shall howl in his ear the bitter taunt, "You first put the poisoned wine-cup to my lips, and thus engendered that fatal thirst which destroyed my usefulness in life, and robbed me of heaven"; and another, all festering with sores, shall hiss the dreadful execration, "It was for *you* that I decked my bed with tapestry and adorned my person with ornaments; for your yellow gold I bartered my body; to your treacherous smiles I betrayed my frailty, and to your pampered luxury I yielded my homely virtue. *Now*, withered, ruined, blighted, filled with that reproachful pain which rots the marrow and consumes the brain, I, whose bed you shared on earth, I am appointed to make your bed in HELL, and heap upon you the 'waves of wretchedness.'" And another and another shall join their voices in the hue and cry, and shall fill the vaults of hell with their accusations. That same company of boon companions shall gather around him once more, not now as before, to admire, applaud, and imitate, but to curse him and curse the day which brought them in contact with his baleful influence. "Some men's sins go before them to judgment, and some they follow after." *And some they follow after.* Forever and anon, as his old associates gather around him, there shall be new accessions of those whom he had never known—of those who were born after he died, that shall join the wretched throng, and identify him as the destroyer of those who in turn destroyed them. Thus, through the long night of a dismal eternity, remorse, the never-dying worm, shall prey upon his guilty soul, and it shall be written on his forehead with the finger of Divine retribution, "That man perished not alone in his iniquity." "Perished," do we say?—He shall live forever, but

" Live like scorpion girt by fire;—
So writhes the soul remorse hath riven,

> Unfit for earth, undoomed for heaven,
> Darkness above, despair *beneath*,
> Around it *flame*, within it *death*."

Oh, young men, if any of you are determined to perish, I pray you to seek to perish by yourself. Go hide yourself in some mountain solitude, fly from this place where so many may be ruined by your example, and if possible avert from your soul the aggravated doom of that " man who perished not alone in his iniquity."

But if there be one depth of woe deeper than all, it will be reserved for the unfaithful minister who, charged with the high commission of a watchman to warn the wicked of his way, has healed slightly their hurt, and cried *"Peace," "peace"* to the wicked, when there is no peace, saith my God, to the wicked. There will be a peculiar aggravation in his case, for it will be that of a man who had no motive to deceive either himself or others; of one who had every opportunity of doing good, every opportunity of knowing the truth, and yet with the lamp of life in his hands, only used it to illuminate the broad road that leads to destruction. And as he is plunged down, down into the bottomless pit of perdition, methinks his very cry for mercy will be stifled, when he casts his eye upwards and beholds the long train of lost spirits, once members of his admiring flock on earth, dragged down by his perverted influence to the lowest hell. Oh that a merciful God would save us from hell; but if we must perish, may we at least be saved from the unspeakable woe of that man who perished not alone in his iniquity!

XXI.

STEWARDSHIP.*

"Give an account of thy stewardship."—LUKE xvi. 2.

THE explanation of the Parable of the Unjust Steward has been by some commentators abandoned in despair, they affirming that a solution of its difficulties is impossible. That it presents great difficulty is evident from the fact that it has received innumerable and most opposite interpretations. A parable is very often a locked edifice, and its correct interpretation requires a master-key. As in a great house there may be many doors, some of which will be unlocked by one key, while others will not; so in the parable there are many parts which one theory of interpretation will explain, while there are other parts that refuse to yield any meaning whatever. And as in a great house all the doors will open to the touch of the master-key; so, too, if we can get the master-key to the parable, all its intricacies become plain as day.

Without wearying you with a detail of all the labored efforts of the commentators to explain how our Lord could derive a lesson of instruction from the conduct of a dishonest man, and how the lord of the steward could commend him for his dishonesty, I proceed at once to put into your hand the master-key which will open all the doors of this long-closed treasure-house.

Let us first consider the parties. They were "a certain rich man," his "steward," who is called "unjust," and the "debtors" of the "rich man."

The man must have been very rich in order to need a steward. His wealth did not consist of money, but of land—large farms,

---

* A New-Year's sermon.

the rent of which was paid in the produce of the soil. The large landed proprietor committed the management of his estate entirely to his steward. This steward farmed out the land for such price as he thought fit, without every particular in the contract being made known to his lord. All that the latter cared to know was the gross revenue which his estate yielded. Up to this time the rich proprietor had not required any accurate reckoning with his steward, until, informed of the man's dishonesty, he determined to displace him. He had bestowed on him full confidence, and invested him with plenary powers in the making of all contracts with the small farmers who rented the land.

Now let us look at the steward. He was accused to his lord of having "wasted his goods." It is clear that he was not accused of such peculation as would have enriched him; for, in prospect of his displacement, he contemplates the alternative of going to work, or of begging, as the means of future support. No, the man had only lived extravagantly and sumptuously, and as he had no property of his own, his malicious neighbors, who did not fare so well as he (just like many people now, when they see a man living better than themselves and know not where he gets the means), jumped to the conclusion that the steward was misappropriating his lord's revenues, and so they went and told on him. They concluded, of course, that he had been wronging his lord, and, with a great deal of virtuous indignation, they determined to put a stop to it. At this point the lord is struck with their representations, and at once calls him to account. He says: "Give an account of thy stewardship." Bring me all the bonds of my tenants and let me compare them with the amounts which you have annually rendered to me. If the papers are produced his lord will be able at a glance to see whether the revenues annually accounted for tally with the farm contracts for the current year. And now at this point we see why he is called an "unjust steward." Observe, if the charges against him had been true he would not have been called unjust, but unfaithful; his breach of trust and want of fidelity would not have been thus characterized. But he had not been unfaithful to his lord; he had rendered to him every year what was a fair rental for his lands. His *unjustness* appears in that he extorted from the farmers more than he had stated and paid to his lord. "He demanded of them an *excessive* rent, and paid to him only a fair amount, so that the difference between what he received and what he rendered constituted a clear gain to himself," and enabled him to support the style and display which excited the envy of his poor neighbors; perhaps, of these very farmers themselves. Hence, in casting about what he shall do, he determined to have two strings to his bow. He will smooth over his accounts with his lord and prove to him by written evidence that he has never wronged him; that the bonds of the farmers correspond exactly with the annual revenue rendered him, and which was, in fact, an equitable revenue; and he will make fair weather with the farmers themselves by an abatement of his customary extortion from them. Hence, he calls the farmers together and says to each in turn, "How much owest thou unto my lord?" The first says, "A hundred measures of oil." Then said he, "Well, I have been conferring with my lord, and he agrees with me in thinking that this is an exorbitant rent, and I have prevailed on him to reduce it fifty per cent. I will exchange your old note of a hundred for a new one for fifty." Well, you see, that farmer went away, saying, "This steward is a good, upright man. I will never fail to do him a good turn, if the time ever comes when he shall need it." He then called a second, and said, "And how much owest thou?" And he said, "A hundred measures of wheat." With the same apparent show of moderation and uprightness he says, "I will exchange your old note for a new one with *eighty* instead of a hundred." And so he goes through the whole list of debtors. They all go away applauding the integrity and moderation of the steward. None of them will join now in defaming him. He has made fast friends of them. Now he comes to his lord with all his accounts ready for inspection, and no discrepancy between the amounts due from the tenants and the amounts rendered is found. And now the "lord commended the unjust steward." This verse has always troubled the commentators; for they never could understand why the rich man would commend his steward for doing that which, upon their theory, was only adding to the wrong he had already done in wasting his goods. They have all persisted in representing the steward as *unfaithful* to his employer, and never seem to have gotten the idea into their heads that he was unjust to the debtors, but faithful to his lord. Hence they never could explain the commendation which his lord bestowed upon him. But upon the interpretation which I have just given all is clear as noonday. His lord commended him because upon the examination of the papers he found that he himself had nothing to complain of. And as long as his own interests were not compromised he was not careful to inquire into the wrong inflicted on his tenants. Indeed, while he was no doubt informed of it, he commended the shrewdness of his steward. . . . . The lord of this steward, so far as we know, retained him in his service as a wise and shrewd manager. He would hardly have dismissed him after commending him for his sagacity.

In commenting upon this parable, our Lord says to His disciples, " Now, I say unto you, make to yourselves friends of the mammon of unrighteousness, that, when ye fail, they may receive you into everlasting habitations." This verse also has been a great stumbling-block. And it is not without its difficulty. In the first place, the meaning is obscured by the inaccurate rendering of a preposition. The translation ought not to be " friends *of* the mammon of unrighteousness," but " friends *by means of* the mammon of unrighteousness" (*vide* Winer's Grammar, p. 460, and Lange on Luke xvi. 9). In the second place, the Greek text upon which the English version is based is generally conceded not to be the true reading. Our version very correctly translates " that when ye fail they may receive," etc. But the best manuscripts in Greek and the New Version read, " that when *it* fails," *i. e.*, when the *mammon* fails, or *is exhausted*, etc. A paraphrase of the verse which conveys its exact meaning may aid you to understand it : " I say unto you, make to yourselves friends by means of the mammon of unrighteousness; so that when this mammon is exhausted, these friends thus made may receive you into the everlasting tabernacles."

Having translated the passage, it remains to be seen how it is to be explained. Does our Lord mean to commend the unjust steward? Does He hold him up for imitation? I answer, He does not commend him for his conduct in so far as it was unjust toward the farmers, but He does commend it at the point where it began to be just; at the point when he began to make his friends. He in effect says: "Where this steward ended do you begin. He ended his career by using his place and power, his control over the mammon which, up to this time, he had unrighteously appropriated to his own selfish ends—he ended his career by using these things righteously, justly, and thus made a host of friends. Do you the same with the mammon which may be under your control. Use it wisely; do not appropriate it to your own selfish gratification, but act like him, and make friends, who, going before you to heaven, will welcome you, when you get there, with outstretched arms. True, his motive was a bad one, but his conduct was wise. Do likewise, only do it with the right motive. Use your means not for yourself, but for others, and you shall reap the eternal reward."

I have thus explained this parable at length, because I know that it is unintelligible to the vast majority of the thoughtful readers of the New Testament, and he renders a great service to his hearers who can succeed in clearing up for them any of the dark sayings of our Lord. I hope that this parable will shine with a new light into your souls; for rightly considered, especially when taken in its historical connection, it is one of the most striking examples of the elevated didactic wisdom of our Lord.

Turning away from the exegetical consideration of this passage, I wish to make a homiletical and practical use of only one part of it. We are entering now upon the work and toil of a new year. And it seems especially appropriate before we launch out upon it to inquire, what have we done for God? And this is suggested by the text: "Give an account of thy *stewardship*." For it may be that our Lord, seeing we have been unfaithful, may be saying: "Thou mayest no longer be steward."

When applied to us the text assumes that God is the paramount owner of all that we are and all that we have; that in all his activity man is called on earth to be the steward of God; that he is not to live for himself at all; that as steward he is placed in a dependent position; that he is pledged to a conscientious faithfulness; that he will be held to a strict account. "Give an account of *thy* stewardship."

Against you as God's steward on earth, there are several accusations preferred by the world, by the devil, and by your fellow-members of the church, and He who hears them all will examine them impartially and carefully to the last one, and before He renders His decision He is saying to you at the opening of a New-Year's account, "Give an account of last year's stewardship."

Over what things has God appointed you His steward?

First. As suggested immediately by this parable, He has made you steward over a certain amount of property, more or less, as the case may be—some of you more, some less. "It is a striking proof of the practical tendency of the Gospel morality that our Saviour has regarded the use and possession of earthly riches as a subject of sufficient weight to be particularly handled by Him in a triad of parables: viz., the parables of the 'Rich Fool,' of the 'Unjust Steward,' of 'Dives and Lazarus,' not to reckon a number of hints occurring here and there in His discourses." How, then, have we employed our Lord's money? There is often a great deal of vague declamation about giving *all* to God and exercising stern self-denial and refraining from this unnecessary luxury, and from that needless expense; and while there is a great deal of truth in what is said, the principle involved in it all would, if carried out to its logical results, bring the whole community down to prison fare—a bed of straw and bread and water. This is not Scriptural; it is at variance with the dictates of the enlightened Christian conscience.

Let us see how, as stewards of God, He would have us expend the means He puts into our hands.

There are three great objects to which our means ought to be appropriated so as to meet the Divine approval. These are:—

1. A certain proportion ought to be taken for defraying personal and family expenses.

2. Another portion may be allowed to accumulate as capital.

3. A fixed proportion ought to be devoted to God.

No one doubts that the first of these objects ought to be attended to. Every one must be housed and clothed and fed. This duty need not be urged; the danger is that this duty be the only one attended to.

In regard to the second there is difference of opinion. Some fanatics go so far as to say that a Christian has no right to acquire property. They say it is a distrust of God's providence and care to store up money for the future provision for themselves and families. They support their opinions by the wresting of such Scriptures as these: "Lay not up for yourselves treasures upon earth"; "Woe to him that ladeth himself with thick clay"; "Go to now, ye rich men, weep and howl for the miseries that shall come upon you," etc. The common sense of mankind, as well as Scripture compared and interpreted, is so totally opposed to these views that no one carries them out in practice. The Scriptural authority for this common-sense view is very decisive. The meaning of the passages I shall quote is that property in itself is a blessing, and only becomes a curse if improperly employed: "The hand of the diligent maketh rich"; "He that gathereth in summer is a wise son"; "The blessing of the Lord maketh rich, and He addeth no sorrow with it"; "And the Lord hath blessed my master Abraham greatly, and he is become great, and He hath given him flocks and herds and silver and gold"; "And Isaac sowed in that land, and received in the same year one hundredfold, and the Lord blessed him, and the man waxed great and went forward and grew until he became very great." It would be hard to prove against such Scriptures as these that it is a sin to die rich.

I thus frankly and fully declare that the Scriptures teach the propriety and necessity, not only of adequately providing for present wants and comforts, but also of accumulating property for commercial and useful purposes and for the future wants of ourselves and families. These apparent concessions, some might think, will counteract or weaken the arguments to be used to enforce the third department of our duty as stewards: viz., the portion to be allotted to the service of God. Truth requires no concealment or suppression of anything. It is our whole record as stewards which is under review, and we are to remember that the same authority which says, "Honor the Lord with thy substance," also says, "But if any provide not for his own, and especially for those of his own house, he hath denied the faith, and is worse than an infidel" (1 Tim. v. 8).

The third department of stewardship, viz., that part of our property to be devoted to the service of God, includes three divisions:—

First. Almsgiving, or charitable contributions to the poor, or to benevolent institutions—such as orphanages, widows' homes, and so forth.

Second. The support of the ministry, both in our country and in foreign lands.

Third. Free-will offerings.

In regard to the first of these divisions, the money which we give to the poor, God has been pleased to designate a *loan* to Him. "He that giveth to the poor *lendeth* to the Lord." "Blessed is he that considereth the poor; the Lord will deliver him in time of trouble."

But in order that we may perform this duty intelligently, the Holy Spirit led the Apostle to lay down a special rule.

"Upon the first day of the week let every one of you lay by him in store as God hath prospered him, that there be no gatherings when I come." This passage has been grievously misunderstood, and made to teach the propriety of Sunday-morning collections in church for the support of the Gospel. Whereas it was Paul's direction to the Corinthians how to provide in a special emergency alms for the suffering saints in Jerusalem, so as to avoid taking up a collection when he should come to preach to them. In effect he says: "Do this in order that there be no necessity for a collection when I come."

Let us now analyze this rule for almsgiving: (*a*) "Let every one of you." This shows that the duty of almsgiving is incumbent upon all, rich and poor, young and old. There is nothing in the Bible that exempts even the poor from giving alms.

(*b*) "Lay by him in store." Literally, "Lay by him at home" (the *para cauto* of the original, being the idiomatic equivalent of the French, *chez moi*, and the German, *bei sich selbst*). This shows that it is the duty of every one to give alms not simply when he is asked or when occasion arises, but to store up beforehand a certain portion of his gettings, so as to be ready to give liberally upon a sudden call. The advantages of this plan are obvious. Things done without premeditation are generally ill-done. So when there has been no deliberate comparison of the claims of different objects and no settled determination of what sum to give, the amount must be left pretty much to chance or to the impulse of the moment.

The passage does not mean that the proportion should be mentally set apart, but that it should be *actually* set apart. Those who are disinclined to keep written accounts should literally comply with the rule, and have a box appropriated to the keeping of their alms separate from their other moneys.

A great man and a great scholar, who certainly is not averse to the use of the pen, told me many years ago that he kept in his study a little treasury-box with three apartments—one marked "Tithes," another "Free-will Offerings," and a third "Alms." There was a holy philosophy in this. It is much harder for a man to quiet his conscience after appropriating to himself actual money once dedicated to God than after making a fraudulent cross-entry in a ledger.

But business men and merchants who keep all their money in banks ought to have openings in their ledgers in which to credit "Alms" and "Tithes" and "Free-will Offerings," each with its due proportion of "Profit and Loss," and to credit each with all paid out to God and the poor.

(*c*) "On the first day of the week." There is no phrase in the Bible that has been so grievously and mischievously misinterpreted as this.

First. It has been made the foundation of the doctrine that collections should be taken up *every* Sunday. But the Greek does not read, "on the first day of the week," but "on *one* of the Sabbaths." Paul was ordering a specific contribution for a single object, viz., the poor saints at Jerusalem; and he says "on one of the Sabbaths"; that is, some of you on one Sabbath and some on another, or each of you on every Sabbath, if he chooses.

Secondly. This has been made the foundation for the false doctrine that the support of the ministry and of the church is to be derived from these public contributions, whereas the object for which the Apostle ordered this contribution was ALMS.

But this clause shows that the Sabbath is an appropriate time for carrying out the injunction to " lay by at home." It does not mean that it is the proper day for inquiring how much a man has prospered. But it means that it is a religious act, appropriate to the Sabbath, to consecrate to God's poor the amount determined on at the close of the preceding week. The inference from the passage is that the practice of storing up for future distribution among the poor should be adopted as a person receives his wages or income, be it weekly, monthly, quarterly, or yearly; and with respect to those who live by irregularly accruing profits, such as of agriculture, trade, or commerce, this duty should be immediately performed after taking account of the year's work, or after making the balance-sheet and determining the debit of " Profit and Loss."

(*d*) " As God hath prospered him."

In this is involved the idea of *proportion*. This is the New Testament rule in regard to alms. In this matter Christ has not bound His people down to any limit. When He gives much He expects His people to give more and more, in proportion to the growth of their incomes. Indeed, if He had laid down an iron rule on this point, it would have been in direct contravention to His specific command that alms should be given so secretly that nobody should know anything about the amount thus bestowed. But the Apostle, carrying out the spirit of the sermon of our Lord, says: " In proportion as God has prospered you." You know how great has been your prosperity, and nobody has any business with your alms. That matter is between you and your Father in heaven. " Thy Father, which seeth in secret, Himself shall reward thee openly."

It is clear that the whole passage teaches the duty of systematic laying aside of your earnings *at home,* in order that you may be able to contribute to the poor saints as often as their necessities require, without resorting to collections in the church assemblies, when one would give by impulse, or caprice, or accident, or give nothing at all.

Second. The second division of religious giving comprises the portion of our substance which *we owe directly to God*. In this, God claims of all His people His right. In giving to the poor, He says, we "lend to the Lord"; but in withholding from Him what He claims as His right, we are said to "rob God." We do not "rob" by refusing a loan, but we do rob when we fail to pay a debt. Now, does God in His Word tell us precisely how much He claims as the portion He will accept from His people as His share? The plain answer is that in all ages of the church, from Abraham to the present moment, He has indicated that the rendering of less than a tenth of a man's income is a robbing of God. Now, in the Jewish church this tenth was devoted exclusively to the maintenance of the ministry and the ordinances of God's house. And Paul, in allusion to this provision for the ministry under the old economy, says: "Even so hath the Lord ordained that they which preach the Gospel shall live of the Gospel." That is, as under the old economy, God prescribed that the ministry, and all who aided them in the service of religion directly, should be supported by the contribution of a tenth of the income of His people; so God expects the ministry of the church and the eldership of the church to be supported now. You may be startled by the proposition that the elders of a church ought to receive pecuniary compensation for their church work, but it is the teaching of the Apostle Paul. He says: "Let the elders that rule well be counted worthy of double honor, for it is written, 'Thou shalt not muzzle the ox that treadeth out the corn.'" All the scholars agree that this has reference to pecuniary compensation for the time abstracted from their secular business in the service of the church.

I mention this, however, now, only incidentally, lest you should think a tithe of your incomes would be too large a provision for the salaries of the ministers of the church.

There is the greatest ignorance among ministers, and great

misapprehension among the people on the subject of the Jewish tithe. It was not collected under stringent regulations. On the contrary he might, and the covetous Jew did, often fail to "bring" his tithe to the storehouse. If he did not bring it voluntarily, there was no compulsory process by which it could be wrung from him. It was a matter which rested between him and his God. The rulers of the people took no cognizance of his dereliction. But God, whom he "robbed," did. Thus you see that what is called the "Law of the Tithe," was only the rule of proportion by which God taught His people what amount of their yearly income He would accept as a token of their acknowledgment of His right to all their possessions. And in the degenerate days of the church, when piety was almost extinct, and when the priests failed to teach the people their duty in this matter, God visited them with drouths and all manner of agricultural disaster, and caused the priests to become "contemptible and base in the eyes of the people," because they had, in the language of Malachi, "corrupted the covenant of Levi"; that is, because they had relaxed the demand for the tithe, which was "the covenant of Levi." In precisely the same way the ministry in our day, by their failure to indoctrinate the people as to the demand which God makes upon them for the support and maintenance of all His ministers and the ordinances of His house, have, in a manner, become "contemptible and base" before all the people. Instead of fearlessly proclaiming their right to live of the Gospel, they too often stand, like beggars, hat in hand, entreating that they may be permitted to starve on the meagre pittance doled out to them by a covetous and selfish people. And hence it has come to pass that most people look upon money paid for the support of the minister at home or for the missionary to the heathen as a charity, instead of a debt owed to God himself.

I wish, while on this subject, to explain briefly the "free-will offering." It is absolutely distressing, as well as amusing, to hear some people talk of their "free-will offerings."

A free-will offering was brought by the pious Jew on a particular emergency as a thank-offering for deliverance from some special peril, or on the experience of signal blessing. It was never appropriated or intended to supplement any deficit in the support of the priests; and there was no room for a free-will offering on the part of any one *who had not brought his tithe.* A free-will offering was something over and above what the offerer owed to God. Only after all obligations were discharged could one dare to present a free-will offering.

You are now prepared to see for yourselves whether any of you could, if you desired, bring to God a free-will offering in acknowledgment of His signal mercies to you during the past year. If your givings to the support of the Gospel in this church and in our missionary work in foreign lands have not been one-tenth of your income in the past year, you are in no condition to respond to the loud call made by the Committee of Sustentation, which you find on a circular put in your pews to-day, in a free-will offering. You must be just to God before you can be generous.

Some, I know, have given more than a tenth of their gains; some only a portion; some nothing. The account is between all and God. Be assured God has a controversy with all who have fallen short. God says by Malachi: "Ye are cursed with a curse, for ye have robbed Me."

The present is a favorable moment for God's people to give an account of their stewardships.

But how can you *give* an account of that of which you keep no account? If your offerings to God have been made simply upon impulse, or only incidentally when you happened to be at church, without any systematic calculation of your resources, you may be perfectly sure that you have not given one-hundredth part of what will be acceptable to God.

I therefore advise every one to go home and make up a strict account of his income for the year 1881; then a statement of all he has contributed to the support of the Gospel in this church and in the missionary fields, and if the amount falls below one-tenth of the income, to bring the difference to the deacons, to be applied at once by them in raising the amount asked for by the Secretary of the Missions. Then you will be prepared to render an account of your stewardship unto the great "Lord" to whom all you have belongs.

The adoption of this rule of voluntary tithing is recommended by four considerations.

First. It has the sanction of Divine authority.

Second. It was practiced by the early church for more than a thousand years after the Apostles.

Third. It is the only equitable plan for distributing the burdens of a church according to the abilities of the people.

Fourth. It is the certain condition of worldly prosperity. It is impossible for God to lie. He says: "Honor the Lord with thy substance and with the first fruits of all thine increase; so shall thy barns be filled with plenty and thy presses shall burst out with new wine." "Bring ye all the tithes into the storehouse, and prove me now herewith, saith the Lord of Hosts, if I will not open the windows of heaven and pour you out a blessing that there shall not be room enough to receive it."

If the time permitted, I could give you extracts from more than a hundred letters, testifying in substance to the fact that God has fulfilled this promise in a wonderful manner to the writers of them. One of these letters I have never been able to read without tears. In the course of it the writer says: "My practice for years had been to devote the tenth to God. But closer investigation convinced me that the tithe and free-will offering together claimed one-third of my income, and alms a tenth of the remainder. And although by reason of an insufficient salary I am often straitened, yet a covenant God keeps me up and bestows His help in various ways. I could not feel satisfied to come short of this, and am often troubled by the thought that I came so late to the knowledge and practice of my duty."

I close this part of this discussion with the following extract from an article written by a minister of our church who has studied this subject more profoundly than any other man in this country:

"The census of 1870 discloses some amazing facts.

Cost of dogs in the United States	$10,000,000
Support of criminals	12,000,000
Fees of litigation	35,000,000
Cost of tobacco and cigars	610,000,000
Support of grog-shops	1,500,000,000
Whole cost of ardent spirits	2,200,000,000
Salaries of all the ministers	6,000,000

"Consider this country's estimate of the Gospel ministry; the ministers of all the denominations grudgingly supported on a sum less by $4,000,000 *than the dogs of the land!* What an insult to the King of kings! Enough to perpetuate the curse upon a God-forsaken land!" Hear old Andrew Fuller: "The love of money will, in all probability, prove the eternal overthrow of more characters among professing people than any other sin, because it is almost the only crime that can be indulged and a profession of religion at the same time be supported." "What the Church of Christ most lacks is faith in God. Her unbelief dishonors God and impoverishes herself. Were it not for unbelief and covetousness, what advances might she not have made! Did her fidelity correspond in the lowest measure with the transcendent position she occupies and the glorious privileges she possesses; did she freely give as she has freely received, the dark places of the earth which are now full of the habitations of cruelty would long since have been illuminated by the glorious sun of the Gospel, the conquests of divine truth would have been complete, the empire of Satan would be dismantled and overthrown, and the glorious shout would now be thundering through the temple of God, Alleluiah! The kingdoms of the earth are become the kingdoms of our God."

But it is not only as the stewards of money that God calls you to account. This is only one, and by no means the most important one, of the Master's goods, which many are accused to Him of wasting.

There is another talent which has been committed to you for improvement, and that is your *personal influence*. There is a difference between this trust and the preceding in this, that while God only claims *part* of your money, He demands that *all* of your influence shall be employed for His glory. He demands that every act of your daily life shall illustrate the doctrines you profess. He demands that nothing you do shall misrepresent the Lord Jesus, whom He has set before you, and whom you profess to have taken as your example. Every part and property of your nature and every moment of your existence have been bought—paid for with "precious blood." And as the interest to which you are pledged is opposed by every other, you cannot yield to any claimant, even for a moment, without lending yourself during that moment to a hostile party, so that there is no alternative but this of devoting yourself exclusively to Christ—your character is to be the reproduction of the character of Christ. The disinterestedness which appeared in Christ, the purity of Christ, the harmlessness of Christ, the separation of Christ from sinners—all these ought to reappear in your character and external conduct, and if tempted to lend but a particle of influence to any other claimant than Christ, your reply is at hand, "I am not my own, I am Christ's; He has put it out of my power to give Him more than belongs to Him, for He has purchased and demands the whole through every moment of time." Now let us enumerate rapidly the means of influence which all possess in a greater or less degree.

Knowledge is a means of influence; *Scholarship* is a means of influence; *Scientific attainments* are a means of influence; *Professional skill* is a means of influence; *Official position* either in the State or in the Church, or in the University, is a means of influence; *Social position* is a means of influence; *Speech* is a powerful force and a means of influence. The most casual remark lives forever. There is not a word you have uttered during the past year that has not a moral history, and we are specifically warned that in the final taking account of our stewardship, by our words we shall be justified or condemned.

Relationship, whether natural or artificial, is a means of influence—of parent to child, of wife to husband, of sister to brother, of teacher to pupil. "There is no relation of life which does not invest the person sustaining it with some degree of influence, and which does not afford him the power of exerting an influence in it which no other being on earth possesses."

Self-denial is a means of influence. It is a means of influence both directly and indirectly. Directly it increases the means of benevolence which self-indulgence would have lavished on itself, and these by increasing usefulness are augmenting influence. But the influence which a man acquires by this increase of actual means is as nothing compared with that which he obtains by the fact when it comes to be known,—that he denies himself in order to obtain it. The amount which he saves by his self-denial may be only an additional mite; but the fact that he habitually denies himself in order to obtain it as a means of doing good, will ultimately invest him with a greater moral influence than the stranger to self-denial, though the giver of thousands, can ever possess.

"*Compassion* is a means of influence. And the deep anxiety which the earnest Christian ought to feel and does feel to snatch the firebrands from the flames and quench them in the blood of the cross, imparts a depth of tenderness to his tones and an energy to his efforts which give them a power over the hard heart beyond that of the most original truths unfeelingly spoken, or the stern authority of law itself." *Prayer* is influence. All those other things which I have described as means of influence become spiritually useful only by that power which descends in answer to prayer. Other means may be influential; but the amount of their influence is calculable, bearing some proportion to the power employed; but prayer, by engaging a Divine power, sets all calculation at defiance.

And now the Lord and Master is saying to you all, "Give an account of thy stewardship in the employment of all these means of influence and usefulness which I have placed in thy hands." How have you, who have acquired influence over the young men of these institutions, by your knowledge, your scholarship, your scientific attainments, your professional skill—how have you used your influence? Have you hidden your light under a bushel or under a bed? or have you caused it to shine upon them with baleful fires? Have you rendered tippling and drunkenness respectable in their eyes, because they see them associated with high literary and scientific attainments?

How have you that occupy official position in the State used your influence derived from such position? How have you who are conspicuous members in the Church of God used the influence which your elevation above the ordinary members of the church has given you? The Lord of the unjust steward said, How is it that I hear this of thee? And in the name of our Lord and Master I repeat the question, How is it that I hear this of thee, that you frequent bar-rooms, and drink whiskey, just like men who have not the fear of God before their eyes?

"Give an account of thy stewardship," ye that have social position, ye that have the power of speech, ye that have money, ye that have heard the oft-repeated injunction, Deny thyself and take thy cross, ye that have had unbarred access to a throne of grace, if ye would only choose to go there. "Give an account of thy stewardship." "Give an account of thy stewardship," all ye that have named the name of Christ and are therefore expected to depart from all iniquity. Have ye, as in duty bound, avoided all appearance of evil, even when there might have been no real evil in all your conduct? Have ye given no occasion to the enemies of the Lord to blaspheme? Have ye given no occasion for the vulgar sneer, and the ribald jest at the "elect" of God, in countenancing by your presence a scene of excess and unwarrantable hilarity? "How is it that I hear this of thee," that ye have been eating meat offered to idols? Do ye not see (if it is all true) that in these concessions which you may have made to the spirit of the world, and of good fellowship, that you have been casting your pearls before *swine;* and what can you expect but that they shall turn again and rend you?

What husbandman would not be discouraged in his work if, as fast as he sowed a field in corn and the good seed had begun to sprout, one-half of his laborers should go into the field by night and pluck up the expanding germ and sow tares in its place? And yet this is no unfair representation of the case of many a minister of the Gospel. One day in seven, he plants the good seed of the Word, and warns men against covetousness, against drunkenness, against worldly conformity, against all ungodliness, and the other six days, many of those whose lives ought to be the living exemplification of his teachings, are engaged in nullifying all his teachings by lives of covetousness, intemperance, worldly conformity, and practical godlessness. "How is it that I hear this of thee?"

"*Give an account of thy stewardship.*" What if in view of your neglect of these things and of your failure to use righteously the Mammon over which God has given you control, He should say, "Thou mayest no longer be steward!" The solemn reckoning cannot be evaded at the last, when the stewardship of the whole life is to be accounted for.

Some merchants make a "trial balance sheet" every month in order that they may know their financial condition all through the year. The reckoning to which I invite you resembles these "trial balances." When life is ended, it will be too late to correct errors. There will be no room on the page for "E. E." But now, before the final account is rendered, you have the opportunity of reviewing and correcting the past. If, in looking back over the year just ended, you find in regard to disbursing your Lord's money that you have been criminal, now is the time to begin to do better.

Renew your consecration to Him; and then you will not "lie to the Holy Ghost" when you sing:

> "Were the whole realm of nature mine,
> That were a present far too small;
> Love so amazing, so divine,
> Demands my soul, my life, my all."

XXII.

CONSOLATION.

"And the cup was found in Benjamin's sack."—GENESIS xliv. 12.

THE story of Joseph in Egypt, as recorded from the forty-second to the forty-ninth chapters of Genesis, is one of the most beautiful and touching narratives in all literature. Let me recall as much of it as will enable you to see the bearing of the text.

There being famine all over the face of the earth, the aged Jacob sent his ten sons down into Egypt to buy corn. Joseph, who many years before had been sold into slavery in Egypt by these very young men, was now in authority; and after selling them the corn, kept one of the young men in prison, but promised to release him, if upon their return to procure another supply they would bring their youngest brother, Benjamin, with them. This they did, although it nearly broke Jacob's heart to suffer the lad, who was very dear to him, to go with them. For after Joseph had been sold into Egypt, the affection which Jacob had for him was transferred to his brother Benjamin. Upon their return to Egypt, they were royally entertained by Joseph; and then dismissed with their sacks full of corn, and the purchase-money secretly deposited in their sacks' mouths Joseph also instructed his steward in like manner to put his silver cup in the mouth of Benjamin's sack.

The next day dawned auspiciously, and full of high spirits on account of the happy termination of their expedition, they turned their faces homeward. Everything had turned out well. They had been graciously received; had been honored with a sumptuous banquet; their brother Simeon had been restored to them, and their fear of being obliged to go home without corn, completely dispelled by knowing that their sacks were full. And now the obelisks of Egypt were disappearing behind them, and the pyramids were sinking in the distance. Congratulating each other on their happy escape from the distress into which they had been placed by the demand which Joseph had made about Benjamin, they were full of exuberant joy.

But as they look back over their shoulders, lo! a cloud of dust and a band of pursuing horsemen! They are overtaken, are commanded to halt, but although alarmed, their fears are quieted by recognizing in the captain of the pursuing band no other than Joseph's steward—the man who the day before had treated them with the highest consideration. But his countenance is severe. He at once charges them with robbing his master. They indignantly deny the charge. They denounce such ingratitude. They remind him of all their previous honest dealing—their bringing back the money for the first purchase, which they supposed had accidentally been taken away.

"The matter may be easily settled," say they. "Search us and search our sacks. With whomsoever of thy servants the cup is found, both let him die, and we also will be my Lord's bondsmen." Secure in conscious rectitude, " they speedily took down every man his sack to the ground. And he searched and began at the eldest, and left at the youngest; and the cup was found in Benjamin's sack."

Utterly overwhelmed, they go back to the city, silent, downcast, despairing, each one asking himself, How did this cup get into our baggage at all and why was it put into Benjamin's sack?

There are few of us who have not been called more than once to pass through just such a trial as this. We have often said, Why in Benjamin's sack? A railroad accident occurs, and while hundreds have escaped, our darling child is among the dead. A great shipwreck happens, and our loved one is among the lost. A tornado sweeps over the town, and our dwelling is demolished. There is a great bank robbery and the thieves have gotten our package of bonds.

Two questions occur to every thoughtful mind in connection with the subject of human experience. Why is it that everybody is sooner or later in life called to pass through a fiery furnace of affliction? And why, when God smites us, does He always strike the tenderest spot?

I. That there is a vast amount of sorrow in the world, everybody knows. The crowds that gather on festivals, or that congregate in theatres or opera-houses, or that flock to the hilltops on a summer's evening, seem to be happy, because they wear smiling faces; but these are their society faces. Let the excitement of the moment subside, and shadows darken them. There is a skeleton in the closet at home.

A wayward son, a dissipated husband; a faithless, jealous, or undutiful wife; a recreant lover, disappointed hopes, buried loves, defeated schemes of ambition, bodily pains, chronic ill-health, nervous prostration, and ten thousand causes of sorrow are present in one or another form in all our houses.

Those religious teachers who tell you that God designed you to be happy; that you must look at the bright side of things, and not suffer yourself to be overwhelmed by these evils, prove by their shallow consolations that they have not solved the mysteries of human life. It affords me very little comfort to know that the nerves of my body are adapted to give me pleasure, while I am racked with neuralgia and tortured with toothache.

But some will tell you that the ills of life are not half so numerous as its joys; that, on the whole, the happiness outweighs the misery; that pain is only incidental; that pleasure could not be appreciated without pain as a foil to set it off; that blessings in order to brighten must sometimes take their flight. It may do for the philosopher to account for the existence of sorrow by this explanation, but the sufferer himself will not receive it.

Then, again, they will tell you that suffering is accidental; that in the constitution of the universe the benevolent Creator did not intend or expect His children to be afflicted. This is the most absurd of all the hypotheses I have noticed. It ascribes to God boundless benevolence, but limited intelligence and power. If anything can be demonstrated, it is that the sorrows we experience are not accidental, but designed by Him whose kingdom ruleth over all. That silver cup of Joseph did not fall into the sack; it was put there.

We need not stop here to inquire into Joseph's motives for doing this. Perhaps it was to try the faith, loyalty, and love of his brethren for their father. And Jesus puts the sorrow into our hearts, to try our faith, loyalty, and love for our Father. Let us endeavor to unravel this tangled mystery of pain a little further.

(*a*). We know in regard to many forms of pain that its design is beneficent. It is sent in order to prevent greater suffering. Like the thorns on the rosebush, which prevent our grasping the flower too hastily, so pain warns us against the too eager pursuit of forbidden pleasures. It would be impossible for us to conceive of the excesses into which human nature would plunge, were it not for the restraining influence of pain. Suppose that wrong-doing were not checked by remorse, or that sins against our body were not followed by disease in the body, or that crimes in violation of social order were not followed by penalties—why, the whole world would become a vast pandemonium. It is because the fire burned him, that "the burnt child dreads the fire." The pain, therefore, was beneficent in its effect on him. The retributions of nature in the production of sorrow are salutary lessons to those who heed them.

(*b*). Human suffering gives occasion to those who look on it, for the exercise of virtues that otherwise would be impossible. How could you find occasion for the grace of benevolence, if there were no widows, and orphans, and destitute? or of sympathy, if there were no bereaved? or of tenderness and gentleness, if there were no "sick and in prison" to whom you might minister? Son, daughter of affliction, be of good cheer. Not for ourselves are we always smitten. By the blow upon you, God may be doing more unto others than you can ask or think.

(*c*). But this of itself would be a poor apology for suffering, if the lesson were taught only for the benefit of the spectator. We shrink with instinctive horror from the cruelty of the ancient sculptor who gloated over the dying agonies of a tortured criminal, because they afforded him a lesson in depicting the contortions produced by mortal pain. This may have been a valuable contribution to art, and a spectacle quite improving to the skill of the artist,—but how about the poor malefactor? Here is the explanation: "The suffering that tends to beautify another life with graces, tends also to bless the sufferer with piety." What occasion would he ever have for resignation, submission, faith in God, if God never crossed his will, nor smote him with His rod, nor plunged him into the depths of dark, inscrutable providences?

(*d*). All this, however, does not serve to explain satisfactorily the mystery of human sorrow. It shocks our sense of justice to admit for a moment that the beneficent and loving Father inflicts suffering upon His creatures for the sake of attaining such ends. If they are indeed the results of sorrow, they must be regarded as incidental and subsidiary; and not as the final cause. The real formal cause of all sorrow *is sin*. It would be wrong to inflict suffering on an innocent being.

No human authority would do this, even for the man's own good. And God does not do it. He does not send pain and death to any innocent human being.

The pangs of infancy are no exception to this universal proposition; for although young infants are sinless, they are not guiltless. They have a corrupt nature; and, on account of the sin of our first parents imputed to them, share a heritage of pain. The sufferings of the Holy Son of God constitute no exception to the proposition. For, while He was personally without sin, He was accounted, by the imputation of our sins to Him, the most guilty being in the universe. "He who knew no sin was made sin for us."

Only upon this ground can God be justified in the infliction of those untold agonies upon His well-beloved Son. Here, then, in human sin, we have, in general, the only satisfactory explanation of human sorrow.

II. Why does God smite us in the most sensitive part? Why did Joseph put the cup in Benjamin's sack? If it had been Simeon's or Judah's, it would not have been so hard to bear. But Benjamin! Leave *him* in Egypt! Go home without *him*, and bring down the gray hairs of our father in sorrow to the grave! Did we not tell the man, "The lad cannot leave his father, for if he should leave his father, his father would die"? And now, that which we most feared has come upon us. Benjamin, in whom our father's life is bound up, Benjamin must be left a prisoner in Egypt!

Just so, many of you have often felt; and you have moaned under the smiting of God's hand. "Take everything else—my houses, my lands, my friends, my other children, but oh! my Benjamin! I cannot live without him. Why was the cup put into the sack of my Benjamin?" I answer, *just because it is Benjamin's*. Sorrow is the medicine with which God cures the spiritual maladies of His children. If the cup had been put into some other sack, you would not have felt the pain which is designed to do you good. God rarely gives sugar-coated pills. The medicine He administers is usually bitter.

The confession which Judah made, "God hath found out the iniquity of thy servants," and his previous distress, show that these troubles came upon them in order that their sin in selling Joseph might be brought to their remembrance. This is always the effect of afflictions.

You have committed some great sin, and for a long time it troubled you; but gradually, the remembrance of it faded out of your mind. And you have never gone with it to God to confess it, and obtain the assurance of forgiveness. Suddenly you discover that God has a controversy with you. God brings your sin to remembrance by one stroke of His providence; and then you are brought to repentance.

Or again, you have been uniformly prosperous; you have all that heart can wish; and you love the world and the things of the world. You have forsaken the fountain of living waters, and sought to slake your thirst at other streams. God dries them up in order to bring you back to Himself. Or you have set up some one object of idolatrous worship. God dashes it from its pedestal, that your heart may be wholly set on Him. Or you have been trying to serve two masters; you have been living partly for earth and partly for Heaven; and this divided allegiance has been the occasion of your present grief. Begin to live wholly for Christ.

There is still another aspect in which we are to look at this matter. It is very certain that notwithstanding the keen sorrow which Joseph inflicted on his brethren by the stratagem he devised, his heart was yearning toward them with an inextinguishable love. His purpose at the time, although concealed from them, was to bring them all into Egypt and save them from the thick-crowding calamities which threatened them in Canaan. When Jacob cried out, "All these things are against me," and when in their profound consternation at the circumstantial evidence which convicted them of robbery, they rent their clothes, he did not dream, they did not know, that all their apparent ills were really straightforward steps to a career of prosperity and honor.

Thus, thus it is with us. In all His dealings with us,

> "God moves in a mysterious way
> His wonders to perform."

Though we cannot comprehend how it is, yet He assures us that "all things work together for good to them that love God, to them who are the called according to His purpose." It is with this precious panacea for all the woes of life that God equips all His ministers when He says to them, " Comfort ye, comfort ye my people." "How am I dumb in the presence of the wailings and complaints of the broken-hearted without this! How can I face this David, as he comes wringing his hands and crying in his agony, 'Oh! Absalom! my son, my son! Would God I had died for thee.' What can I say to this poor Rachel, weeping for her children and refusing to be comforted, unless I may say to them : ' This affliction cometh not by chance—it comes as the outworking of His adorable purpose who worketh all things together for good to them that love Him!'"

Again, it is evident from the sequel, that it was Joseph's plan to recall his brethren in order to make himself known to them. He might have adopted some other method. But he did not choose to do it. So Jesus wants us to become acquainted with

Him, and it is His plan to bring this to pass through the medium of sorrow. We are so busy in our chase after the butterflies of the world, that He maims us, so that we may stop in our hurried pursuit of them, and sit down awhile and talk with Him. Many a man has never seen the Son of God, till he finds Him walking by his side in the furnace of affliction.

Lastly. Joseph longed to gather his loved ones around him, that they might share his good fortune and see his honor. And so Jesus wants to fill heaven with His friends. "Father, I will that they also, whom Thou hast given me, be with me where I am; that they may behold my glory." Oh! is it not enough to console us amid all the sorrows of our troubled life to know, that the whole course of our discipline here is intended to prepare us for the full enjoyment of the society of Jesus there? To know that He will never see of the travail of His soul and be fully satisfied until He shall gather all His redeemed ones around Him in heaven? If "the Captain of our Salvation was made perfect through sufferings," and "for the joy that was set before Him, endured the cross, despising the shame," surely we can cheerfully submit to the conditions of our future elevation to a place by His side, knowing that "if we suffer with Him, we shall also reign with Him." *

---

* This was the last sermon Mr. Pratt ever preached.

XXIII.

RESURRECTION.

"The Power of His Resurrection."—Phil. iii. 10

"The resurrection of Christ is the most important and the best authenticated fact in the history of the world." Paul says that he counted all things but loss, and suffered the loss of all things, that he might know the "power of Christ's resurrection."

What is this "power of His resurrection" that is an object of such intense and eager curiosity? The Apostle does not mean by this expression, the power by means of which Christ's resurrection was effected; that we know was the mighty power of God, the Father, Son, and Holy Ghost. But he has reference to the resurrection itself as a source of power. He means the force which the resurrection exerts since it occurred.

Now one mode of attaining a conception of the power of any force, either moral or physical, is to picture what would have been the state of the sphere in which it has operated, if that force had never existed. For example, in order to gain an idea of the power of the sun, we imagine what would be the condition of this earth if the sun had never shone, or should cease to shine.

In like manner we may form some conception of the "power of His resurrection" if we consider what would have been the condition of the world if Christ had remained in the tomb of Joseph and never risen in His body from the grave.

If Christ had not risen from the dead, the Gospel would have been proved false; the whole of His life, all His miracles, all His doctrines, all His promises, all His threatenings would have been a palpable and notorious imposture and delusion. All the prophecies, all the Psalms, all the Old Testament types and symbols and sacrifices would have been proved to be a tissue of cunningly devised fables; His claim to being the Divine Son of God would have been exploded as a falsehood; "the whole scheme of redemption would have been a failure; and all the predictions and anticipations of its glorious results in time and in eternity, for men and for angels of every rank and order, would have been proved to be chimeras." It is almost impossible to conceive of all the consequences which would have followed His failure to rise from the dead. There could have been no Christian Church; for its existence is based upon the continued life of an incarnate Saviour: there could have been no Bible; for the whole Old Testament would have been demonstrably false: and the New Testament would never have been written. Men would live and die without hope; for they would have no Saviour. The hopes which a living Jesus had kindled in the bosoms of those who looked for a Messiah would have been extinguished in the tomb of a dead Jesus, who had not the strength to burst the prison bars of His grave. Universal skepticism must have engulphed the universal mind of the race. All that had been received as true for ages would have been proved a fable; for the whole revelation of God, from Moses to John the Baptist, pointed to Jesus as Him who was to save mankind by His death *and* resurrection; and if His resurrection failed, His death was the death of a man, and not of a great God and Saviour. His life of beneficence and holiness, His death of agony and shame, so far as we are concerned, would have no more significance and value than the life and death of Socrates, unless they were followed by His triumph over death, to prove that a greater than Socrates had been crucified. This resurrection of Christ was thus the keystone in the arch of the plan of Redemption. Had it been a-wanting, the whole structure must have tumbled into a heap of shapeless and *unreconstructible* ruins.*

"St. Paul, writing to a Gentile Church, expressly makes Christianity answer with its life for the literal truth of the Resurrection: 'If Christ be not risen, then is our preaching vain, and your faith is also vain. Then they also which are fallen asleep in

---

* Hodge.

Christ are perished.' Our Lord's honor and credit were staked upon the issue, since He had foretold His resurrection as the sign which would justify all the claims He had set up during His life." For the Scribes and Pharisees had said, We would see a sign from Thee, and He said that He would give them no other sign than this: "As Jonas was three days and three nights in the whale's belly, so shall the Son of Man be three days and three nights in the heart of the earth." The stupendous truth that Jesus, after predicting that He would be put to a violent death and then rise from the dead, did actually so rise, forces every man to accept the whole of Christianity as true. The Resurrection has all the force of an *a fortiori* argument. The proof of this as a historical fact, of necessity demonstrates the truth of the whole Gospel history. And it is because its proof is essential to the establishment of Christianity that God, in His providence, has so authenticated it that the man who doubts it is a fool or worse than a fool. If, then, Christ did rise from the dead, He is the Son of God, equal with the Father, "*God manifest in the flesh.*"

Having thus seen the power of His resurrection by glancing at what would have been the condition of the world without it, let us look more directly at the effects which the Scriptures ascribe to it.

I. The power of the resurrection in quickening our souls is asserted by Paul in the 2d chap. of Ephesians, ver. 5: "*Even when we were dead in sins, God hath quickened us together with Christ.*" This does not refer simply to the impartation to us of spiritual life; this was given to us by the Holy Spirit in regeneration. Spiritual life was received by believers long before Christ came in the flesh, and hence before His resurrection. The quickening, therefore, to which the Apostle refers, is something different from this. He does not mean that our souls are quickened as His body was:—that there is an analogy between His resurrection from the grave and our spiritual resurrection; but the truth here taught is the same as that taught in such passages as these: Rom. vi. 6, 8, "*Our old man is crucified with Him: Now if we be dead with Christ, we believe that we shall* *also live with Him*"; Gal. ii. 20, "*I am crucified with Christ: nevertheless I live, yet not I, but Christ liveth in me*"; 2 Cor. v. 14, "*If one died for all, then all died*"; 1 Cor. xv. 22, "*For as in Adam all die, even so in Christ shall all be made alive*"; *i. e.*, "that in virtue of the union, covenant and vital, between Christ and His people, His death was their death, His resurrection their resurrection, and His exaltation theirs. These passages all express what has already taken place; not what is future or merely in prospect. The resurrection, the quickening, and raising up of Christ's people, were accomplished when He rose from the dead and sat down at the right hand of God. The life of the whole body is in the head; *and, therefore, when the head rose, the body rose.*" *

II. Another effect of the power of the resurrection is *the strong assurance it gives all believers of the resurrection of their mortal bodies;* "*He that raised up Christ from the dead shall also quicken your mortal bodies by His Spirit that dwelleth in you*" (Rom. viii. 11). The mystery of our future resurrection exceeds our reason; but it is as clearly revealed, as it is inexplicable. The Apostle distinctly connects the final resurrection of believers with the accomplished resurrection of Christ. As His body was raised by the power of the Spirit that dwelt in Him, so our bodies shall be raised by the Spirit that dwells in us. As His body was sanctified by having been the residence of the Holy Spirit and therefore could not be the prey of the grave forever, so our bodies, being once honored as the temple of the Holy Ghost, cannot remain under the dominion of death. And as the indwelling of the Holy Spirit in Him secured His rising from the dead, so the indwelling of that same Spirit in us secures our rising from the dead. And the fact that He did thus rise, is the pledge and security to us that we shall rise also. It may be because we cannot understand the mystery of the resurrection of our mortal bodies that we think so little of it as a source of joyful expectation. But it is one of the most exhilarating and glo-

---

* Hodge on Eph. ii. 5.

rious truths revealed in Scripture. If we realized it as we ought, we could not, as so many do, regard the cold, damp, dark grave with any sense of aversion or repulsion. If we knew the power of His resurrection in securing our own, as Paul desired to know it, then we should long to be conformed to His death, so that we might attain to a similar resurrection from the dead. The ordinary comments upon this latter clause of the verse seem to me to eviscerate it of all its meaning. I do not believe that it has any reference to the fact that Paul was conscious that he was exposed to a violent death similar to that of Christ. But it means that being dead *like Christ* and lying in the grave *like Him*, being thus conformed to His death, he would in like manner attain to a similar glorious resurrection by the same power that raised Him up. Bishop Pearson "on the Creed" has expressed this idea in the following words: "The resurrection of Christ is the cause of our resurrection by a double causality, as an efficient and as an exemplary cause. As an efficient cause our Saviour, by and upon this resurrection, has attained power and right to raise all the dead. 'For as in Adam all die, so in Christ shall all be made alive.' As an exemplary cause, in regard that all the saints of God shall rise after the similitude and in conformity to the resurrection of Christ: *For if we have been planted together in the likeness of His death, we shall be also in the likeness of His resurrection* (Rom. vi. 5)." This then is a second power of the resurrection; that it confirms and proves the resurrection of believers: Christ rising from the dead has obtained the power to effect, and is become the pattern of our resurrection. We are the members of that body of which Christ is the head; "And if the head be risen, the members cannot be far behind."*

III. A third power in the resurrection of Christ is that by means of it believers are *justified*. "He was delivered for our offences, but was *raised again for our justification*" (Rom. iv. 25). This truth is not fully grasped by the Church in general. It is more frequently the case that the consciousness of believers

---

* Pearson.

turns to the death of Christ as effecting their justification. But the death of Christ was only a demonstration of the *guilt of those whom He represented*. The work of their justification was only begun in His death. Had it been arrested at this point by His failure to rise, *they never could have been justified*. He wrought their justification by His death, but its *efficacy* depended on His resurrection. By His death He *paid their debt*, in His resurrection He *received their acquittance*. He was quickened by the Spirit and by this Spirit was *justified Himself* from every charge that could be alleged against Him as the party and covenant head of those whose iniquities He bore. The resurrection of Jesus is therefore something more than a mere *proof* of our justification. It *was*, in fact, our justification. It was an integral, essential part of the thing itself. His resurrection was the justification of *Jesus himself* as the Head of the Church; it was the actual discharge of the prisoner on account of His satisfaction of the debt which He had assumed. If Christ had remained under the power of death, the curse of the law could not have been removed from us; we should have been left to die in our sins. He was delivered for our offences and raised again for our justification. "Jesus bowed beneath that death which the law demanded and which sinks angels and men to everlasting ruin; and He came victorious from the conflict. If He had been a creature, He would have been crushed, sunk, lost; if He had been less than God, the bitterness of death could not have been passed; never, never could He have emerged from that thick darkness into which He entered when He made His soul an offering for sin. The morning of the third day—and a more glorious day never dawned upon our earth—forever settled the question of our justification. When our great Substitute had given up the ghost and 'descended into hell,' the possibility of His return to us depended upon His ability to meet and *exhaust* the infinite wrath of the Infinite God. When the terrific cup was administered, and He drank it and died, His slumbers in Joseph's tomb could never have been broken, unless He could thunder with a voice like God, and bear the burden of infinite woe. The third day, which proclaimed His triumph, declared

Him to be the Son of God with power, 'according to the spirit of holiness' by His resurrection from the dead. He had died a death which none could die but one who was almighty." * And when He rose from that death in triumph, *He arose justified*, and drew with Him in His train all His people for whose sins He had undertaken the conflict; and *thus He rose for their justification*.

IV. In close connection with this thought, I call your attention to a fact recorded by Matthew, about which you rarely ever hear anything said: first, because few really believe it, and secondly, because it is only once mentioned in the New Testament. But it is a most amazing fact and is strikingly illustrative of what may be called the *physical* power of His resurrection. On the first day of the week after Christ's burial, at early dawn, there was a *great earthquake,* and the body of Jesus was restored to life, and He walked forth from His grave a living man. Now, an earthquake is a *physical effect,* involving the play of tremendous physical forces. This earthquake was no mere coincidence; it was *actually produced* by Jesus rising from the dead. It was only one among the many proofs of the "power of His resurrection." The earth in giving up the dead was convulsed with mighty throes, and thus the forces of nature were made to attest the power of His resurrection. But this was not all; He burst the prison of the grave not only for Himself, but for many others—the graves all around Him were opened, "and many bodies of saints which slept, arose and came out of their graves after His resurrection, and went into the holy city, and appeared unto many." Now, here is a stupendous physical fact: that as soon as Christ arose He drew others from the dead and brought them with Him into the living world. It proves that the "power of Christ's resurrection" "reached down into the domains of the dead. Even in the appalling regions of physical corruption He overthrew the empire of him who, according to the Scriptures, 'had the power of death,' and acquired the authority not only to

---

* Thornwell, II., p. 298.

conduct the *souls* He had redeemed to the mansions of eternal peace, but also to wrest their bodies from the bonds of the curse, and present them to His Father in *bodily* as well as spiritual glorification." We do not know who were these first trophies of the glorious conqueror of the king of terrors. Was Abraham among them, to whom it was promised that he should see in a very peculiar manner the day of the Lord? Was Moses, of whom Jude relates that Satan strove with the heavenly powers, about his body? Was Job, who said, "I know that my Redeemer liveth, and that He shall stand at the latter day upon the earth: And though after my skin worms destroy this body, yet in my flesh shall I see God"? The narrative leaves us without a reply, and is also silent as to the appearance presented by the risen saints; and when and where, and in what manner, they were afterward taken up into heaven. The mission of those who were thus called from the dust of the grave, was limited to one thing: viz., to represent the resurrection of Jesus as an event that operated with creative physical power, in the past, the present, and the future; and not less in the depth than in the height; and to give actual proof of the exceedingly abundant and well-grounded cause we have to glory in "the *power of His resurrection*."

V. The power of His resurrection is exemplified in that it is presented by the Apostle as the motive or stimulant to all holy living. "If ye then be risen with Christ, seek those things which are above where Christ sitteth at the right hand of God; set your affections on things above and not on things on the earth." The fact that we are identified with Christ in His resurrection, should fill us with lofty aspirations, and should wean us from the love of earth. Here is the Apostle's argument:

(1.) Being raised up with Christ, we ought to seek things above. Any other search or desire would be very inconsistent. "The image is this:—the region of the dead is beneath; they are let down to their final resting-place. Should a man then rise from this dark and deep receptacle, and ascend to the living world, would *he* set his desires on the gloom and chill and rottenness he had left behind him? Would he place the objects of his search among the coffins and the mean and creeping things that live in putrefaction? Would he still seek for things below? At the very idea and memory of that locality, would not his spirit shudder? And if Christians have been raised from a yet lower condition and by a nobler resurrection, should not similar feelings and associations rule their minds? Why should they be gazing downward from their position, and groping among things so far beneath them? Their past state with its sin and guilt, its degradation and misery, can surely have no attractions for them now. And

(2.) "Christ is *above*, in a station of glory. Their union with Him will lead their thoughts to Him. As He is in heaven, holding it in their name; as their present life and peace originate in union with Him—a union to be realized more vividly when He shall bid them 'come up higher,' therefore should their desires stretch away upward and inward toward Him, and the scene He occupies 'on the right hand of the glorious Majesty.' The Apostle does not urge any transcendental contempt of things below; but simply asks that the heart be not set upon them, in the same way and to the same extent in which it is set upon things above. The pilgrim is not to despise the comforts he may meet with by the way; but he is not to tarry among them, or to leave them with regret. Things on earth are only subordinate and instrumental; things above are supreme and final. Attachment to things on earth is unworthy of one who has risen with Christ; for they are beneath him, and the love of them is not in harmony with his position and prospects. What can wealth achieve for him whose treasure is in heaven? or honor, for him who is already enthroned in heavenly places? or pleasure, for him who revels in 'newness of life'? or power, for him who is endowed with a moral omnipotence? or fame, for him who enjoys the approval of God?"*

Thus the power of His resurrection is displayed in weaning the heart of the Church, which is His bride, from the world, from which she has been divorced; and in raising her affections to heaven, her destined home.

---

* Eadie on Col. iii. 1, 2.

VI. The power of His resurrection is evinced in the fact that by means of it believers are made to "walk in *newness of life.*" I wish to call your attention specially to this doctrine—*All holy living flows from the life of Christ.* "To live in sin," and "to walk in newness of life," are two opposite characteristics of two different conditions. While a man is still alive to sin, *i. e.*, under its guilt and condemnation, he goes on living in sin, and he cannot help it; he must of necessity sin and keep sinning, for that condition has no life to produce a walk according to God's mind. But when such a man has become incorporated into Him who bore his sin, he is, just because his judgment has been borne, and by virtue of his union with Jesus risen and living forever, a partaker of Christ's life; and this is "newness of life." When the Apostle speaks of this newness of life as connected with the resurrection of Christ, he simply declares that they who died in Christ have become righteously and really living in Him, in whose death they died, and *this is a new life to them.* Being then made partakers of life in Christ, who was raised from the dead, they are called to walk "in newness of life." The conclusion is obvious: that whatever deliverance from the power of sin, or whatever attainment may be made in holiness, these are the outgoings and manifestations of the life of our risen and exalted Lord. "The holy walk of the believer, in this world, is not the result of his death to the power of sin, nor is it the result of the evil principle being dead in him, but it is the fruit of a life which has been given him in Christ Jesus, as the reward of his obedience unto death. And the truth of this,—our death to the guilt of sin in His death, and our life unto God in *His* life, is ever more offered to the faith of living saints as the directing motive of their life." This is what the Apostle means when he says, "Therefore, WE," *i. e.*, all believers without exception, (not one class of believers who have made high attainments in piety, as distinguished from some who have not yet "got the blessing" from a want of "unreserved consecration"—we, any of you and all of you), "are buried with Him by baptism* into death, that like

---

* "Buried with Him by baptism" has no reference to immersion, as Baptists teach.

as Christ was raised from the dead by the glory of the Father, even so we also should walk in newness of life" (Rom. vi. 4). This, then, is another power of His resurrection, that it *actually* imparts to all believers a *new spiritual life*.

VII. I have dwelt so long on the power of His resurrection in believers as individuals, that I have left time for only one remark as to the "power of His resurrection" as manifested in the course of human history. If you will read the Acts of the Apostles carefully, you will see that the chief element in their preaching was their personal testimony to the resurrection of Jesus. You will see that Matthias was chosen in the place of Judas, to be with the rest a witness to the resurrection of Jesus. This was an essential qualification of an Apostle. And in order that Saul of Tarsus might be thus qualified to be an Apostle, it was necessary to bring him to a personal interview with the risen and ascended Saviour; so that he might be able to say he had "seen" the risen Lord. Now, as I said in the beginning, that the resurrection of Christ was the key-stone in the arch of the plan of redemption, so now I say, from another point of view, that it is the foundation on which the Church is built. Hence all the victories of Christianity in the world are the direct result of the *power of His resurrection*. The Christian Church is the colossal structure reared upon this foundation, deep as the granite basis of the world. "If Christ be not risen, then is our preaching vain and your faith is vain." But preaching has not been vain; faith has not been vain. The preaching of this risen Christ has revolutionized human history; it has brought a new power into social, domestic, and political life. Of the two doctrines, the Crucifixion and the Resurrection,—the one inspired among all men indignant horror, the other unbounded scorn. Consider what these doctrines have overcome: First, "Judaism with its long and splendid history, rolling back from the heroic struggles of the Asmonean princes to the magnificence of Solomon; nay, backward to the day, when, with uplifted spear, Joshua had bidden the sun to stand still on Gibeon; and Abraham, obeying the mysterious summons, had abandoned the gods of his fathers in

Ur of the Chaldees. The rod of Moses, the harp of David, the ephod of Samuel, the mantle of Elijah, the graven gems on Aaron's breast, the granite tables of Sinai, the living oracles of God—all these were the inheritance of Judah; and who was this crucified Nazarene about whom some miserable Galileans testified that He had risen from the dead, that He should dare to assail an immemorial faith like this! But still, Judaism survived His resurrection for only forty years. The blood of the King whom they had crucified, fell like a rain of fire from heaven upon them and their children."

Secondly, they encountered *Paganism*, with its mercenary priests, its proud philosophy, its favorite vices, its tyrannous politics, and its abominable and debauched social life. Yet, unaided by anything external, the doctrine of a risen Jesus won. "Without one earthly weapon, Christianity faced the legionary masses, and tearing down their adored eagles replaced them by the sacred monogram of her victorious *labarum;* made the cross, the instrument of a slave's agony, more glorious than the laticlave of consuls or the diadem of kings"; without eloquence, silenced the subtle dialectics of the Academy; and without knowledge, the encyclopædic ambition of the Porch. And when, after essaying argument, and rhetoric, and railing, and irony, and invective in vain, Paganism resorted to brute force and crushing violence, even then Julian, the last of the persecuting pagan emperors, died prematurely in the wreck of his broken powers with the despairing words upon his pallid lips, as he flung toward heaven a handful of his clotted blood, "*Vicisti Galilæe,*" "O Galilæan, thou hast conquered!" Then after triumphing over external foes the doctrine of a Divine Risen Redeemer encountered foes in its own household, and the Arian apostasy threatened the very existence of the Church, while Athanasius seemed to "stand alone against the world." But there were thousands of the true people of God who constituted the church that had not bowed to Baal, and mouths that had not kissed him; and the great heart of the Christian multitude remained sound.

Then came the avalanche of the northern barbarian invasion; and it seemed to the eye of man as if the church must perish.

But in the language of Gibbon, "The progress of Christianity was marked not only by a decisive victory over the learned and luxurious civilization of the Roman empire, but over the warlike barbarians of Scythia and Germany, who first subverted the empire and then embraced the religion of the vanquished."

Then in the seventh century came Mohammedanism, with its trooping beauties and heaven of lust; then Atheism in the fifteenth century, when Christendom had ceased to be Christian, and priests, turned atheists, made open scoff of the religion they professed; when a Cardinal Bembo could speak of Christ as "Minerva sprung from the head of Jupiter"; and Pope John jested with his secretary on the "profitableness of the fable of Christ." All seemed lost and dead, when the voice of Luther's indignation shook the world. The hierarchy fell; but the power of His resurrection, by which we are justified, saved the Church.

And so I might go on, did time permit, and show you how down to this very moment the energy of Christ's resurrection has been reforming apostate civilizations; and when it did not reform, has been purging out pestilence from the reeking atmosphere with fire and storm. Other religions have withered into dishonored decrepitude; but Christianity, with continuous rejuvenescence, has renewed her strength like the eagle, has run and not been weary, has walked and not been faint. If ever, through her own faithlessness, she has fallen before her enemies, she has risen, Antæus-like, with new vigor, and "shaken her invincible locks." She cannot die, because, by the power of His resurrection, she is endued with the "power of an endless life."

The power of His resurrection has left its imprint upon the very calendars of all Christianized nations. As His birthday was the beginning of a new era, so that in every letter you write, in every legal document you pen, in every legislative enactment that is engrossed, in every historical event that is recorded, even infidels are compelled to acknowledge the "year of our Lord": so at the beginning of every week all Christendom recognizes the "power of His resurrection," in observing as sacred the day when He entered into His rest and ceased from His labors, as

God did after the first creation. When busy commerce in all our crowded marts folds her arms, and the din of trade is hushed in the still Sunday morning; when church-bells ring out their gladsome tones in honor of the day; when even law refuses to enforce contracts made in violation of the sanctity of this *dies non*, how can we doubt the power of His resurrection? Yes! the Christian Sabbath, with all that this involves, observed by 300,000,000 of the human race, attests the "power of His resurrection."

"'Christ the Lord is risen to-day,'
Sons of men and angels say;
Raise your joys and triumphs high,
Sing, ye heavens, and, earth, reply.

"Vain the stone, the watch, the seal;
Christ has burst the gates of hell;
Death, in vain, forbids Him rise,
Christ hath opened Paradise.

"Hail the Lord of earth and heaven!
Praise to Thee by both be given!
Thee we greet triumphant now!
Hail the Resurrection Thou."

XXIV.

HEAVEN.

"In my Father's house are many mansions: if it were not so, I would have told you. I go to prepare a place for you."—JOHN xiv. 2.

IF we were informed by a competent authority that a large part of our present life on earth is to be spent in another country, different in every respect from the land of our birth, where greater happiness than we ever experienced would fall to our lot, where the society with which we should associate would be more agreeable and congenial, the employments in which we should engage more interesting and exciting, the range of our thought more extended, and the objects of desire and affection more elevated and exalted,—we should certainly be most deeply interested in learning beforehand all that might be known in regard to that untried country of which we were to become the denizens. How eagerly would we read every book which could give us any information respecting it! How anxiously would we interrogate every pilgrim returning from that distant shore! How carefully would we treasure up in our memories every piece of intelligence which might reach us in regard to the climate, the society, the politics, the laws, the government, the religion, the fashions, the customs of our future home!

Now, what I have presented in the form of a mere supposition is in reality a sober fact. We are informed by a competent authority, that each one of us who is a Christian, will, after a longer or a shorter period, be immediately transported to another and a better country than that which we now inhabit, where our condition, character, associations, and employments will be materially modified and changed. We are informed that the place to which we are thus destined is called *Heaven*. And it is not strange that we should be anxious to know all that may be known about this, which is to be our future eternal abode.

While we speak of *heaven* as if it were a place of which we know everything, is it not true that many of us have very vague, shadowy, dim, unsatisfactory conceptions of the state of the blessed dead and of the place where they are to spend their eternity? Perhaps this incertitude is unavoidable and pertains of necessity to our present imperfect intellectual development. All the knowledge we can have of heaven must come to us through a written revelation. But a revelation can be made to us only in words; and human language is a very imperfect medium for the conveyance of conceptions which have no pattern on earth with which we can compare them. Another reason for the vagueness of our notions respecting heaven is that the Scriptures nowhere undertake to give us a description of it, except in the highly figurative language of the Revelation of St. John, which no one understands, and which it is probable it was not meant that we should understand. While these figurative descriptions are unintelligible, they are not on that account to be neglected or despised, for they convey to us some general idea of the splendor, the beauty, and the bliss of the New Jerusalem.

Now, while all this is true, it is clear that God has not left us entirely in the dark with respect to the place and state of the soul after death. He has revealed so much as is necessary to excite our desires to reach that heavenly abode, and to stimulate us to that patient continuance in well-doing by which we shall reach glory and honor and immortality beyond the grave.

Let us endeavor to gather together the scattered rays of light and bring them into one focus.

I. The Scriptures clearly teach that *heaven* is a *place;* i. e., that somewhere in the universe there is a central spot, where are congregated together holy angels and the spirits of just men made perfect. "We sometimes hear and read such statements as this: Heaven is a *state* as well as a *place.* Such propositions have no meaning."* They are words which are not intended to

---

* See Harbaugh on Heaven.

convey thought, but are used simply to conceal the absence of all thought. I do not know what is meant by saying *Heaven* is a *state*. To my mind, it is equivalent to a negation of thought. Now, let us look at the proofs from Scripture that heaven is a place.

(1.) In the text, our Lord says, "I go to prepare a place for you." This language is not figurative; the word I GO implies an actual departure from one *place* to *another*. If the point *from which* He departed was a place, the point toward which He went must be a place also. So, too, the word *"place"* is used in its literal sense. It is the ordinary Greek word for a *locality*, used constantly to designate a precise spot or situation. From this passage alone, then, we are warranted in concluding that heaven is a place.

(2.) But again, that heaven is a place, is proved by the revealed truth that the *bodies* of *Enoch*, of *Elijah* and of our Lord are in heaven. Now, a body is a substance which has relations to place. It is bounded by limits; it is *here*, and not there. It has spatial relations. As the bodies of Enoch and Elijah did not experience death, they were not chemically decomposed. They did not see corruption. The particles which composed those bodies were never separated from each other; the flesh and bones and muscles and nerves must have retained their organic connection with each other, and do retain them to this very day and hour.

The statement in Genesis with regard to the translation of Enoch is not decisive—there it is simply said that Enoch walked with God and *was not*, for God took him; the same form of expression is applied to those who died—that *they were not*. But St. Paul relieves us of all doubt by the distinct assertion that on account of his faith Enoch was translated that he should not see death and was not found, because God had translated him; *i. e.*, his actual physical body was removed *from this earth* and carried away; and if it was carried away it must have been carried to some place, and that place must be heaven. The narrative of the translation of Elijah is succinct and clear. Standing with Elisha on the bank of the river Jordan, and in view of fifty young men who composed the school of the prophets, he is visibly placed by angels in a fiery chariot drawn by horses of fire and forcibly separated from his companions and in a whirlwind carried up to heaven. He wore a *mantle;* that mantle was composed of *woolen* or *silken* fibres—it was *matter*, and Elijah's body was *matter*, consisting of flesh and bones and blood. The *mantle* which he wore was thrown out of the chariot and fell upon Elisha, symbolically to denote that he inherited from his master the prophetic spirit, and also because no doubt this fabric of wool or silk could not be carried up to heaven. Now, the mantle came back to the earth and was taken up and worn by Elisha; but the flesh and bones and blood of the translated prophet went with his soul into heaven. The young prophets asked permission to hunt for the body of Elijah. Elisha, who knew that the body of Elijah was taken away from the earth, discouraged the search, but after being importuned by them consented to it, and after an unavailing search of three days, in his case as in Enoch's, Elijah was not found: because God had translated *him*, i. e., *his body to heaven.*

Now the body of Elijah was a substance, having relations to *space* and *place;* it was not annihilated; it was not decomposed; it underwent no corruption; in its physical entireness it was snatched away *from* this earth and borne to some other place through the air. It was seen 926 years afterward by Peter, James, and John, in company with Moses, on the Mount of Transfiguration, in familiar conversation with our Lord. It went and it came back; and it must have gone somewhere and come from somewhere—that somewhere must have been a *place*, and that *place* was *heaven.*

(3.) Again, it is a matter of history that our Lord died and was buried and rose from the dead in His own proper body. He in this body appeared to two of His disciples, sat at meat with them in this body, broke bread and gave it to them and suddenly vanished out of their sight. Astonished at His presence and still more at His sudden exit, they came in haste to Jerusalem, and finding the other disciples gathered together, told them of their interview with Him, and while they were yet speaking, Jesus stood in the midst of them and said, "Peace be unto you." They were terrified, supposing that they had seen a spirit. He distinctly disclaimed being a spirit, and said, "Behold my hands and my feet, that it is I myself; handle me and see, for a spirit hath not flesh and bones, as ye see me have." And then, in further attestation of His *physical* existence, He called for food and ate a piece of broiled fish and of an honeycomb. Here were all the evidences of a natural body. It could be *seen*, and *felt*, and *handled;* it took food and ate it and satisfied its hunger. On a similar occasion, Thomas, who had been informed by the other disciples that they had seen the risen Lord, said, " Except I shall see in His hands the print of the nails, and put my finger into the print of the nails, and thrust my hands into His side, I will not believe." Eight days after this, Jesus came in His body through closed doors, and invited Thomas to reach forth his finger and reach forth his hand and thrust it into His wounded side, *i. e.*, to prove to his sense of touch the *material existence* of the risen body of his Lord. Now, after a period of something more than a month, this same visible, tangible person, standing with His eleven apostles upon Mount Olivet, is taken up into heaven, and a cloud receives Him out of their sight. And while the wondering disciples stand gazing up after Him in mute astonishment, two men stand by them dressed in white apparel, and assure them that " this same Jesus shall so come in like manner as ye have seen Him go into heaven." Here then, again, was a body that had flesh and bones, and that had recently eaten food, that was visibly snatched from this earth and carried away to a place somewhere beyond the clouds; and at the instant of its departure angels inform those who behold the prodigy that it has gone to heaven and will remain there a human body for ages, and will return one day to this earth in like manner as it went. And that *human*, visible, material body *is* now somewhere in the universe, and although the wisest of us know not where it is, yet we are bound to believe, in view of all these concurring testimonies, that it is a *place*, and that where He is, there is heaven. Let no sophistry of philosophy, let no jugglery of metaphysics cheat you out of the well-founded belief that heaven is a place prepared for you, and that there are many mansions in the Father's house. We may not go farther in our deductions from the known to the unknown, nor inquire how visible and tangible bodies subsist in this abode. The Apostle tells us that there is a natural *body* and that there is a spiritual *body*—a natural body, *i. e.*, a body adapted to the principle of animal life; a spiritual body, *i. e.*, a body adapted to the principle of spiritual life, and not as the words interpreted according to the letter would mean, *immaterial matter*. A natural body consists of flesh and blood, is susceptible of pain and decay, and needs air, food, and rest; it is an animal body adapted to the conditions of an earthly existence. What a spiritual body is, we know only from Paul's description and from the manifestation of Christ to His disciples after His resurrection in His glorified body. But spiritual does not mean *ethereal*, refined, or *made of spirit*, which would be a contradiction; but a body adapted to the principle of spiritual life as distinguished from animal life. The Apostle teaches us that flesh and blood cannot inherit the kingdom of God; and although at the resurrection those will be there who will join the Lord at His second coming, who, being alive at that time, shall not sleep, that is, die; yet they, too, shall be "*changed*," *i. e.*, their animal bodies will become spiritual bodies. Now the point of all this is to suggest the idea that as the spiritual body is a body adapted to the spiritual life, so heaven is a *place*, but not a place in the gross sense of being a material abode, but a spiritual place adapted to the residence therein of the glorified and spiritual bodies of Enoch and Elijah and Christ. Now into this place we are to be introduced as disembodied spirits immediately upon our release from our mortal bodies. This is the paradise of God in which the dying thief met the spirit of Christ immediately after the crucifixion. Into this paradise Paul was introduced, whether in the body or out of the body he knew not, and there saw sights and heard words which it was not lawful for him to utter. In this great house of God not made with hands there are many mansions, and Christ went thither to prepare a place for all them that love Him.

II. I come now to the inquiry, who are the inhabitants of this Paradise of God? I answer first of all, it is the place where Jesus—the man Christ Jesus in His glorified resurrection body—the same body which His disciples saw and handled, dwells. Secondly, it is the abode of all the angels who worship around the throne of God. Thirdly, it is the abode of Enoch and Elijah in their glorified and spiritual bodies. Fourthly, it is the abode of the spirits of just men made perfect. If speculation were allowable in this connection, we might add a fifth class of intelligent beings composed of the inhabitants of other worlds than ours, who may be presumed to have been translated from their starry homes to compose a part of the shining retinue of the King of Glory.

But we are not to be wise above what is written. We are nevertheless entitled to be wise up to what is written. And Scripture justifies us in asserting that heaven *is* the abode of *Jesus*, of *angels*, of translated men, and of the spirits of just men made perfect.

The Apostle Paul, in the 12th of Hebrews, in describing the glorious privilege of believers, enters into a detailed description of the Church on earth and the Church in heaven; and in speaking of the latter, he describes it as composed of an innumerable company of angels and of the spirits of justified men made perfect. The prophet Daniel, in a vision of the night, saw heaven opened, and "thousand thousands and ten thousand times ten thousand ministered unto and stood before the Ancient of Days."

Here imagination shrinks abashed and droops its palsied pinion when it would attempt to body forth in language a description of the splendid scene. An innumerable company of created spirits, older than time; mysterious cherubim and burning seraphim, principalities and powers, hosts of inferior angels ranked in endless files; and all the armies of the sons of God; the glorious company of the Apostles, the goodly fellowship of the prophets, the noble army of martyrs, and among ten thousand times ten thousand saints, some whose very names are familiar to our ears; the father and mother of mankind, our primal ancestors; Noah and his children who by faith condemned the world; Abraham, the friend of God; Isaac, the child of prayer; the princely Jacob, who prevailed with God; Joseph and the patriarchs; Moses, the man of God; Joshua, the son of Nun; Deborah, the warrior prophetess; Samson and Jephtha; David, the sweet singer of Israel; the kingly Hezekiah; plaintive Jeremiah; the rapt Ezekiel and Isaiah, whose lips a seraph touched with a live coal of fire; the saintly Daniel "and the three who walked unsinged and scatheless through the fiery flame"—but the time would fail me to mention the names of thousands who we know are there. And last in the enumeration, but not least in point of interest to each one of us, our own blessed dead are there—the little nurslings that smiled for one brief hour on their mothers' breasts; the tender lambs that nestled by our sides, "the dove whose gentle cooing echoed in our hearts," the gentle sister, the brave and gifted and beautiful,— all, all our loved and lost ones whose memory dwells in our souls like a departed glory, are there; *they are there.*

III. Let us turn to consider the nature and character of these inhabitants of the heavenly abode.

(1.) They are all intelligent beings; of this there can be no doubt. The Scriptures everywhere ascribe lofty intelligence to the angels, everywhere investing them with the attributes, actions, and emotions of self-conscious beings. They praise God continually, they rejoice over repenting sinners. They hearken to the voice of God's Word, they talk with each other, they are employed by God as the ministers of His providence and as the executors of His judgments. So too the Scriptures everywhere ascribe intelligence to the souls of departed saints. All that the Scriptures say on this subject is based upon the assumption that the souls of believers at the very instant of death enter at once upon a state of quickened intellectual activity. There is no such doctrine as that implied in the expression, "the sleep of the soul," taught in that which is revealed to us.

(2.) But if heaven is peopled with intelligent self-conscious beings, it follows from the very necessities of the case that they must hold intercourse with each other. Man and all intelligent beings are constituted to be happy in society. Place a man in solitude, and however exciting and felicitous his circumstances in other respects, he will wither and pine away. And if heaven is a place of perfect bliss, then this element of happiness will not and cannot be wanting there. With the entire heaven of angels and the whole host of the redeemed, we shall have sweet and improving fellowship forever. The wise and the good, the great and the pure, the benevolent and the active from every region will be our companions and associates, with whom we shall live, and love, and know, and obey, through one eternally enduring day. Of all the afflictions to which we are liable, there is none so painful as the death of our friends. And oh, how consoling the doctrine that we shall in the realms above be restored to their fellowship! This doctrine is involved in many passages of Scripture; in the account of the last judgment,—in the language of David on the occasion of the death of his infant child,—in the parable of the rich man and Lazarus,—in the consolation which our Saviour gives to the penitent thief on the cross,—in the assurance administered by Paul to the Thessalonians that they should be his joy and crown of rejoicing in the presence of our Lord Jesus Christ at His coming and in his forbidding them to sorrow for such as had fallen asleep as though they had no hope of being united with them and of being together with the Lord,—and in the general use which the sacred writers make of the word *sleep* for death,—a simile which would be flagrantly incorrect, if our recollections, our friendships and affections were not renewed in a future state. And in general the same doctrine is taught through the whole book of the Revelation of St. John. Happy prospect that exalts friendship into religion! What blest society there will be above!

(3.) On the question *how* intercourse shall be conducted in the future state, it were easy to speculate or to refer to the speculations of ingenious and pious minds. These, however, conduct us to no certain results. With what rapidity and to what extent spirit may communicate with spirit, what new faculties adapted to communication it may be the purpose of God to impart, or what existing but undeveloped faculties may be brought into play in that state of intellectual maturity and perfection—what channels of communication accessible to the blessed, and established between the throne of Him who is "Head over all things" and all parts of that creation which He governs, it is not for us to say. We may believe that a thing is, without knowing how it is.

(4.) But if there is intercourse between the inhabitants of heaven, we may reason farther that it shall be very *intimate*. The society of heaven is called by the Apostle a family—"*the whole family in heaven*." The inhabitants are a family convened in the domestic mansion of their Father. This conveys the idea of the most endearing intimacy. When do we feel such unreserved ease; when do we unbosom ourselves with such unsuspecting confidence, thinking aloud with one another; when do we experience such an identity of unconflicting and stirring interests, drawing forth and mingling all kindred streams of thought and feeling, as in our homes? On earth we can hardly reach intimate intercourse with many. We have no time to cultivate it, in a state in which "our days are but as an hand-breadth." When death so soon divides us, we can enjoy direct intercourse only with a few, separated as we are by natural and artificial barriers, by language, by distance; and indirect intercourse is never very intimate. Among those near us, many will not let us know them, keeping always on the reserve, and, as it were, behind the curtain; many are not worth knowing; and after we think we know others well, we find by events which bring out character that we have been grievously mistaken. Society on earth is formed into an infinite variety of little coteries, or cliques, arising from station, wealth, literature, or religious party; each of these has its peculiarities, its usages, its language, its prejudices, its intellectual and moral customs; notwithstanding the expansive and combining influence of true religion, these distinctions remain; and in passing from one party to the other, the individual feels as a stranger, receiving and rendering many agreeable civilities indeed, in the large halls of promiscuous entertainment, but excluded from the private and smaller circle of interior and intimate converse, and departing, in a great measure, unknowing and unknown.

Suppose that at a period remote as the creation, the human race had reached the number in which it exists at this moment on the globe, and had remained unchanged until the present period, and suppose that no obstructions to unrestrained intercourse, individual and national, such as have arisen from sin, had existed; suppose that such tendencies, inducements, and facilities for communication as a sinless world, accomplished in every improvement, would exhibit, had been continued for 6,000 years, who can calculate the degree of acquaintanceship which would have existed among men at this day? Who can conceive the intimacy of that intercourse which must already have embraced a large proportion of the whole family of man? Now transfer these thoughts to the society of that world where all the obstructions to intercourse which exist on earth shall vanish—when common interests and pursuits shall animate, and the bond of love shall bind the whole—when means of intercourse shall be multiplied, and when the fellowship of the blessed shall be eternal.

(5.) And this leads me to speak of another element in the state of the blessed dead in heaven.

How evanescent is society on earth! Pleasant are the endearments of home—pleasant the interviews of hallowed friendship. They come like sunbeams on the soul. But how soon are they darkened by the shadow of death! The sweetness of intercourse in this land of affliction and mortality is only the antecedent to the bitterness of separation. In heaven we meet, but not to part. There are no mournful, tremulous adieus—no empty places of friends who once were with us, no vacant chairs at the festal board, no lamentation for those who are not, no solitary survivor longing in sadness for his own dismissal. Heaven is the land of immortality—no more death, no more sorrow nor crying. The society of the blessed shall be, like their existence, eternal.

IV. What shall be, what are the employments of the inhabitants of this blessed abode?

Some light is thrown on this inquiry by the Scriptures, but it must be confessed it is very scanty. All our meditations on and descriptions of heaven want balance, and are, so to speak, pictures ill-composed. It was not ill-said by a great preacher, that most people's idea of heaven is that it is to sit on a cloud and sing psalms. Others again strive to fill this out with the bliss of recognizing and holding intercourse with those from whom we have been severed on earth. And beyond all doubt such recognition and intercourse shall be and shall constitute one of the most blessed accessories of the heavenly employment; but it can no more be the employment itself than similar intercourse on earth was the employment of life itself here. "To read some descriptions of heaven one would imagine that it were only an endless prolongation of some social meeting, walking and talking in some blessed country with those we love." Is it not clear that this does not provide the renewed energies and enlarged powers of man with food for eternity? Nor if we look in another direction—that of the absence of sickness and sorrow—shall we find any more satisfactory answer to the question. Nay, we shall find it more difficult, and beset with greater complications on this very account. For, think how much of employment for our present energies is occasioned by, and finds its very field of action in, these anxieties and vicissitudes. They are, so to speak, the winds which fill the sails and carry us onward. By their action hope and enthusiasm are excited. But suppose a state where they are not, and life would become a dead calm; the sail would flap idly and the spirit would cease to look onward at all. So that unless we can supply something over and above the mere absence of anxiety and pain, we have not attained to, nay, we are farther than ever from a sufficient employment for the life eternal. Now, before we seek for an answer to the question, let us think a moment thus: *Can* we know, are we able in our present state of the infancy of our spirits to know or understand much about the employments of heaven? What does the child at play know, what *can* he know of the employments of the man? Such portions of them as are merely external and material, he may take in and represent in his sport; but the work and anxiety of the student at his book, or the man of business at his desk—these are of necessity hidden from the child, and so it is onward through the advancing stages of his life, of each of them it may be said, "We know not with what we must serve the Lord until we come thither" (Ex. x. 26). So that we need not be utterly disappointed if our picture of heaven be at present ill-composed; if it seem to be little else than a gorgeous mist after all. We cannot fill in the members of the landscape at present. If we could, we should *be* in heaven. For we walk by faith, not by sight. Now we see through a glass, *i. e.*, in a mirror, darkly; but then, face to face; now I *know* in part, but then shall I *know* even as I am known.

Although little is actually conveyed by the words, do they not give a glimpse by suggestion of the possible employments of the blessed? This immense accession of light and knowledge must of course be interpreted partly of keener and brighter faculties wherewith the blessed shall be endowed; but do not words also point to glorious employment of those renewed and augmented powers? How could one endowed with them ever remain idle? What a restless, ardent, many-handed thing is genius here below. How the highly-endowed spirit searches about and tries its wings, now hither, now thither, in the vast realms of intellectual life. And if it be so here with the body weighing on us, with the clogs of worldly business and trivial interruptions, what will it be there, when everything will be fashioned and arranged for this express purpose that every higher employment may find its noblest expansion without let or hindrance. What power mind shall acquire there, to what a distance the intellectual eye shall reach, over what a field and over what a crowd of glorious objects it shall range, and with what distinctness its perceptions shall be accompanied in that bright region, it is not for us at present to conceive. With what accuracy the judgment shall act; with what power and rapidity reason shall conduct its most involved and sublime processes, and at what magnificent results it shall arrive; with what stores memory faithful and strong shall be enriched, as it shall amass intelligence from all parts of the universe and the transactions and discoveries of past duration; amidst what boundless amplitude of varied and glorious being, of whole regions of truth yet undiscovered imagination shall travel, and what its creations shall then be, and with what promptitude and fullness mind shall communicate itself to mind! How consoling and at the same time how exciting and exhilarating is this view of heaven, considered as the scene of perfect intellectual strength, activity, acquirement, and communication. Remember that in heaven we are to be "forever with the Lord"; and if we are fit companions for the Lord, we must be like Him as He is there, and this alone seems to mark out employment sufficient for eternity. For what is, what will the Lord be doing in that state of blessedness? Will He be idle like the gods of Epicurus, sitting severe above all and separate from all created things? No, indeed; no such glorified Lord is revealed to us in Holy Scripture. "My Father worketh hitherto, and I work." The created universe will be as much beholden to His upholding hand as it is now. If we are to be forever with Him, attending and guiding His steps, we shall doubtless be fellow-workers with Him as we are here. Look abroad on a starry night—and behold a field of employment for those who shall be ever with the Lord. And who can tell what works, not of creation only, but of grace also, the blessed may have to search into, works wrought on themselves and others, which may there be brought back to them by memory entirely restored, and then first studied with any power to comprehend and be thankful for them?

Then again, the glory of God himself, there first revealed to them—the redeeming love of Christ—the glory of the mystery of the indwelling of the Spirit,—dry and lofty subjects to the sons of men here,—will be to us, when there, as household words and as daily pursuits. It seems to me, when we look at all these sources of blessed employment, though we are unable from our present weakness to follow them out into detail—and when we think that perhaps after all we may be omitting some which shall then constitute the chief,—it seems to me, I say, as if we should not have to complain of insufficient employment for the ages of eternity, but rather of an infinite and inexhaustible variety for which even endless ages of limited being hardly seem to suffice.

V. And now consider that this *place* of many mansions and of such infinite employments is not far from us in reality. The nearness of heaven is suggested by the word veil. Our forerunner, Jesus, is said by the Apostle to have retired behind the veil. There is then only a veil between us and heaven. "A veil is the thinnest and frailest of all conceivable partitions. It is but a fine tissue, a delicate fabric of embroidery. It waves in the evening zephyr; the touch of a child may stir it, and the slightest accident may rend it; the silent action of time will moulder it away. The veil that hides heaven from our eyes is only our embodied existence, and though fearfully and wonderfully made, it is only wrought out of our frail mortality. So slight is it that the puncture of a thorn, the touch of an insect's sting, the breath of an infected atmosphere may make it shake and fall. In a bound, in a moment, in the twinkling of an eye, in the throb of a pulse, in the flash of a thought, we may start into disembodied spirits, glide unabashed into the company of great and mighty angels, pass into the light and amazement of eternity, know the great secret, gaze upon splendors which flesh and blood could not sustain, and which no words lawful for men to utter could describe. Brethren, there is but one step between you and what lies behind that curtain; between you and heaven there is but a veil." "This day shalt thou be with me in paradise," said the dying Saviour to the penitent thief. It is not far to heaven; it is not a day's journey. The angel came all the way from heaven in a few minutes to Daniel while he was speaking in prayer. The Saviour ascended from Olivet to heaven, and was soon out of sight. The dying saint closes his eyes in death, sleeps in Jesus, and opens them in heaven. Sometimes the departing Christian hears the songs and music of heaven even before his immortal spirit stretches its wings for its final flight. How far, then, is it to heaven? You may be already within the sound of its happy voices, and but for the "veil of humanity" they might even now fall upon the ear.

VI. *Lastly.* There is one more thought which I desire to present, although I have already detained you too long. But it is one immediately connected with this theme, though not necessarily growing out of it. It is suggested by what a lovely Christian woman once said to me, just before she fell asleep: "I do not fear death because I have any doubt or misgivings as to my safety in Christ, but I shrink from the thought of standing so suddenly in the awful presence of the great and glorious and holy One." Her idea was that the entrance of the soul into heaven would be accompanied by a shock of surprise, and that the infinite sublimities of the new and glorious state would overwhelm and well-nigh annihilate the soul. Great excitement has sometimes driven reason from her throne; and verily, the joy and splendor of that moment might seem more than enough to confound the bravest and holiest spirit. But no, beloved, it shall not be so. Be comforted; be assured it shall not be so. There will be no stunning shock to your spirit; there will be no sense of embarrassment; no shame, no fear, no painful awe, no confusion of face, no sinking of the spirit, no shrinking of the soul—*nothing* to disturb the calm serenity with which the soul shall enter the blessed abode. "A troop of angelic beings, unseen, crowd around the bed of the dying Christian in the chamber of death, and are ready, with outstretched wings, to bear the spirit home to God; the last quiver gasped from the bloodless lip, the last sigh breathed out, and swifter *than the beams of the morning*, or the flash of the lightning, they tower with it to glory."

> "Oh change! oh wondrous change!
> Burst are the prison bars;
> This moment, there—so low,
> So agonized—and *now*
> Beyond the stars!
>
> "Oh change, stupendous change!
> There lies the soulless clod;
> The sun eternal breaks,
> The new immortal wakes—
> Wakes with his God."

But He who has protected it from all evil, also shields it when disembodied amidst that opulence of celestial glory, so that it feels serenely calm and perfectly at ease the moment it crosses the threshold of its heavenly home, and is encompassed by the stupendous realities of an eternal condition. Wherefore, my beloved, "Let not your heart be troubled, neither let it be afraid; in my Father's house are many mansions; if it were not so, I would have told you. I go to prepare a PLACE for YOU. And if I go and prepare a place FOR you, I will come again and receive you unto myself, that where I am there ye may be also." *

---

* "By a happy coincidence Mr. Pratt's ministry closed where it may be said to have begun. On the 15th of January, 1888, a few months before his death, he stood among his old friends in Tuskaloosa, and amid the tender memories of the home of earlier years (the last Sabbath morning he ever preached), spoke to them of 'Heaven,' the other and eternal home he was so soon to enter."

PRAYERS.

A COMPREHENSIVE PRAYER FOR MORNING SERVICE.

ALMIGHTY GOD, we are glad to be found again in Thy sanctuary, for our feet are weary and our hearts long for rest. We have been all the week in the cold world, and have sighed over its sinfulness and disquietude. And yet *we* see only the outside deformity and blemish; but Thine eye searches the recesses of the corrupt heart. There is nothing hid from Thee. Our service in the world has quickened our desire to enter into the praises of Thy sanctuary, for we have felt as men who sigh in a far-off land for the sweetness and comfort of home. Now we are in Thy house, and a sense of safety makes us glad; we feel that we are in a City of Refuge, into which no man-slayer may enter. This is our Father's house, and the enemy has no place in it. Thou dost shut the gate upon all our foes. Come, then, and meet us; speak comfortably to our hearts, and by the infinite tenderness of Thy love, rather than by the alarming thunder of Thy law, do Thou bow down our hearts in the joyful sorrow of penitence. What shall we say of our sin? We cannot speak of it without shame and confusion of face, especially when we think of all the mercy Thou hast shown to us. God be merciful unto us sinners!

We lay our hand upon the cross, and find all our hope in the blood of Thy Son, which cleanseth from all sin. Think of us in Jesus Christ's name, and our sins shall not shut Thee out. Thou seekest to dwell in us as in a holy temple; come and be the only guest in the whole sanctuary of our love. While we are yet speaking of our sin do Thou forgive it; and though we would not have our sense of its enormity diminished, we would see Thy love overshadowing and exceeding our great sinfulness. Even now while we are in this, Thy house, let us hear Thee saying that all our sin is cast behind Thee. We know not how to tell Thee of our many wants; our joy is that Thou needst not to be told. As Thy great waters flood all the beds of the sea, and Thy rains fall even upon the desert and the rock, and the light of Thy sun shines upon all the earth, even more doth Thy love pour itself down upon the poverty of our needy and anxious hearts. We would be wise in Thy wisdom; we would love according to the measure of Thy love. We would be high above the world, as Thou art. We would partake of Thy riches. Thou hast given us all that has ever been for our good—every clear idea of truth, every tender emotion, every aspiration which has raised us above grovelling pursuits—nor have we exhausted Thee: Thou art the everlasting Father, full of riches which Thou offerest to the children of men; therefore we come again to the overflowing river of Thy loving-kindness. We aspire very high this morning, encouraged to do so by Thy providential mercies. Thou hast given us the joy of early harvest; Thou hast made a way for the lightning, and through the paths of the thunder Thou hast poured the cool and refreshing rain upon the parched fields.

Thou hast also showers of blessings for Thy church; yea, even a blessing which the church has not room enough to contain. Excite in our hearts intense longings for this blessing, that we may give Thee no rest until Thou hast opened the windows of heaven. Give us a firmer hold of Thy truth and a truer experience of Christ's unspeakable peace. And may we prove that Thou hast heard us by living a godly and more heavenly life among men.

We believe that the effectual, fervent prayer of the righteous man availeth much, and we would not forget to make intercession this day for all those for whom Thou hast commanded us to pray—for our rulers of every grade, from the President to the humblest officers of the law. Counsel our counsellors, and teach our Senators wisdom. May they rule us in the fear of the Lord, and through their wise governance may we become that happy people whose God is the Lord. Pour out Thy Holy Spirit on all schools and colleges and seminaries of learning, so that from these fountains may issue streams which shall make glad the city of our God. Illuminate the printed page, and bless all Bibles and tracts and religious newspapers. Impart heavenly wisdom to those who conduct them. Bless all the inmates of hospitals, the deaf, the dumb, the blind. Restore to soundness of mind all who are bereft of reason. Heal all who are tossing on beds of languishing. Smooth with Thine own soft hand the couch of the incurable sufferer, and give her grace to show by her patience that the Gospel is the power of

God not only to save the soul, but to sanctify the heart. Comfort all Thine afflicted, sorrowing, bereaved children. Be the God of the widow, the father of the fatherless. Extend the shield of Thy protection over all who travel by land or by sea. Bless all sailors who do business on the mighty waters; all soldiers who are far removed from the means of Grace; all commercial travellers, and all railroad employés who, through the avarice of great corporations, are constantly breaking Thy laws,—may they remember the Sabbath day to keep it holy. Bless all policemen, those trusty guardians of our homes, who watch for us while we sleep; and all firemen, those brave men who rescue our property from the flames, and who are often exposed to peril on our behalf. And, O God, bless all prisoners and such as are appointed to die; and the poor, the outcast, and the homeless. We beseech Thy tender compassion for all prodigal sons over whose waywardness pious parents are mourning in heaviness of heart. Recall them from their wanderings. We make intercession for this world which lieth in wickedness. Hasten the day when all flesh shall know Thee, when Jesus shall see of the travail of His soul and shall be satisfied; hasten the reign of universal peace throughout the world, the prosperity of the Church universal, when Zion shall shake herself from the dust and arise and shine, the glory of the Lord being risen upon her. Bless the Jews, Thine ancient people. Give success to all missionaries at home and abroad; may their lives be precious in Thy sight. Bless Thy Word; may it not return unto Thee void. And bless, we beseech Thee, all who are persecuted for righteousness' sake, our brethren among the heathen, who are exposed to the temptation of renouncing their faith. Pour out Thy Holy Spirit upon all our Sunday-schools, and from these nurseries of the church may there be transplanted stately trees to adorn the garden of our Lord. And now we pray for a blessing upon us—as we wait before Thee—upon this church, its elders, deacons, and all its members, and upon the strangers who may be with us; may they feel at home in this their Father's house. Finally, we pray for all the unconverted members of the church, and for *all* sinners, that the Holy Spirit would this day rend the heavens and come down and save their souls; and all the praise shall be to God the Father, Son, and Holy Ghost, in a world without end. Amen.

MORNING PRAYER.

O God, Thou art our God and our Father. Doubtless Thou art our Father, though Abraham be ignorant of us and Israel acknowledge us not. Thou, O Lord, art our Father, and we will exalt Thee. Thou art very great, clothed with honor and majesty. Thou coverest Thyself with light as with a garment, and in Thee is no darkness at all. Thou art God alone, and beside Thee there is none else. The heavens declare Thy glory. Thou art worthy, O Lord, to receive blessing and honor and glory and power, for Thou hast created all things, and for Thy pleasure they are and were created. The earth is full of Thy riches; Thy kingdom ruleth over all. A sparrow falls not to the ground without our Father, and the hairs of our head are all numbered. Thou hast made us and not we ourselves. We are not our own, but Thine, Thy people and the sheep of Thy pasture. In Thee we live and move and have our being. Thou hast redeemed us from evil, we are bought with a price. It is of Thy mercy we are not consumed, because Thy compassions fail not. Thou hast appointed a High Priest in whose name we come boldly to Thy throne of grace. We make mention of the righteousness of Christ and of His only.

CONFESSION.

Most merciful God, we come to Thee in humble dependence upon His atonement and intercession, and confess our sins which are many and great. Against Thee, Thee only have we sinned; to us belongeth shame and confusion of face. Behold we are vile; what shall we answer Thee? We have ruined ourselves, but in Thee is our help. If Thou, Lord, shouldst mark iniquity, who could stand? But there is forgiveness with Thee, that Thou mayest be feared. With Thee is mercy; yea, with our God there is plenteous redemption. We thank Thee that Thou hast so loved the world as to give Thine only begotten Son, that whosoever believeth in Him should not perish, but have everlasting life.

SUPPLICATION.

In the all-prevailing name of Jesus of Nazareth, a name with which Thou art ever well-pleased, we present our prayers and supplications to Thee. And now, Lord, what wait we for? Our eyes are unto Thee and our hope is in Thee, through Jesus Christ our Redeemer. Deliver us from our transgressions; and, O God, be merciful to us sinners. Wash us thoroughly from our iniquity and cleanse us from our sins, for we acknowledge our transgressions, and our sins are ever before us. Justify us freely by Thy grace through the redemption that is in Jesus Christ our Lord. Work in us the work of faith with power. Give us a goodly sorrow and true repentance. Shed abroad Thy love in our hearts. May our conscience be always tender; may we abstain from the appearance of evil. Enable us to be circumspect in all our conversation, watching over our thoughts, our lips, and our lives. May we be diligent in every duty, performing it with a ready mind and with joy and gladness of heart. Grant that we may increase in godliness, that we may grow in grace, and in the knowledge of our Lord and Saviour, Jesus Christ. O Lord, Thou who art the confidence of all the ends of the earth, preserve us from temptation, support us under afflictions, comfort us in sorrow, make us useful in life, prepare us for death, and when we have done serving Thee here below, admit us, we beseech Thee, to that state of rest and perfection which Thou hast prepared for Thy people in the heavenly world.

THANKSGIVING.

We thank Thee for Thy Son, for Thy Spirit, for Thy Word, Thy ministry, the Sabbath, and sanctuary blessings; for life and breath, and all things; for sweet communion with Thee, for gracious answers to our prayers, for succor in temptation, support under trouble, and for the joyful hopes of a glorious immortality. Hear our supplications and accept our thanksgiving for Christ's sake.

INTERCESSION.

For President, Congressmen, Governor, and Magistrates; Policemen, Firemen, Travellers by land and sea, Sailors, Soldiers, Railroad employés, Steamboat men, Commercial travellers, Blind, Deaf, Dumb, Insane, Prisoners and those appointed to die, Poor, Outcast, Homeless, Widows, Orphans, Fatherless, Sick and Afflicted, Sunday-schools, Colleges, Prodigal Sons, Missionaries at home and abroad. Church Universal, This Church, Elders, Deacons, Private members, Strangers with us, etc.

NOTE.—We have heard of a minister who said "if he had only five minutes to pray he would like to spend four of them in preparation." As this seems to accord with Mr. Pratt's habit, on that account we are able to comply with the request of those ministers who asked that some of his prayers be included in this volume.

"And I heard a voice from heaven, saying unto me, Write, Blessed are the dead which die in the Lord from henceforth: Yea, saith the Spirit, that they may rest from their labors; and their works do follow them."

REVELATION xiv. 13.

www.ingramcontent.com/pod-product-compliance
Lightning Source LLC
Chambersburg PA
CBHW030819230426
43667CB00008B/1284